Diamond Hitch

What would one not give to be young again, riding with a pack-train through the Canadian forests? To emerge from the jackpine shadow on to gravel flats beside a sparkling river. To pass through a kaleidoscope symphony of fireweed and paintbrush, while, through rifts in the clouds, gleaming peaks burst out in their upward soaring. Scarcely differing from the scenes beheld by explorers of long ago, the cayuses enter the rushing ford led, as if by a centaur: The Man of the Trail.

—J. Monroe Thorington

Diamond

the pioneer guides and

by E. J. Hart

Hitch

outfitters of Banff and Jasper

EJH Literary Enterprises Ltd.

Printed in Canada

Copyright E. J. Hart 1979 & 2001

ISBN 0-9699732-7-6

Originally published by Summerthought Ltd., 1979

This edition published in 2001 by
EJH Literary Enterprises Ltd.
Box 2074
Banff, AB. T0L 0C0
(403) 762-4194

Table of Contents

Preface to the New Edition

I originally became enthralled with the story of the early guides and outfitters of the Canadian Rockies shortly after going to work as an archivist at the Whyte Museum of the Canadian Rockies in 1972. At that time I became familiar with the collection of the great mountaineer and mountain historian J. Monroe Thorington, which contained correspondence and information about such famous individuals as Tom Wilson, the Brewsters, Bill Peyto, Jimmy Simpson and Curly Phillips. Reading this grist of Rockies' history convinced me to do some writing about these men and set me off in quest of more information. My odyssey led to additional collections at the Whyte, to other archives with treasure troves of documents relating to guides and their clients, to the original writings and publications of intrepid mountain explorers and, best of all, to the very homes of many trailmen to interview them on their youthful exploits when they were pioneers in the Rockies.

In the intervening quarter-century, I have written often about these unique individuals. In addition to *Diamond Hitch*, my books on the subject have included: *The Brewster Story, from pack train to tour bus* written in 1981; *Jimmy Simpson, Legend of the Rockies* produced in 1991; and *Ain't it Hell, Bill Peyto's 'Mountain Journal'* which appeared in 1995.

Recently, in re-reading *Diamond Hitch*, I noted how I might have improved the work had I known then what I know now, but I was equally struck by how well many of the stories had stood the test of time and had become part of the lore of Banff and Jasper. These realizations have led to the production of this new edition, and I hope that those of you being introduced to these legendary mountain men for the first time will enjoy reading about them as much as I did revisiting their lives after so many years.

E. J. Hart

Introduction

*T*he history of exploration in the Canadian Rockies is replete with accounts of the daring and intrepid men (and occasional woman) who have been successful in meeting the rugged mountain landscape on its own terms and, if not always conquering, at least surviving to tell the tale. In earlier times, before roads and well-trodden trails penetrated their most secret recesses, the Rockies demanded that only the strong, the skilled and the most tenacious could lay eyes on their wilderness mantle. Each period of exploration has had its share of these individuals. During the fur trade of the early nineteenth century, mapmakers such as Peter Fidler and David Thompson probed the chain's passes in order to made the geography understandable to the North West and Hudson's Bay Companies and aid them in their desire to penetrate to the Pacific slope and claim its furs for their corporate interests. Following at mid-century were other early travellers, running the gamut from missionaries such as the Reverend Robert T. Rundle and Father Pierre J. de Smet, to scientists like Dr. James Hector of the Palliser Expedition, to Pacific coast colonizers such as James Sinclair. Not until a quarter-century later did the next group of seekers appear in the guise of the surveyors for a national railway, the Canadian Pacific, which in 1885 was to make the previously remote landscape part of the new country's national transportation route. They were quickly followed near century's end by individuals such as George M. Dawson and J. J. McArthur employed by the government in the work of the Geological Survey of Canada and the Dominion Topographic Survey to identify and map the natural resources and the rugged topography of the newly revealed mountain fastnesses.

The subject of this work encompasses the last great period of exploration in the Canadian Rockies, that carried out by tourist-explorers during the period from the completion of the Canadian Pacific Railway in 1885 to the waning of their influence in the

Diamond Hitch

1920s. An initial reading of the plentiful literature that these pleasure-seeking and often wealthy self-styled explorers had produced led to some interesting conclusions. While they were extremely competent individuals in their business and professional backgrounds and were successful in achieving first ascents of unclimbed peaks, in discovering unreported valleys and in rafting across alpine lakes where no white man had preceded them, they had a tendency to take most of the glory for themselves. Indeed, in many cases there was little extended to those responsible for getting them there — the pioneer guides and outfitters who supplied the wherewithal, the knowledge and the skills with horses, pack outfits and mountain trails necessary for their clients to acheive their goals. It was apparent that the story of this exciting and important period of exploration would not be complete until these individuals received their just due.

Though it was with the intention of rectifying some misconceptions that the task began, it soon became more complex. Initial research indicated that rather than being merely vehicles for the early tourist-explorers to carry out their desires, the guides and outfitters had actually played major roles in the development of transportation in the mountains and in the economic growth of the Banff and Jasper National Park areas. Similarly, as I probed more deeply into the lives of the men involved, it became obvious I was dealing with a group of very unique individuals. Rather than being drawn exclusively from backwoods environments, as I had supposed, I discovered that many were from fine English, American and Canadian backgrounds, some were well-educated and most appeared to be of higher than average intelligence. This seeming contradiction fueled the fire and spurred on my investigations.

Hoping to shed some light on these matters, I spent many enjoyable hours hearing the stories and yarns of those of the old trailmen who were still among us and listening to tape recorded interviews of those who had crossed the last divide. This book was the result of these unforgettable experiences, and it is dedicated to the spirit and zest for life that was so evident in all of them.

Introduction

I would like to extend my thanks to all who took the time and made the effort to help me in this project. The staffs of the archives of the Whyte Museum of the Canadian Rockies in Banff, the Glenbow Museum in Calgary and the Jasper-Yellowhead Historical Society (in particular the late Mrs. Constance Peterson) constantly supplied me with new sources of material. Numerous people took the time to respond to my queries by letter or agreed to meet with me and, although too numerous to mention here, I owe them a tremendous debt of gratitude. However, I would be remiss if I did not extend particular thanks to three men who, while no longer with us, were at the time always agreeable to answering my rather persistent questions — F. O. "Pat" Brewster of Banff, Joe Woodworth of Calgary and George Camp of Salmon Arm, B. C. I would also like to thank Mrs. Maryalice Stewart for reading the manuscript for historical accuracy, and Mrs. Lillian Wonders for her fine work on the maps.

Chapter I
The Oracle at Banff

W hen Canadian Pacific Railway (CPR) general manager William Cornelius Van Horne looked at the shocking construction costs for the Mountain Section of the line after its completion in 1885, it was apparent something had to be done. Countless steep grades, expensive blasting and tunneling work and the bridging of innumerable chasms and rivers had driven them skyward, and now the section appeared to his trained eye as likely being uneconomical to operate. Unlike the adjacent prairies, where agricultural settlers were to be carried west and the fruits of their labours shipped back east, the Mountain Section promised little in sustained traffic. Van Horne's solution was to "capitalize the scenery," a plan which provided the backdrop for the appearance of the Canadian Rockies' most interesting characters and the creation of some its most enduring legends concerning their exploits on the trail. How this came to pass had its origins in one man who began life as a simple Ontario farm boy but who fate would lead to a fascinating career as the discoverer of some of the Rockies' foremost beauty spots and the repository of knowledge about their farthest reaches and hidden recesses. This was Tom Wilson.

Thomas Edmonds Wilson was born on August 21, 1859 at Bondhead, a small town north of Toronto, but at a young age moved with his Irish-Canadian parents to a farm at Holly, near Barrie, Ontario. Living the normal life of a country boy, he attended the local public school and then completed his formal education at Barrie Grammar School in 1875. While his father wished him to attend Guelph Agricultural College and his mother hoped he would train for the ministry, Tom would hear of neither. Nurtured on romantic tales of the North West, he instead fell victim to the spirit of wanderlust so common to the youth of his time. A rangy lad of sixteen already nearing his full height of five foot nine inches, he set out in search of adventure, his travels taking him to Detroit, Chicago and as far west as Sioux City, Iowa over the next three years. On returning home, he helped fill the time by vounteering for a militia unit, the Ontario Field Battery, in October, 1878 and served until March, 1879. While not apparent at the time, his service was a good decision, for when he heard the six-year-old North West Mounted Police (NWMP) force was recruiting for their undermanned western posts, he would possess exactly the background they were looking for. Upon applying for service at Barrie on July 19, 1880, he was immediately engaged at the rank of constable as Regimental Number 506.

Tom was assigned to Fort Walsh in the Cypress Hills of present-day southwestern Saskatchewan, one of fifty-two recruits sent to the storied post in 1880. After an arduous journey, which included a steamer voyage across Lake Superior, a train trip from Duluth, Minnesota to Bismarck, North Dakota, a river boat voyage up the Missouri to Coalbanks and a horseback ride to Fort Walsh, he began his service on September 22, 1880. Life at Walsh mainly revolved around surveillance of a large concentration of Indians who, due to their destitute condition, had gathered in the hope of receiving relief from the force. The focal point of police attention was the self-exiled Sioux chief Sitting Bull and his followers who had fled to Canada after Little Big Horn and were still vacillating about returning to the United States, despite several years of efforts to convince them to do so. As Tom recalled it, the high point of his police career came when he accompanied a detachment to meet with the stubborn Sioux and spent some time in conversation with "the wily chief."[1] However, apart from this brief interlude, the life of a police constable was rather routine, and boredom soon set in. According to Tom, it was at this point, early in 1881, that word reached Fort Walsh that the CPR was hiring men at Fort Benton, Montana to assist in surveying a route through the mountains. Although he claimed to have purchased his discharge in order to join them, his official record shows that he was invalided from the force on May 16, 1881 suffering from pleurisy.

In any case, he headed for Fort Benton and, after a short time working with a cattle outfit, was hired on as a packer by P. K. Hyndman, chief engineer for Major A. B. Rogers, engineer-in-charge of the Mountain Section for the CPR. An American with a stellar reputation as a locating engineer on U. S. lines, Rogers had been hired by the CPR Syndicate with the objective of having him find a route through the southern Rockies and on through the rugged Selkirks. He had not only been promised a five thousand dollar reward for discovering a suitable Selkirks pass but, more importantly for the posterity-conscious major, the honour of having his name attached to it. When Tom joined the survey, Rogers was already engaged in this task, and the survey outfit departed for Old Bow Fort, the former fur trade post at the junction of Old Fort Creek and the Bow (on today's Stoney Indian Reserve) and the proposed survey headquarters and rendezvous site. Most of the supplies and equipment were freighted by the ox teams of the I. G. Baker Company of Fort Benton, while the packers rode their own saddle horses and herded the eighty pack animals that would be used in the mountains after the freight wagons could go no further. The pack horses were mostly Indian-bred stock, commonly known as "cayuses," and were chosen in preference to the mules used in American railroad building because of their larger hooves, a consideration in negotiating the treacherous muskegs known to exist in the Canadian mountain valleys. Although Tom already possessed a considerable knowledge of horses, he had to quickly acquaint himself with the unpredictability and quirks of this unfamiliar breed at the same time as he mastered the tools of the packer's trade.

Foremost among these was the pack saddle, or "sawbuck," constructed of two pieces of strong wood about fifteen inches long, five to seven inches wide and about an inch deep. These pieces of wood, which were rounded or slightly contoured to fit the horse's back, were connected at each end by the arms of a wooden "X," the upper arms of which were considerably smaller than the lower.

From these arms hung the sling ropes, which were tied using basket hitches to support the packs. The packs were of several varieties, the two most popular being sturdy wooden boxes used for smaller and more fragile items and large cowhide bags, or "alforjas," which could carry goods of any size and shape. Each pack was loaded to weigh about 100 pounds, as 200 pounds, with one pack balanced on either side of the saddle, was the maximum burden for most horses. Over the top went the pack mantle, or cover, a large piece of heavy canvas measuring about six by eight feet. With everything in place the cinch and lash rope, which was a half inch thick and about fifteen feet long with an eye spliced into one end, was brought into play. Using an intricate series of loops and twists, the lash rope was tied over the load into either the diamond, double diamond, three-quarter diamond or squaw hitch to secure it tightly to the saddle and the horse. These knots had to be practiced religiously as they were the key to the whole packing operation and their secrets were jealously guarded by the initiated. Their importance was perhaps best described some twenty years later by A. O. Wheeler, the famous surveyor of the Rockies and Selkirks, in his book *The Selkirk Range*: "The diamond hitch, or rather series of hitches the shape of a diamond, is the combination of rope twists by which a load is kept in positon on the back of a pack animal. I am not aware who invented it — he should have been knighted."[2]

The trek to the foot of the mountains proved to be an adventure in itself. Because the outfit left towards the middle of June, high water time in mountain-born streams, it had to contend with several hair-raising fordings. Added to the excitement was a stampede of the stock at the NWMP post of Fort Calgary when some of the Montana packers became a little too boisterous in their celebration of the Fourth of July. Despite these delays, the time passed quickly and the survey party soon found itself at the end of the regular wagon road at the Stoney Indian mission settlement of Morley on the Bow River at the foot of the mountains. Here they were greeted by pioneer Methodist missionary Reverend John McDougall, who agreed to guide them on to Old Bow Fort where the Baker company's freight contract ended. However, Hyndman had decided that the headquarters should be established as close to the mountains as possible, and McDougall's brother was hired to freight the remainder of the way to the mouth of the Kananaskis River. Near a location called "Osade" (the forks) by the Stoney, a commissariat was established and named Padmore after F. W. "Paddy" Padmore, the assistant commissary, who Tom recalled "was sincerely liked by all the men." While they awaited Major Rogers, Tom and the other packers began sorting the supplies and equipment and alloting them to the horse whose strength and temperament was thought to be the best suited to the individual load.

On July 15th Rogers finally arrived after an unsuccessful attempt to find the key pass through the Selkirks, having completed an exhausting ride from Spokane by way of Pend d'Oreille Pass, the Kootenay and Columbia rivers, the Brisco Range, the Cross River and finally down from Whiteman's Pass by way of the Spray River and Lakes. Tom's first sight of "Hell's Bells" Rogers was one that would forever remain engrained in his memory as "his voluminous sideburns waved like flags in a breeze; his piercing eyes seemed to look and see everything at once" and "every few moments a stream of tobacco juice erupted from between his sideburns."[3] Shunning any rest, he immediately split the party into separate gangs, each charged with the investigation of a different pass that could hold the key to accommodating the construction of a rail line over the backbone of the continent. Tom was assigned to the crew accompanying the irascible, profanity-spouting major himself and was soon herding his pack animals up the Bow Valley deep into the mountains on an old Indian trail. As he rode along, he made his first acquaintance with the topography which would soon become second nature to him — the towering peaks, the broad U-shaped glacially-scoured valleys and their smaller hanging tributaries, the verdant forests and flower-mantled meadows, the rushing blue snow-fed rivulets which joined to form bawling streams, and the gem-like lakes and tarns. But he had little time to enjoy the matchless scenery on this occasion as the major was bent on reaching the Great Divide as quickly as pos-

14

sible to await the arrival of his nephew, Al Rogers. To this young man he had given the difficult task of taking a pack train from the confluence of the Kicking Horse and Columbia rivers up the rugged and boulder-strewn channel of the former to the height of land, where it was believed to connect to the upper Bow River.

Meanwhile, Major Rogers had determined that he needed a personal attendant who he could trust to be at his beck and call to carry out orders without hesitation. As his perennial bad temper and abrupt manner had already become apparent to the men as they made their way up the Bow, there was no immediate takers when he asked for a volunteer. Finally, Tom stepped forward and agreed to take on the role, perhaps against his better judgement. But, if so, it was nevertheless to prove one of the most fateful decisions of his life, for it provided the basis upon which his knowledge of the mountains would be built. Travelling with the major as he made his way from camp to camp or explored possible new routes gave him the opportunity to gain an understanding of the geography that would never have otherwise been possible.

This education began immediately on reaching Kicking Horse (Wapta) Lake at the summit of the Divide and finding that Al Rogers had not yet arrived. Concerned about his nephew's welfare, Rogers took Tom and began searching along the north side of the river, feeling that he may have reached the rendezvous before them and continued eastward along the opposite bank. Reaching a fast flowing creek swollen with meltwater, Tom suggested that they postpone their crossing until morning when its crest would have subsided. Impatient as always, Rogers hurled oaths upon his companion's head and plunged directly into the swirling, bone-chilling water and was immediately swept from his mount. Luckily, Tom found a strong branch close at hand and was able to fish him out. The incident not only provided proof to the major of the wiseness of his choice in a travelling companion but also gave the creek its name. Whenever it ran high and dirty the men of the survey would jest, "Hello, the old man must be taking another bath," and before long it was known to all and sundry as Bath Creek.[4] The search for Al Rogers continued and two days later

15

Tom and another packer found him exhausted and close to starvation near the confluence of the Yoho and Kicking Horse.

For the remainder of the 1881 season, Tom accompanied Major Rogers to the various survey camps and packed in provisions and equipment from the commissary headquarters at Padmore. The work provided further valuable experience but was not without its hardships, as the packers lived on a lacklustre diet of sowbelly and beans and slept out covered only by a tarpaulin slung between pack saddles no matter what the weather. On one of these overnight stops he made camp close to the site of what would later become the town of Banff. His campsite was on the banks of a small creek and the area was referred to as "Aylmer Park" after Fred Aylmer, chief of one of the survey crews. The creek subsequently became known as Whiskey Creek because near the springs at its head an individual named Gosling manufactured a "snake bite cure" from potato peelings. In later years, Tom recalled "two drinks and the snake died if it bit you."[5]

Having heard of some trapping possibilities in the Little Snowy Mountains of Montana, Tom left the survey before the end of the season, scoffing at Major Rogers's prediction that he would be unable to resist returning. But, sure enough, by the following spring he was hearing the call of the Rockies and in May, 1882 reappeared at Fort Benton ready to sign on. Soon he was at work on the seemingly monotonous chore of hauling supplies from Padmore to the survey camps with fourteen to sixteen horse pack trains. But, as it turned out, the summer was to prove anything but uneventful. On the return trip from packing his second load of the season to the Divide, he camped at the usual spot at the mouth of the Pipestone River near the present-day hamlet of Lake Louise. While sitting around the campfire with a group of Stoney Indians also stopped there, the thunder of several large avalanches was heard. Tom enquired of an Indian known as Gold Seeker (Edwin Hunter) as to their source and was told they originated on a mountain above "the Lake of the Little Fishes." His interest aroused and the next day being wet and unsuitable for travel, Tom was able to convince Gold Seeker to guide him to the spot. After a steep climb through the forest, the pair emerged on the shore of the lake and, given the packer's usual penchant for rough language, Tom probably muttered something along the lines of "sonofabitch, that's beautiful." But, because of the importance and public profile this discovery was to take on and the number of times he had to repeat its story, Tom later developed a more palatable version:

As God is my judge, I never in all my explorations saw such a matchless scene. On the right and left forests that had never known the axe came down to the shores apparently growing out of the blue and green waters. The background, a mile and a half away, was divided into three tones of white, opal and brown where the glacier ceased and merged with the shining water. The sun, high in the noon hour, poured into the pool, which reflected the whole landscape that formed the horseshoe.[6]

Surmising that he was the first white man to lay eyes on this beautiful sheet of water, he named it Emerald Lake, due to its colouring caused by suspended glacial silt, and so it appeared on Dr. George M. Dawson's reconnaissance map published for the Geological Survey of Canada in 1886. Later it was changed to Lake Louise by Dawson and Sir Richard Temple during a visit to the site in 1884 in honour of Princess Louise Caroline Alberta, daughter of Queen Victoria and wife of the Marquis of Lorne, Governor-General of Canada. Although he did not protest the change, in later years Tom variously agreed and disagreed with the supposed origin of the name Louise. At times he acknowledged that it had indeed been Princess Louise who inspired the nomenclature while at others he insisted it was a daughter of Temple who deserved the credit.

A second exciting discovery followed close on the heels of the historic visit to Lake Louise. During one of his regular trips to the Divide, Tom left some of his extra horses at the bottom of the hill leading to the summit of Kicking Horse Pass and on going to retrieve them found they had wandered off. After being unable to locate them at a favourite feeding spot, he picked up their trail and followed it over the Natural Bridge on the Kicking Horse and through the thick forest to the north. Eventually it led to a small stream (Emerald River) which, when traced to its source, was found to emanate from a lake whose charms rivalled those of Lake Louise. This body of water eventually became known by the name originally applied to his earlier discovery — Emerald Lake.

Despite the interest of these two side trips, they in no way compared with what was to be Tom's most arduous journey in the 1882 season. Major Rogers had staked his faith almost entirely in the Kicking Horse Pass route for the line, all but ignoring other likely paths. One of these, Howse Pass at the head of the North Saskatchewan River, had been the traditional fur trade trail from Rocky Mountain House to the Columbia River country until 1811 when David Thompson discovered the henceforth more popular Athabasca Pass. Because of its historic importance and the reports of Walter Moberly, an earlier CPR surveyor who had investigated it, Rogers began to have second thoughts and decided that the Howse warranted investigation. With Tom accompanying him, he spent two days toiling through the interminable muskegs and burnt timber of the upper Bow Valley before concluding that the exploration would be a long and difficult one. Consequently, he excused himself on the pretext of the need for his immediate presence in the Selkirks, but convinced his companion to continue on foot with the offer of a fifty dollar bonus. The trip was to prove Tom's trial by fire and came near to being one he didn't survive.

Estimating the amount of food needed to complete the remainder of the journey, Tom agreed to a rendezvous at the confluence of the Blaeberry and Columbia rivers ten days hence and set off with only a light pack. It was not long before he realized he had seriously underestimated the difficulty of traversing the pass. Crawling over downed timber, swimming across swollen streams and frequently having to retrace his steps after following the wrong path, he found himself close to exhaustion by the time he reached the summit. Again, the descent of the western slope proved harder than anticipated due to heavy timber and undergrowth and two narrow canyons whose passage required some precarious rock climbing. Lost time stretched his scant rations to the limit contributing to his weakening condition, and it was not until thirteen days after taking leave of Rogers that he stumbled into his camp on the Columbia half-starved, bruised and battered.

Tom undoubtedly felt that no advantage other than the major's promised fifty dollar bonus would result from his labour, but, if so, he was mistaken. The trek brought him into contact with some of the country that hunters, climbers and tourists of future days would find among the most interesting in the Canadian Rockies — the upper Bow Valley, the Waputik Range, the Bear Creek (Mistaya) Valley, the forks of the North Saskatchewan and the Forbes and Lyell groups. His forte was a keen eye for detail and once over a piece of ground he never forgot its every nuance, possessing almost a photographic memory in this regard. The value of this gift would become apparent in the not too distant future.

After the completion of memorable 1882 season, Tom made for Calgary intending to continue southward and again winter in Montana, but his plans quickly changed. Probably because of his police experience, when he reached Calgary the CPR offered him the job of helping to deal with some unruly Blackfeet who were holding up the work of surveyor Charles Shaw near Medicine Hat. After helping to assuage the natives, he returned to Calgary and was immediately hired on as part of a crew surveying near Padmore on a timber lease belonging to Colonel James Walker, a former NWMP officer and manager of the famous Cochrane Ranch. When the timber limit was laid out in mid-winter, he decided to remain in the area and await the arrival of the CPR survey in June, boarding with the David McDougall family at Morley.

In June, 1883, Tom began his last season of work with the CPR survey. His unfavourable report on the Howse Pass route had had its effect, as Rogers was again focusing his attention exclusively on the Kicking Horse Pass. Advancement of the survey to near the mouth of the Kicking Horse required lengthy pack trips early in the season, but new distribution centres were soon set up close to his campsite of 1881 at Aylmer Park and about fifteen miles further west at Hillsdale. The high point of this season occurred with Tom's first real guiding activity when he was assigned to accompany Sandford Fleming, a one time engineer-in-chief of the railway, and Reverend George Grant, principal of Queen's University, over a part of the surveyed route. Fleming, who had been asked by CPR president George Stephen to ascertain the viability of Rogers's route through the pass that he had now discovered in the Selkirks, later published the story of their journey through the mountains as part of his book *England and Canada, A Summer Tour Between Old and New Westminster*. It provided a rare description of the daily problems faced by the CPR packers.

After travelling by wagon from Calgary to Hillsdale, the Fleming party met Wilson[7] on August 26th and discussed his instructions, which were to escort them to Rogers's camp at the mouth of the Kicking Horse. The following day the party took a short, toughening up excursion to the vicinity of Vermilion Pass, but the next morning they were underway in earnest with Tom in charge of the six packers and the pack string. Freight wagons were taken part of the way over the rough tote road before the load was shifted to the backs of the ten most trustworthy pack animals for the trek down the rugged Kicking Horse. During the course of the descent, Fleming noted the rapport between the packers and their charges, stating "there is always a wonderful link between the man and the horse, and the kinder the man the more gentle the quadruped." This somewhat suspect observation was followed by a classic understatement of the manner in which the packers, cultured gentlemen by no stretch of the imagination, addressed these "gentle quadrupeds:" "The names of our horses are Black, Coffee, Blue, Calgary, Coaly, Buck, Pig, Bones, Strawberry and Steamboat, and each creature knows perfectly the reproof or cheering cry addressed to him."[8] Although somewhat genteel in these descriptions, Fleming was nonetheless accurate in his observation about the link between the packer and the horse, born of shared trials and tribulations evident on this particular trip.

Notorious for its hazards to both man and beast, the so-called "Golden Stairs" trail along the Kicking Horse consisted for most of its length of a ledge high up on the canyon wall requiring nerves of steel to travel. Fleming found the experience almost intolerable:

To look down gives one an uncontrollable dizziness, to make the head swim and the view unsteady, even with men of tried nerve. . . . We are from 500 to 800 feet high on a path from ten to fifteen inches wide and at some points almost obliterated, with slopes above and below us so steep that a stone would roll into the torrent in the abyss below. There are no trees or branches or twigs which we can grip to aid us in our advance on that narrow precarious footing. . . .[9]

While these conditions were difficult for Fleming, the situation was far worse for the men who had to see to the horses' welfare as well as their own. Trouble occurred when in the course of ascending one particularly steep spot a horse slipped and somersaulted over the side of the hill. Fortunately, the animal's pack caught on a rock, halting the fall after a short distance but necessitating some back-breaking work for Tom and one of his assistants. The two scrambled down to the prostrate animal, and after laboriously unfastening his packs were able to get him to his feet and shoulder him back up the slope. Next, Calgary's footing gave way and he plunged over a fifty foot embankment, requiring a similar rescue operation, and disaster struck again when the pack train ran into a hornet's nest. These winged devils, the bane of many a packer's existencce, sent the horses in paroxysms of agony causing untold confusion and the abandonment of the regular trail. Eventually, though, persistence paid off and the gentlemen were delivered safely to Major Rogers's camp. Reflecting on the path, one that the packers were forced to travel regularly, Fleming concluded that "for my part I have no desire to retrace my steps by the path I have followed in the descent of the Kicking Horse Valley."[10]

When reminiscing about this trip in later years, Tom joked, "I never knew how hard a time we had until I read the book." But he did recall another occasion when one of his fellow packers had a much worse time of it on the same trail. As Tom told it, the packer was taking a string of eleven horses along the Golden Stairs 700 feet above the river after a few inches of wet snow had fallen. The horses' hooves quickly balled up and the bell-mare lost her footing, plunging to her death in the canyon below. Immediately the other horses panicked and within a few seconds seven more animals had followed her over the precipice, leaving three shaking horses and an ashen-faced packer "standing on the edge of nothing."[11]

Although Tom couldn't recall anything particularly extraordinary about the Fleming-Grant trip, it did provide him one of the most embarrassing moments of his life. Often when faced with crossing a swollen stream it was the packers' practice to cut trees and construct a makeshift bridge to prevent the wetting of the packs. At one particularly bad crossing after building such a bridge, Tom found that one of his animals had avoided the structure and had taken to the water. The animal had soon sunk to its knees in the mud and to stop from sinking further simply lay down on its side. Tom had to prepare himself to wade into the mire and attempt to heave the recalcitrant to its feet. As the day was warm and the mosquitoes and flies were taking advantage of the fine weather for an outing, his temper quickly got the better of him. He addressed his charge "in the language he was accustomed to hear" and armed himself with a stout club. To his amazement, the horse suddenly leapt to its feet and scrambled free of its muddy prison. Still fuming, Tom turned to extract himself and glancing up was surprised to see Reverend Grant standing on the makeshift bridge above him:

I guess I turned seven or eight shades redder than I had been before. I hadn't the sand even to apologize for my talk. But I felt kind of glad when he looked at me with a laugh and said: 'It seems to help sometimes, Tom.'[12]

So much for Fleming's "reproofs" and "cheering cries."

This important journey was one of Tom's last duties on the CPR survey. Early in November he accompanied Major Rogers from the Kicking Horse summit to the end of steel at Cascade Mountain by sleigh and then joined him riding the caboose of a work train as far as Calgary. There his employment ended. It had not only provided him with the opportunity to gain considerable knowledge of packing and guiding in the mountains, but also allowed him to gain an understanding of the country along the line's right-of-way. However, it was time to look elsewhere for a livelihood and he immediately began to put his knowledge to work. During the course of his travels, he had on several occasions found traces of minerals, and a bit of prospecting seemed like a possibly lucrative course of action. Accordingly, he first located at the base of Castle Mountain where the boom town of Silver City, fed by rumours of fabulous silver and copper deposits in the near-by mountains, was beginnng its shortlived existence. But this field proved too crowded for his liking and looking for better pros-epects further west he soon pushed on to Holt City (later renamed Laggan and eventually Lake Louise). After spending the remain-der of the winter there in a fruitless search for a paying proposi-tion, he went into partnership with fellow prospector Jim Wright in 1884.

Apparently, the first locale to be prospected was around the base of Mount Stephen, but attention was soon shifted to an area that had attracted Tom while packing for the CPR, the North Fork of the Wapta River. This Tom called "Yoho," meaning "its won-derful, " the word the Stoney used for the valley. A foot trail was blazed up it and it was investigated intensively, but without suc-cess. But the effort was not to prove a complete waste, as Tom gained his first glimpses of the striking Takakkaw, Laughing and Twin Falls to add to his repertoire of mountain beauty spots. Following this, the partners pushed on west and spent the month of August at a mineral claim on Quartz Creek, a tributary of the Columbia near Donald, although the weather proved too inclement to make any headway on mine work.

At the end of this fruitless season of prospecting, Tom returned to Silver City and turned his attention to more romantic pursuits. Over the winter he made the acqaintance of Minnie McDougall, a native of Owen Sound, Ontario, who ran a boarding house known as "The Miner's Home" with her brother Mose. Given the over-whelming majority of males in the town, 237 compared to just five women, Tom must have been persistent in his advances as before the snow left the ground he had become engaged to the striking young relative of the McDougall family of Morley. Part of that winter was also spent working at the sawmill on Colonel Walker's timber lease near Padmore that he had helped to suvey in 1882.

The spring of 1885 found Tom beginning one of the most eventful years of his life. In April he received a wire from Major Sam Steele, who had been in charge of the NWMP at the CPR construction camps, requesting that he join Steele's Scouts. This unit was being organized to take part in subduing the recent outbreak of Métis and Indian violence known as the second Riel Rebellion, and Steele felt that with his packing experience Tom would be an ideal candidate to assist with the transport of the mounted corps. Tom made for Calgary to answer the call, and most of his service was spent in pursuit of the renegade Cree chief Big Bear north of Fort Pitt in Saskatchewan. With the cessation of hostilities in early July, Tom returned to the mountains for a short time but soon departed for Edmonton where some unfinished business awaited him. On October 19, 1885 Tom Wilson and Minnie McDougall were married by Reverend John Howard with the bride's two cousins, D. M. McDougall and Clara Hardisty, acting as witnesses.

While already sufficiently interesting to make it noteworthy, 1885 still had one more historic event to offer. After their wedding the Wilsons were visiting their McDougall relatives at Morley when Tom received word of the special excursion trains heading for Craigellachie, B. C. for the driving of the CPR's last spike. Joining some of his fellow survey workers on one of these trains, he completed his first journey over the extent of the line on which he had laboured for three years. Undoubtedly his thoughts were much like those of Sandford Fleming, a fellow passenger, who recalled that "for my part I could not help contrasting the luxurious travelling which the railway afforded with the experience of my little party journeying westward through the mountains in 1883."[13] When Craigellache was reached on the cold, raw morning of November 7th, Tom disembarked with his fellow workers and watched Donald Smith, one of the partners in the CPR Syndicate, complete the line. In perhaps the most famous of all Canadian photographs, his stetsoned head is just barely visible peering over the crowd of onlookers as Smith drives home the historic spike.

As if symbolic of his own history with the construction of the CPR, the driving of the last spike marked the end of an era in Tom's life. Only five years had elapsed since he had come west, but they had proven exciting for a young man in search of adventure and equally profitable for the experience and knowledge gained. His bachelor state had allowed him to move freely without worry of responsibility during this formative period. However, from the end of 1885 onward the need to support a wife and soon a growing family demanded a more permanent and dependable mode of life. He and Minnie first returned to Silver City to run the boarding house for the winter of 1885-86, but even though Tom's income was supplemented by some blacksmithing they could not make a go of it when the town's population sunk to just twenty souls when word of a new mineral strike near Golden resulted in a general exodus. Consequently, they began searching for a homestead near their relatives at Morley and in the spring of 1886 found a suitable location to the northeast of the settlement. Here they built a log home, a stable and corrals and, after registering the subsequently famous powder horn brand, settled down with the intention of devoting themselves entirely to the raising of horses and cattle. But soon the memory of the mountain trails and news of developments along the line lured Tom back to the scene of his old exploits.

On returning to the mountains early in 1887, Tom must have been amazed at the transformation of his old camping grounds. A small community huddled around the railway siding at the foot of Cascade Mountain, known as Siding 29, had been the only habitation when left for Morley a year earlier, but now it was being rivalled, if not outstripped, by another settlement further to the south around the base of Tunnel Mountain. The reason for its presence lay in the hot springs on the lower slopes of Sulphur Mountain which Tom had first become aware of while with the CPR survey in 1882. During the intervening years, several squatters had located at the springs, each trying to develop them for commercial purposes, resulting in conflicting claims of ownership.

In September, 1885 William Pearce, Superintendent of Mines for the Dominion Government, visited the area and after interviewing the claimants returned to Ottawa and recommended that a crown reservation be established in order that the "sanitary advantages" of the springs be made available to the public. With visions of tourist spas on the order of those at Hot Springs, Arkansas and Baden, Germany, the government complied, setting aside a ten square mile reservation by Order-in-Council on November 25, 1885. During the same year a preliminary survey of the springs was carried out by P. R. A. Belanger of the Dominion Topographic Survey and in 1886 fellow surveyor George Stewart was instructed to lay out a townsite and roads on the north side of the river. The town was named Banff after the birthplace in Scotland of George Stephen, president of the CPR. Soon it became the headquarters for Canada's first national park after an 1887 Act of Parliament extended the reservation to 260 square miles and named it Rocky Mountains Park, with George Stewart placed in charge as the first superintendent.

Tom had been attracted to Banff by the possibilities it presented for employment for one with his skills and knowledge of the mountains. Van Horne's aforementioned policy of "capitalizing the scenery," encapsulated in his famous pronouncement when speaking of developing traffic for the Mountain Section that "if we can't export the scenery, we'll import the tourists," had resulted in the decision to build a series of railway hotels at such key locations on the line as Fraser Canyon, Rogers Pass and Field. These were modest affairs, meant mainly as dining stops so that passenger trains didn't have to haul heavy dining cars over the steep grades, with the addition of a few guest rooms for those wishing to stop over. But word was already circulating that Van Horne intended on building a far grander hotel at Banff, one that would attract the world's touring elite to the glories that his line had opened up. Tom's relationship with the CPR was a sound one due to his work with Rogers and his completion of several special assignments carried out the year he left the survey. One was the blazing of a foot trail to Lake Louise and escorting Madames Ross and Brothers, wives of the chief engineer and assistant superintendent of construction for the Mountain Section and the first ladies to visit the beauty spot. Another was the blazing of a new foot trail to the lake to accommodate the visit of a group of scientists associated with an excursion of the British Association, which had just met in Toronto under the presidency of Sir Richard Temple.

It is also likely that Tom was acquainted with Van Horne himself, the general manager having frequently visited survey and construction camps along the line and both being present at the last spike ceremony. In any event, the story goes that Van Horne was searching for the best location for his new hotel when he was advised to seek Wilson's opinion. Tom said he knew exactly the right spot and introduced Van Horne to a site overlooking the confluence of the Spray and Bow with its grand vista down the Bow Valley to the Fairholme Range beyond. Here construction began on the Banff Springs Hotel, which Van Horne stated was to be the "Finest Hotel on the North American Continent," early in 1887.

Meanwhile, the railroad company had also decided that the attractions of Lake Louise warranted development and as a preliminary measure sent in a construction gang in the summer of 1887. As the man most familiar with the territory, Tom was hired to blaze a new and larger trail so that a boat could be taken along. The construction gang erected a rough log shelter, a forerunner of the Chateau Lake Louise, and the boat was the first to be used on the lake. Both were milestones for the CPR, but for Tom there was an even more important event later in the year. Van Horne's policy had resulted in the production fo the CPR's first piece of tourist promotional literature, *The Canadian Pacific, The New Highway to the East Across the Mountains, Prairies & Rivers of Canada*, which invited the English traveller to enjoy the scenery and promised that "if you are a sportsman, you will meet with unlimited opportunities and endless variety, and no one shall deny you your right to hunt or fish at your sweet will." In September, an English party appeared at Banff anxious to take up the company on its offer. The obvious choice for someone to guide them was Tom, and his hiring marked the launching of his career in the guiding and outfitting business and the establishment of this henceforth celebrated profession at Banff.

His first task was to decide exactly where to take the Englishmen, H. W. Calverley and Arthur Brearley, so the the CPR's assurances of success might be fulfilled. Indeed, while working for the survey he had been struck by the lack of game in such seemingly ideal habitat. This he had attributed to overhunting by Indians in the Bow Valley, to the numeous forest fires created by construction activity and to the presence of the huge body of workers engaged in building the line. However, there was one region he was sure was the haunt of substantial populations of bighorn sheep and perhaps some bear, goat and deer as well — the headwaters of the North Saskatchewan River which he had visited during his crossing of Howse Pass in 1882. Therefore, when he departed from his homestead early in September with three saddle horses and two pack horses, he had made arrangements for his hunters to meet him en route at Laggan, several days closer to their destination than Banff.

Little is known of the details of the trip, except that the Englishmen wished to spend approximately a month in pursuit of big game of all varieties. It is probable that Tom guided them as far as the Kootenay Plains, a favourite Stoney hunting grounds on the upper reaches of the North Saskatchewan, and it is certain that the return was made via Howse Pass. Apparently this part of the journey proved no more enjoyable than Tom's previous passage, as the downed timber and steep canyons that had caused him so much grief in 1882 again brought progress to a virtual standstill. Finally the horses had to be abandoned because of the bad going and the three hiked the remaining distance down the Blaeberry to Moberly. Here, in a rather inauspicious ending to his first private guiding venture, Tom had to hire some axemen to return and free his animals from their timbered prison. Nevertheless, despite its setbacks this initial guiding and outfitting venture was to mark the beginning of a whole new career.

As was so often the case in a life where he seemed to be in the right place at the right time, the moment Tom chose to enter the guiding and oufitting field was one of great promise. Following the completion of the CPR, Prime Minister John A. Macdonald had set out to prepare western Canada for development in line with his "national policy" of supporting the Canadian economy. In order to exploit the riches of the west, an identification and mapping of its lands and resources was required, work to be carried out by such agencies as the Geological Survey of Canada and the Dominion Topographic Suvey. It is possible that Tom packed for some of the geological work carried out by Dr. George M. Dawson and other scientists in the Bow Valley in 1883-84 and it is certain that he performed the same task for Dominion Land Surveyors J. J. McArthur and W. S. Drewry in their chore of mapping the mountain landscape along the line from 1889 to 1893.

Under the direction of Surveyor-General Edouard Deville, the Dominion Topographic Survey had developed a new method of mapping mountain terrain based on the use of cameras that had to be taken to the summits of mountains of known altitude to establish stations for a variety of photographic views. Accordingly, the surveyors had to travel through rough mountain country where few, if any, trails existed to visit the large number of mountain peaks required to carry out their triangulation and phototopographic work. For example, in 1891 alone J. J. McArthur ascended forty-three peaks between 8,000 and 10,000 feet and travelled over 400 miles of wilderness terrain to accomplish this task. Of course, the work required the services of a packer to transport the equipment and supplies, to look out for the welfare of the survey party and sometimes even to assist in carrying the bulky twenty pound camera and plates and the fifteen pound transit to the summit of the chosen photographic station. Tom's familiarity with the Rockies and Selkirks made him ideally qualified for such a task. Although he may have accompanied McArthur at some point between 1886 and 1888, it was not unitl 1889 that it is definite that he joined W. S. Drewry in his summer's surveys. The results of that season included the first ascents of Wind Mountain (Mount Lougheed) and Storm Mountain by Tom and Drewry as well as a visit to Marble Canyon on the Vermilion River, the first recorded by white men. He continued to accompany both Drewry and McArthur in their travels during the four succeeding seasons, taking part in the ascent of several other unclimbed peaks and visiting noteworthy points of interest.

Beginning in 1891, Tom also performed another important function for the Department of the Interior under whose auspices the survey was carried out. Previously it had been the practice of the surveyor to return the government pack horses and equipment to Calgary upon the completion of the season's work, something that caused several days delay in taking the field the following spring. Tom helped to overcome this problem by contracting to keep the equipment and winter the horses at his Morley homestead for the sum of ten dollars per head. This arrangement made it possible for the surveyor to wire ahead his expected time of arrival and proposed scene of operations so that everything would be in readiness on his appearance. Under these terms, Tom was keeping more than twenty head of the Department's livestock on his range by the winter of 1892-93.

Despite the value of the survey contracts in getting his business established, it was to be the support of the CPR that would remain the critical factor. The success of their international advertising campaign meant that an increasing flow of hunters, fishermen and sightseers began to appear at Banff in the period following the opening of the Banff Springs Hotel in 1888. Soon the CPR and the Dominion Government began cooperating in the construction of roads and bridle paths in the town's vicinity to accommodate the less adventurous of these, and the CPR Transfer Company was created to provide livery services in the form of carriages and saddle horses. But the principals of this company, Colonel James Walker and Major John Stewart, were not interested in providing horses and equipment to the visitors wishing to probe the mountain trails away from the main line. Thus when W. L. Mathews, the hotel's manager, was approached by guests seeking information on longer trips he put them in touch with Tom, and before long he was granted the privilege of advertising his services as "Guide to the CPR."

A side benefit of these early tourist trips, particularly the big game hunting variety, was the number of hides and heads procured in the course of huntng for food and trophies. Shortly after 1890, a Banff acquaintance, William Fear, suggested that they go into business selling these articles along with furs that could be gathered in winter trapping. Tom liked the idea and formed a partnership with Fear and his brother George, both of whom had been original inhabitants of Siding 29. Their store became known as Wilson and Fear and occupied a strategic location right in the heart of the developing tourist district on Banff Avenue. However, within a few years the growing demands of his guiding and outfitting required all Tom's time and he was not able to hold up his end of the bargain. The business was dissolved and the Fear brothers turned part of their store into a curio shop which, with the later addition of a photographic department, became a well-known fixture in Banff for many years.

As it became apparent that the tourism side of guiding and outfitting held the most potential, Tom took steps to solidify his position as first on the scene in Banff. To properly outfit parties generated by his association with the CPR, a local headquarters was required for the tourist season. Early in the 1890s he was able to secure the lease on a piece of property near the corner of Banff Avenue and Buffalo Street (Lot 2, Block B, 302 Buffalo Street) on which there was a substantial corral. Some of the horses raised on the Morley homestead were brought to this location to be used as saddle horses and to these were added a number of cayuses bought from the Stoney for pack animals. Henceforth, his corral would be a favourite rendezvous for residents and tourists alike to gather and watch the activities which accompanied the preparation and departure of a pack outfit. These were perhaps best described by Walter Wilcox, one of his foremost early clients:

During the summer season 'Wilson's' is frequently the scene of no little excitement when some party is getting ready to leave. Then you may see ten or fifteen wicked-eyed ponies, some in a corral and the rest tied to trees ready for packing. If the horses are making their first trip of the season there will be considerable bucking and kicking before all is ready. Several men are seen bustling about, sorting and weighing the packs, and making order out of the pile of blankets, tents and bags of flour or bacon. The cayuses are saddled and cinched up one by one with many a protesting bite and kick. The celebrated 'diamond hitch' is used in fastening the packs, and the struggling men look picturesque in their old clothes and sombreros as they tighten the ropes, bravely on the gentle horses, but rather gingerly when it comes to a bucking bronco.

A crowd of the businessmen of Banff, who usually take about 365 holidays every year, stands around to offer advice and watch the sport. Then the picturesque train of horses with their wild looking drivers files out through the village streets under a fusillade of snap-shot cameras and the wondering gazes of new arrivals from the East.[14]

The establishment of this outfitting headquarters was followed in 1893 by the decison to move his wife and growing family of four children from Morley to Banff, joining the approximately thirty families and 450 residents already present. Their first home was a small log house on Banff Avenue near the town's school, but this was quickly exchanged for a more spacious abode built adjoining his corrals. It would soon become the gathering place for travellers from around the world anxious to learn about and experience the mountains, and the welcome and hospitality received there would earn it a reputation as a home "where the latch string hung on the outside."

Tom's future partner, Bob Campbell, would later state that "the history of Banff may be said to have begun with the arrival of Tom Wilson."[15] While this may be somewhat of an exaggeration, there is no doubt that his decision was to play a major role in the subsequent events that would shape its future and gain it its reputation. Already an old hand in terms of his knowledge and understanding of the moutain wilderness, in 1893 he stood ready to introduce the world to the glories of the Canadian Rockies.

Chapter II
Men for the Outfit

*T*he soundness of Wilson's decision to stake his future on Banff and the trail business began to pay immediate dividends as the 1893 season proved to be his busiest to date. Particularly noteworthy was a one month outing taken that fall with Robert L. Barrett, a Chicago paper manufacturer and businessman. Returning in late August from a three week pleasure trip with with CPR Land Commissioner L. A. Hamilton, Tom received word from W. L. Mathews that Barrett was enquiring at the Banff Springs about a new type of trip, one where he could climb a difficult mountain strictly for sport. His curiosity aroused, Tom met the would-be alpinist at the hotel and upon Barrett's query about a suitable objective recommended Mount Assiniboine, the highest known peak south of the railroad. He had learned about the mountain from Dr. Dawson, who had provided its name, and himself had glimpsed it wedge-like 11,870 foot summit in 1889 while working on the topographic survey with Drewry in the Simpson Pass area. Barrett eagerly concurred and arrangements were made to leave early in September.

Acting in the capacity of guide, with George Fear assisting as cook, Tom led the pack train out of Banff and up Healy Creek as far as Simpson Pass on old Indian trails. Once over the pass, the party descended into the valley of the Simpson River and followed it to a point where a south branch joined in. Here no trails existed and the best route to follow was not immediately evident. After locating a good camping spot and resting for the better part of a day, Tom and Barrett struggled up a heavily timbered ridge to get their bearings. They were rewarded with their first close-up view of the "Matterhorn of the Rockies," a sight which would remain indelibly impressed on the memories of both men. As late as 1924, Barrett was still remarking in a letter to Tom written from his camp at the base of the second highest peak in the Himalayas that "I don't think even old K2, the 28,000, looked to me as high and imposing, and as terrible as old Assiniboine when you and I finally won through to where we could have a good look at him."[1] The next day Barrett again mounted the ridge and discovered what appeared to be a suitable pass into an adjacent valley, requiring Tom to do some back-breaking axe work to the top of what would be named Ferro Pass and then down into the valley of the Mitchell River. From there it proved a fairly simple matter to ascend the river to its headwaters in the picturesque lakes at Assiniboine's foot. Unfortunately, due to the lateness of the season, Barrett was to be denied an attempt on the giant, and after a short stay in its environs they retreated by way of the Simpson River and Vermilion Pass, visiting Marble Canyon en route.

While Barrett was the first mountaineer to be guided by Tom, he was not the earliest of that ilk whose acquaintance he had made. Before his departure with Barrett, the outfitter had been approached by two young travellers with a similar interest. They were Samuel E. S. Allen and his classmate at Yale University Walter D. Wilcox, who, particularly in the case of the latter, were destined to play a major role in his future.

Wilcox, a native of Chicago, attended Andover Academy before enrolling in the class of 1893 at Yale, and later he attended Columbia University as well. As a young man he had taken a world tour which included a stop in Cuba, where he would later establish a large mahogany plantation, and in several countries with mountainous terrain. There he had performed some minor climbs, piquing his interest in the sport to the extent that he made an ascent of Oregon's Mount Hood in 1890. In 1891 while returning from a trip to Alaska he visited Banff and Lake Louise and resolved to return at a later date and test his mettle on some of the area's challenging peaks.

Allen was born in Philadelphia and after his early education there became a member of the class of 1894 at Yale, going on to

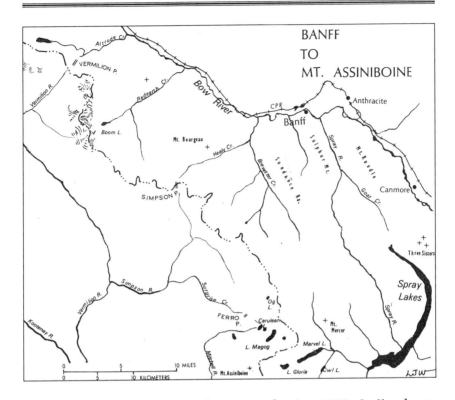

BANFF
TO
MT. ASSINIBOINE

receive a Master's Degree at the same school in 1897. Sadly, shortly afterwards he would become a victim of dementia and would spend the rest of life confined to a mental institution, cutting short a promising career. His first visit to the Rockies and Selkirks was also in 1891 when he attempted some minor climbs, including the Devil's Thumb near Lake Louise. Equally impressed, he too vowed to return but first turned his attention to the Alps, where he ascended the Matterhorn in 1892.

Sometime after their 1891 trips, Wilcox and Allen met at Yale and, discussing their mutual plans to climb in Canada, agreed to combine forces. Allen was the first to disembark at Banff early in the summer of 1893 and while awaiting his companion's arrival climbed Mount Rundle and viewed Mount Assiniboine. Wilcox appeared at about the same moment, as did news of the burning down of the rough lodge at Lake Louise, necessitating the acquiring of camping equipment and "outfit from Mr. T. E. Wilson of Banff." The two then proceeded to Lake Louise where Willoughby Astley, the manager of the new chalet the CPR had under construction, provided them with a horse and a Stoney guide, Enoch Wildman. Wildman quickly concluded that the temperatures at high altitudes were not to his liking and returned to Lake Louise, but Wilcox and Allen remained in the field unsuccessfully attempting the first ascents of Mounts Temple and Victoria. Undeterred, they vowed to return at a later time and attempt the ascents anew when they were better prepared and equipped.

Although it was not immediately apparent, the appearance of sportsmen eager to hunt and fish and mountaineers like Barrett, Wilcox and Allen marked the inauguration of the last great period of Canadian Rockies exploration and discovery — the age of the tourist-explorer. Following on the heels of the fur traders, early travellers and missionaries, railroad builders and government surveyors, this group was to make known over the next three decades most of the remaining secrets of the Canadian Cordillera's geography. The Alps of Europe, the hills of Skye and the Appalachians and Rockies of the continental United States were growing stale for the European, British and American climbing fraternities, who thrived on first ascents and new explorations. The impetus was provided by the CPR's international advertising campaign and by published reports of pioneer mountaineers such as William Spotswood Green, who had begun climbing in the Selkirks in 1888. Anticipation of future mountaineering and exploration was attested to by Wilcox's report upon stopping at the CPR's Glacier House hotel in 1891 that he had found a group of enthusiasts "who were accustomed to gather every evening around a blazing fire and read selections from Green's *Among the Selkirk Glaciers* just as our forefathers were wont to read a daily chapter from the Bible."[2]

In the circumstances, Wilson stood on the verge of a potentially bright future where both his services and knowledge were to be in great demand. But with the increasing number of those coming to experience the Rockies, it was not an opportunity that he could grasp solely on his own. On some occasions he had already relied on Banff acquaintances to provide assistance, such as George Fear's acting as cook on the trip to Assiniboine in 1893. But due to the shortness of the season, full-time, trustworthy and competent men who could take out parties on their own were needed if his venture was to become a paying proposition. One possible source of help was local Stoney Indians who had a good knowledge of the Bow Valley region and an ability with horses. But possibly because they were not always dependable, as illustrated by Wilcox's and Allen's experience with Enoch Wildman, Tom chose not to use them. Instead, he turned to finding capable individuals from among the veritable flood of immigrants who were beginning to flow into western Canada from the British Isles and augmented them with men from the steady stream of eastern Canadians and Americans arriving in search of better prospects and a fresh start. Many of these early arrivals in the west were of an adventurous mien and it is not surprising that some eventually gravitated to the rough-and-ready atmosphere of pioneer Banff. Mainly from rural backgrounds, they possessed exactly the right mixture of toughness, independence and sense-of-humour necessary for survival during long periods out on the trail. They also quickly picked up the skills required to handle their specific roles in the efficient team that comprised the crew of a pack outfit.

The primary position in this team was the guide. While on the trail he was charged with several responsibilities, including the well-being of the clients, or "dudes," and the other members of the crew as well as the care of the animals and equipment. In addition, he was ultimately reponsible for guiding the party safely to its proposed destination and back again. Required attributes were a well-developed sense of direction and ability at route finding, leadership and good judgement and, above all, skill in the handling of horses. An ability at route finding was essential because many early parties wished to go where no formal trails existed and in such circumstances the guide had to make numerous decisions about course on which the whole success of the expedition depended. Leadership and good judgement were needed in order for the party to avoid the many serious situations which could befall an outfit while travelling in such rugged conditions or in extracting it from any difficulties, or "jackpots," it did get into. Death by drowning, starvation or any number of other mishaps was a constant possibility and it took a strong personality to inspire the necessary confidence in other members of the crew when the going got tough. Finally, ability with horses was crucial since the welfare of the party could be directly correlated with the state of the livestock on which it depended. The guide had to know the quirks of each animal to enable him to handle it properly in a given situation; he had to know each one's individual capabilities, its preferences for packing or riding and how to rate it to achieve maximum performance during a typical day's march of five or six hours (about twelve miles); he had to know how to pack each one to prevent the dreaded saddle sores that could make a valuable animal useless when most needed; and he had to know what was suitable pasturage for their needs when picking a camping spot for the night. In short, he had to know each horse as an individual personality and respond to its needs.

Assisting the guide and acting under his instructions was the packer, sometimes also referred to as the horse wrangler, whose desired skills were, to a lesser degree, the same as those required of his boss. The packer's life revolved around the performance of the thousand-and-one chores which were essential to a successful pack trip. Up at the crack-of-dawn, he was out to round up the horses and bring them to the campsite where they were saddled and packed, usually with the guide's help, as the camp was dismantled. When the outfit pulled out for the day's ride, he took a position in the middle or more often at the rear of the string, herding along stragglers, gathering up strays and "eating dust" all day. Usually the only respite from this routine occurred when a dude got into difficulty or when the guide called him forward to assist in chopping out deadfall or clearing a new trail. After the day's march when the guide had selected the camping spot, the packer assisted in unpacking the horses, cutting teepee poles if none were available, setting up the teepee and/or wall tents, chopping a sufficient supply of fire wood for the night and preparing mattresses from freshly trimmed spruce boughs. After the evening meal, the horses had to be taken to the night grazing area, where they were frequently picketed or hobbled, and a smudge had to be lit to keep off the flies. Finally, it was his responsibility to see to it that all the packs and other pieces of equipment were properly covered to prevent wetting from any overnight rain or snow.

Last, but by no means least, in the ranks of the crew was the cook, whose abilities were, of course, slightly different than those of the rest of the men. Anyone could cook if he had to, but the mark of the true trail cook was his success in producing a light and toothsome bannock — a bread substitute made from flour, salt, baking powder and water and baked to a golden brown in the campfire with the aid of a metal reflector. In addition to whipping up a batch of bannock dough every two or three days, the cook also had a busy daily routine. Up with the guide and packer at dawn to start the fire, he had to have breakfast ready by the time the dudes rose and the horses were brought in. Lunch also had to be prepared in advance before quickly washing up and packing the cook boxes. With the exception of the brief lunch break, when a pot of tea or coffee had to be brewed, he could ride along in comparative peacefulness until camp was made. Then his real work for the day began. The evening meal was the heartiest and most important of the day and it had to be ready by the time the rest of the men had finished their chores. Even after cleaning up the dishes from this meal his job was not complete as he had to prepare the rudiments of the next morning's breakfast before joining the evening parley around the campfire.

While these were the usual positions an outfitter had to fill in organizing a trip for a party of two or three, there were many permutations and combinations possible depending on the size of the party, the number of horses required, the men available to send out and the client's wishes. If the party was composed of a single client, as sometimes happened, only one capable man would be required to perform the duties of all three positions. On the other hand, if there were a large number of dudes it would require the assignment of two or three packers and, on rare occasions, two cooks. However, to prevent any disagreements and facilitate decision-making, there was always only one guide.

The individual who carries the distinction of being the first guide hired on by Wilson was a young Irish immigrant named James Tabuteau. His first recorded expedition came in 1895 when he was given the unenviable task of guiding Colonel Robert O'Hara, one of the earliest tourist-explorers in the Canadian Rockies, to the lake which would bear his name. O'Hara was a retired British army officer who paid his first visit to the Rockies at the age of fifty-two in 1887. During a conversation with J. J. McArthur he learned of the lake, which the surveyor had seen from a peak while working in the region of the Ottertail Valley. The colonel successfully reached the lake that year and visited it again in both 1889 and 1894, using a trail which he had discovered leading up Cataract Brook. At the completion of the 1894 trip, he appeared at the recently completed new chalet at Lake Louise where he evidently proved to be a somewhat irascible guest. Wilcox, who was there at the time, later reported with somewhat unconcealed glee that the other patrons were able to have the last laugh at the expense of the reclusive and often ill-tempered O'Hara. On one of his jaunts in the neighbourhood of the chalet he was forced to cross Louise Creek on two slender poles which had been placed there as a makeshift bridge. Although the unfortunate hiker had armed himself with a stick in each hand so as to be sure not to lose his balance, lose it he did and after a plunge in the ice-cold water came into the chalet "all dripping and swearing mad."[3]

On returning to the mountains in 1895, O'Hara had two objectives in mind — to reach Simpson Pass from Vermilion Pass by way of Twin Lakes, and to make yet another visit to Lake O'Hara. Because of a difficult time the previous year when he had been led astray by an inexperienced guide, he approached Wilson to hire better men for his present expeditions. Tom provided two and with them the first objective of reaching Simpson Pass was achieved, but when he attempted to engage them for his second trip they refused because of the strict military manner with which he had insisted his camps be run. Although he had been planning to use Tabuteau with another party, Tom turned to him to guide the tempestuous colonel to his lake, and he only agreed to go on the promise of extra pay for putting up with the expected trouble.

Sure enough, it quickly became apparent as Jim led the colonel up Cataract Brook that their personalities were not going to mesh. The deadfall on the trail demanded some strenuous chopping and after much cussing on his guide's part, O'Hara was moved to comment, "Tabuteau, you swear entirely too much." Jim wryly enquired what he suggested be done about it. The colonel retorted, "When you feel the urge coming on, stop and think once, then think twice, then think a third time and by then the urge will have passed." Seemingly taking the suggestion to heart, Jim did much better until the two reached the lake and made camp. After setting up the tent and lighting a campfire, a strong breeze came up, fanning the flames and sending a shower of sparks flying. Suddenly Jim leapt to his feet with a perplexed look on his face and was about to let loose an exclamation when the colonel, sitting with his back to the tent, stopped him with, "Tabuteau, remember what I told you." Jim stared at him for a moment, pulled himself together and slowly repeated, " Tabuteau, think once . . . Tabuteau think twice . . . Tabuteau think thrice." Then, unable to contain himself any longer and making a wild dash for the water bucket, he blurted out, "Colonel, your goddam tent's on fire!"

The fire was easily extinguished, but not so the colonel's temper, and most of the remainder of their stay in the lake's vicinity passed in uneasy silence. On returning to Banff, O'Hara sought out Tom and delivered what sounded like an ultimatum: "I want that man Tabuteau dismissed — he swears too much and isn't a very good guide." The outfitter was only too aware of the colonel's bluster by this time and paid no attention. But he was somewhat bemused eight months later when he received a letter from O'Hara containing only one short sentence: "Wilson, I've thought the matter over — don't dismiss Tabuteau."[4]

While the O'Hara trip was one of the more challenging expeditions Tabuteau guided, his Irish temperament and thick skin made him invaluable for difficult parties and he was given several other tough assignments. However, he soon decided to leave the trail life to join the NWMP and began a successful career that led to the position of chief of police in New Westminster, B. C. Fortunately, Tom was able to hire his brother Fred a short time later and "Tabby," as he became known to his friends, more than adequately filled Jim's shoes, becoming one of the legendary trail men of the area. Described by a close acquaintance as "wild as a hawk but the kind of man who would stick with you through any kind of trouble," he was noted for a variety of abilities. One of these was an unfailing talent for being able to sing "Show Me The Way To Go Home" backwards when "well-lubricated."[5]

During the O'Hara expedition of 1895, two of Tom's other top trailhands were engaged in a major excursion to Mount Assiniboine. The two, Bill Peyto and Ralph Edwards, were to achieve reputations in the guiding business second only to Wilson himself, especially Peyto who was to become one of the most colourful characters ever to set foot in the Canadian Rockies.

Ebenezer William "Bill" Peyto was born in the village of Welling, Kent, now part of Greater London, in 1869, the third son in a family of nine children. As his father Augustus was a farm bailiff, he spent most of his youth in the country before going on to attend Foster's Endowed Church of England School. Possessed of a wandering spirit, he left England for Canada at age eighteen and landed in Halifax in late February, 1887. From there he set out for the west on the newly completed CPR line and within a month was at work for the company clearing a snowslide in the Kicking Horse Valley. He settled at Moberly, B.C., alternately working for the CPR and prospecting, developing a lifelong interest in and knowledge of geology and paleontology, before moving on to the Cochrane area about 1890. There he homesteaded land in the Montreal Valley west of the town, but before long began to prospect the Bow Valley into the mountains. In doing so, he reacquainted himself with Tom Wilson, whom he had met at Moberly in 1887, and soon had hired on as an apprentice guide with him. Immediately he was favourably impressing the dudes he was assigned to take out, as he did Wilcox who accompanied him on several trips:

I soon grew to admire Peyto. . . . He was efficient, daring, highly imaginative, an excellent man with the horses and a good friend. He spoke in the low, quiet voice of the true westerner, but even so he spoke rarely. His forte was doing things, not talking about them.[6]

It was not only Bill's abilities which impressed Wilcox, as his appearance on the trail was something he found equally interesting and worthy of note:

Peyto assumes a wild and picturesque though somewhat tattered attire. A sombrero, with a rakish tilt to one side, a blue shirt set off by a white kerchief (which may have served civilisation for a napkin), and a buckskin coat with fringed border, add to his cowboy appearance. A heavy belt containing a row of cartridges, hunting knife and six-shooter, as well as the restless activity of his wicked blue eyes, give him an air of bravado. He usually wears two pairs of trousers, one over the other, the outer pair about six months older. This was shown by their dilapidated and faded state, hanging, after a week of rough work in burnt timber, in a tattered fringe knee-high. Every once in a while Peyto would give one or two nervous yanks at the fringe and tear off the longer pieces, so that his outer trousers disappeared day by day from below upwards. Part of this was affectation, to impress the tenderfoot, or the "dude" as he calls everyone who wears a collar.[7]

Peyto's wild appearance was matched by somewhat unusual behaviour, and he soon became known for many of his escapades. One of these occurred when he live-trapped a lynx near one of his prospecting cabins on Sunshine Creek, knocked it out with a dose of chloroform, tied it up securely and packed it in to Banff to a bar where some miners he was known to dislike were wont to have a drink after the day's shift. Nonchalantly walking in, he bellied up to the bar, only to have the bartender ask him what it was he was carrying on his back. Turning so he could see, the barkeep exclaimed "Holy C. . . . boys, he's got a polecat on his back and its still breathing!" The bar emptied in a heartbeat and after finishing his drink Bill proceeded to the Banff Zoo with his prize, where it became a popular attraction for many years.

Another incident, which illustrated his rather bizarre idea of justice, happened when an acquaintance accompanied him to one of his mining cabins in the Simpson Pass region. On reaching the cabin the man was about to enter when Bill told him to wait and began throwing stones in the door. The loud "snap" of a bear trap being sprung soon issued from within and when questioned about it by the amazed guest, Bill told him he suspected that a certain trapper from Banff was stealing his grub. Pointing out that the intruder could have died if caught in the trap, he was further amazed to hear Bill reply, "you're damned right he would have, then I would have known for sure it was him."[8]

Although perhaps not so colourful as was Peyto, Ralph Edwards played an equally important role in the early days of Wilson's business. In fact, although only in his early twenties, he was regarded as Tom's most reliable guide in the years around the mid-nineties and was given the responsibility for escorting many of his major parties. Born in 1869 at Ramsgate, Kent, Ralph received his formal education at the City of London School. Emigrating to Canada in 1888, he spent four years in the east before coming to Canmore to work in the mines. Two years underground proved to be enough and he eagerly accepted Tom's offer of a job in 1894, later relating in his book of reminiscences, *The Trail to the Charmed Land*, the motivation which led him to adopt the trail as a way of life:

Dowered at birth with the itching foot, it was but natural that I should grasp the earliest opportunity of entering the packing business, for, like the Athenians of old, I was ever desirous of seeing and hearing some new thing. Some of my detractors basely asserted that the real reason for my adoption of the life of a trail guide was a rooted objection to real work of any description and that riding around the hills on a horse was about all that I was ever likely to do. In refutation I rise to remark that any one who imagines that following a pack train, in all kinds of weather, over all kinds of country, with the attendant thousand and one jobs that seem to appear from nowhere in particular, does not provide some of the steadiest and most continuous work conceivable is making just about the biggest mistake of his life. But we who followed the lure of the mountain trail loved the life and would not willingly exchange it for any other.[9]

The party taken into Mount Assiniboine in 1895, with Edwards as guide and Peyto as packer, was the largest Wilson had outfitted to date, requiring nine horses, extensive equipment and supplies and two extra men to act as cook and second packer. The dudes included Robert Barrett, making his second journey in three years to Assiniboine, his friend J. Porter and Walter Wilcox, who joined at the last moment. He had spent the summer of 1894 with Sam Allen and three other Yale men in the vicinity of Lake Louise doing some of the pioneer exploratory work of that region. Astley had provided two Indian guides and two horses, but the guides promptly deserted, leaving the alpinists with the difficult task of managing the animals themselves. Despite struggling with loose packs, bogged down horses and lost trails, they had performed admirably and their season was crowned with several notable achievements. Among them were the first ascent of Mount Temple, the discoveries of Paradise and Prospector's valleys and the Valley of the Ten Peaks as well as the first recorded visits to Sentinel, Wastach, Wenkchemna and Opabin passes. Sadly, Wilcox and Allen came to a parting of the ways at the end of the season due to a misunderstanding over the data gathered for a map of the Lake Louise area. This led Wilcox to write Wilson to see if the outfitter could arrange for him to join Barrett and Porter on their trip before Allen could do likewise. Tom was successful in doing so and arrangements were made to leave on the sixth of July. Meanwhile, as they were preparing to depart, the trio of adventurers frequently visited at his home where he related "every detail of swinging stream and ford, of rockslide and lake and mountain pass" on the route into the great mountain.

An examination of this trip points out some of the problems

and situations that Wilson's men had to deal with on the trail. Peyto began by having to ferry the three dudes across the cold, swift-flowing Healy Creek one by one on the back of his horse, Chiniquay, as they had chosen to walk rather than ride, a common occurrence in the early days of tourist exploration. Immediately afterwards he had to take over responsibility for guiding the party when Edwards realized his axe was missing and backtracked along the trail to try locate it. The following day one of the horses became slightly lamed and the next day fell in a soft spot breaking its leg, forcing Bill to despatch it with his revolver and repack its load on the back of his own horse. Next, six to eight feet of snow was found covering the summit of Simpson Pass and the men had to go ahead of the horses and pack down a trail to enable them to get through. After encountering many similar setbacks, the party arrived at the base of Mount Assiniboine and a permanent camp was set up. Then, after a brief rest, Peyto began to retrace the trail to Banff to try discover what had become of Edwards, now long overdue. He reappeared a week later with a replacement horse and the missing guide, who had lost the trail and returned to Banff.

With everything in order, Peyto set out on foot with the now well-rested Wilcox and Barrett to attempt to find a way around Assiniboine to obtain a view of its hiterto unseen southern face. The venture, which according to Wilcox was "attended by considerable hardship," turned out to be a forty-six hour circuit of the mountain covering some fifty-one miles of the toughest country imaginable. Some areas had to be crossed spider-like as miles of downed timber required a passage often ten feet off the ground, while other burnt-over regions turned them "black as coal heavers." At one particularly steep spot where a sheer wall of rock five hundred feet high appeared to block their advance, Peyto went ahead over an old goat trail and forged a path across "a slope that appeared nearly vertical."[10] Before the weary and footsore hikers finally regained their camp, they stumbled on a camp on the Mitchell River occupied by none other than Sam Allen and Dr. Howard Smith, also outfitted by Wilson and with the same objective in mind. It appeared that the Rockies were already becoming a considerably crowded place.

After returning to their own camp and a short day's rest, the Barrett and Wilcox party began their return to Banff by way of Vermilion Pass, once again with Edwards in the lead as guide. Another strenuous journey ensued as the Vermilion River had to be crossed and recrossed, with the men frequently having to ferry the dudes over on the backs of their own horses or rescue endangered horses from the swirling water. Finally, on August 5th , they reached Banff after twenty-nine days of absence, a period which had seen Peyto constantly in action. The exact rate of pay that Wilson's men received at this time is not known, but since he charged two dollars for a man and his outfit per day, it was probably somewhat less than a dollar a day. Whatever the amount, Bill had earned every penny coming to him on this occasion.

Upon his return, Wilcox felt that enough of the season remained for a further outing and again approached Wilson for his advice. He recommended the area around the Waputik Range and the sources of the Bow and Mistaya Rivers, relating details of both his 1882 and 1887 trips. Because Wilcox had found Peyto "most efficient" on the Assiniboine trip, he requested Bill's services again, and the outfit, including a cook and five horses, set out from Banff on August 14th. As it pulled out of town ahead of him, Wilcox was moved to remark on the sight that a Peyto-led pack train presented:

Peyto, as packer, always rode in the saddle, for the dignity of the office never allows a packer to walk, and besides, from their physical elevation on a horse's back they can better discern the trail. A venerable Indian steed, long-legged and lean, but most useful in fording streams, was Peyto's saddle horse. The bell-mare followed next, led by a head-rope. The other horses followed in single file, and never allowed the sound of the bell to get out of hearing.[11]

In the course of the trip Bill was able to show his prowess as a fisherman and hunter, keeping the grub-pile well-stocked with

47

fish, one a twenty-three inch lake trout taken from Bow Lake, and small game. The ever plentiful spruce grouse, or "fool hen," was easy pickings for the sharp-eyed marksman, Wilcox relating that "many a time, when on the trail, I have seen him suddenly take his six-shooter and fire into a tall tree, whereupon a grouse would come tumbling down, with his neck severed, or his head knocked off by the bullet."[12] But the trip was also to provide a new skill for Bill's repertoire — mountain climbing. Notoriously fearless in the face of any danger on the trail, be it enraged grizzly bear or swollen mountain torrent, trailmen were usually skeptical about risking their necks in what most regarded as the utter foolishness of climbing mountains for sport. Bill was no exception, and spent the time his "gentlemen" were engaged in their alpine pursuits either hunting or prospecting for minerals. On this occasion, however, he allowed himself to be convinced, probably because Wilcox would have otherwise had to climb alone, and the two ascended a 10,000 foot peak to the north of the beautiful glacial lake that would later bear Peyto's name. Reaching the summit and viewing the panorama spread out at his feet, he grudgingly allowed that he could now understand "the mania which impels men to climb mountains."

With the unprecedented demand for outfits being made by Wilcox, O'Hara, Allen and several others in the summer of 1895, Wilson soon found himself in the position of being unable to supply enough men and horses for prospective parties. This could have proven serious, as an outfitter's reputation was usually established on the basis of the service provided to a party on their first trip. But the fact of the matter was that he held a virtual monopoly on the business in the Banff area, and the eagerness of mountaineers to bag first ascents was such that they would venture out under almost any conditions. Such was the case with a group of mountaineers from the Appalachian Mountain Club who were to play an important part in the future of his business. This club had been formed in Boston in 1876 for "the advancement of the interests of those who visit the mountains of New England and adjacent regions, whether for the purposes of scientific research or summer recreation." The moving force behind it and the editor of its publication *Appalachia* was Dr. Charles E. Fay, professor of modern languages and dean of the graduate school at Tuft's College in Massachusetts. By the mid-eighties, he had joined with others in the club who wished to see included in its activities an alpine section for members who wanted to ascend major peaks outside the Appalachians. The leading voice among them was Philip Stanley Abbot, a Harvard graduate and lawyer who had become general solicitor for the Milwaukee and Lake Winnebago Railroad Company and was acknowledged as one of the leading mountaineers in America.

When Abbot was giving consideration to areas which might warrant the attention of an alpine section, Fay was able to offer a suggestion. In 1890, while returning from a trip to California, he had visited the Selkirks, stopping for a day at Glacier House in Rogers Pass where he made a partial ascent of Mount Sir Donald. He was so impressed that he returned for a closer look in 1894, and on that occasion went on to Lake Louise where he met Wilcox and Allen returning from their successful first ascent of Mount Temple. The area seemed a natural for Abbot's designs and when the club's annual excursion was being planned for 1895 it was decided that Fay's suggestion of Lake Louise would be an appropriate choice. It would be the first time that a club outing had gone beyond the confines of the Appalachian mountain system.

The Appalachian Mountain Club was progressive in its membership, allowing women to join, and the majority of the twenty partaking of the 1895 excursion were ladies. Understandably, given their lack of experience, most of the group contented themselves with some of the easier scrambles in the vicinity of the chalet. But not so Fay and Abbot, who along with Charles S. Thompson, also a Harvard graduate and at this time a freight contracting agent with the Illinois Central Railroad, looked forward to indulging in more serious climbing. They were informed that the best way to accomplish this was by making arrangements with Wilson:

Our first step was to get hold of Wilson, the best guide and outfitter for that region, and to hold a council of war. Many plans were proposed but none hit our fancy. Finally, for about the tenth time since he joined us, Thompson brought forth his fixed idea. Mt. Hector . . . had never been climbed; better still it had been attempted without success; and it was high, because the Canadian surveyors, when they turned back, had already reached 10,400 feet. It further appeared that Wilson himself had been with that party; and he said he believed the peak could be climbed. He also told us of an enormous snowfield to the west of Hector on the main watershed, and stretching away to the north for fifty miles, which was absolutely unexplored.[13]

The only problem in successfully completing arrangements for this trip was Tom's shortage of men and horses. Nevertheless, the eagerness of Fay, Abbot and Thompson to have their mountain was such that they agreed to take on the trek from Laggan to the base of Hector on foot and without pack animals. Because there was no-one else to guide them, Tom had to take on the task himself and engaged as a porter "an admirably patient individual named Hiland who . . . carried an enormous and shapeless pack composed of tin things and all the other articles which the rest refused to touch."[14]

Apparently, the trio were somewhat dissatisfied with the guide service, probably due to the lack of time that Tom had to devote to it. Difficulties began when he insisted they attempt to reach the shores of Lower Bow (Hector) Lake to camp, a point well past what was in Abbot's estimation the proper place to turn off for the ascent of the peak. The error was compounded when it became obvious that the hikers, fresh from their office desks, could not reach the shores of the lake before dark and were forced to camp on a swampy hummock alive with mosquitoes. After camp was made, Tom chose the opportunity to inform them that because of the pressure of business his return to Laggan the next day was imperative. A further irritation resulted from the directions provided to reach the large snowfield lying to the west of Hector. When they reached the point where they had been led to believe the river could be crossed it was unfordable and Abbot later wrote " we could have hung somebody with pleasure." Fortunately for Tom, despite these hurdles the trip did prove at least partially successful. The ascent of Mount Hector was easily carried out, the first time that an Appalachian party had conquered an alpine peak without the assistance of climbing guides. Given some time to reflect on the accomplishment, Abbot was moved to admit "It certainly was a glorious trip. I think in my present state of mind I should say that the mosquitoes at the foot of Hector soothed us by their melody. . . ."[15]

Taken as a whole, the results of the 1895 season must have proven surprising to the seemingly well-prepared Wilson. Although he had taken measures to ensure that he could handle all the business coming his way, its sheer volume had made his preparations inadequate. Part of the problem undoubtedly stemmed from not knowing in advance exactly which parties were coming or their time of arrival, making planning difficult, if not impossible. Informing his clients of the problem, in the years ahead correspondence between outfitter and dude to make proper arrangements became much more common. Steps were also taken to remedy an insufficient supply of competent men and livestock. During the winter of 1895-96 additional horses were purchased from the Stoney Indians and more men were hired. As formerly, many of them were newly landed Englishmen, but two of the most noteworthy, Fred Stephens and Tom Lusk, were new arrivals from the United States.

Fred Stephens hailed from Michigan where he had been born on a farm in 1868, but had in his early youth gone to work in the state's lumber camps. Later he had headed west to Montana and had made his living at various times as a hunter, trapper and logger. Finding the northwestern United States becoming too populated for his liking, he drifted north until arriving in Banff in 1896 and signing on with Wilson's outfit. The following year, Stanley Washburn, at the time a Minneapolis student but later a noted war correspondent, described him on being introduced by Tom:

Diamond Hitch

Fred Stevens stood six feet and one inch in his stockinged feet. Twenty-nine years old then, he was, with the shoulders and muscles of an athlete, and soft blue eyes that drifted back and forth from the gentleness of a woman's to the glint and fire of a savage's. Big hands, big feet, and a big soul. He was then, and is to-day, a big man, as big a one as I have met in travels in many far corners of this world; big not only in bulk, but big in the qualities of heart and soul that go to make the best type; . . . To be Fred Stevens' friend is all the introduction that a man needs, to get the best that the trail offers in western Alberta and eastern British Columbia.[16]

Soon after becoming a packer, Stephens gained a reputation on two counts that was to make him an invaluable addition to Tom's staff. Arguably, he was the best axeman to work for the outfitter, and he spared no effort in the care of his livestock. Given his early life in the Michigan woods it was not surprising that he was skilled with an axe, but at times his exploits with the tool almost defied belief. When deadfall was particularly heavy he was known to spend ten to twelve hours a day for three or four consecutive days chopping the trail ahead of the pack train. On a lighter note, a fellow guide recalled that "as soon as he got to camp he would take off his boots and socks, grab his axe, which he would later take to bed with him, and go out cutting wood in his bare feet."[17]

While physically hard on himself, Fred felt that the guide who mistreated his livestock deserved nothing but contempt and he would often spend several days letting his horses recuperate when he felt they were becoming run down. Washburn, while on a trip up the Athabasca, was witness to the way in which he justified such delays to the members of his party:

"Now old Sorrel," remarked Fred, as we sat around the pack-cover at dinner, "He's sure gotten skinnier'n h--- these last few days, and I don't think the old devil's got the ginger under his hide to cut the mustard, when it comes to swimmin' this young flood which you fellers see abilin' past. The little Bay now, he's some peaked too since he fell down the mountain and skinned his knees. He ain't a bad horse, the Bay ain't, and I don't want to see him get his'n in this rampagin' river. And then there's

52

the old White — he's just barely been draggin' his hinders over the trail this week, and besides, Nick's saddle horse has been getting' down in the dumps worse and worse every day for a month. Now, fellers, if we was to tackle the job this minute, a lot o' them critturs would just naturally turn up their toes to the surface and drift off down the river to the Arctic Ocean.[18]

Needless to say, such logic usually won Fred his point.

While Fred Stephens came to Banff with a reputation as a competent woodsman, his new co-worker, Tom Lusk, arrived with one of quite a different order. Lusk's background, what little is known of it, may best be described as shady. He seems to have spent the greatest part of his life riding the Chisholm Trail with various cattle outfits before heading across the Canadian border with someone else's steers and a Texas sheriff in hot pursuit. The stock formed the nucleus for a small ranch he established south-east of Morley. Although already in his sixties, in 1896 he went to work for Wilson on the trail to supplement the meagre returns of his spread. Before long he had distinguished himself as the hardest drinking member of Tom's crew, his feats in this regard soon becoming legendary. When introduced to Martin Nordegg, whom he later guided to the discovery of the famous Nordegg coal field, the young German immigrant was amazed at his prowess:

In strutted an old cowboy dressed in buckskins. He was properly introduced to me as the famous Tom Lusk, our head packer. He squatted on the floor. The factor offered him a glass of beer with a knowing grin and a winking eye. Tom declined emphatically with a shudder and pulled from his chaps a large squash bottle of whisky and took a long drink interrupted by gurgling, then smacked his lips . . . . As long as we were at Morley, his eyes appeared to me glassy and I began to believe that this was their natural appearance. But when I noticed the copious drinks which he took frequently, I had my doubts and asked Dowling. He told me Tom never took a drink while on the trail for good reason. Bottles are too fragile and the weight [of] many cases of supply during many months had to be taken into consideration, as they would require a few more pack horses. But at the return to civilization after the season's work, this reason did not exist anymore and then Tom invested his earnings in liquor, retiring with several cases to his cabin near Morley. I never saw his cabin but heard that his outhouse had been constructed from such empty cases. The Indian Agent and Tom's neighbors watch out for the smoke from Tom's chimney. When they could not see any smoke, they pay him a courtesy call to convince themselves if they have to prepare for a funeral or just relight the fire for Tom after his usual carousel. Tom was methodical in his habits: he divided his cases and bottles carefully into the weeks and months of the long winter allowing to himself double quantities for Christmas and New Year, thus constituting a whisky budget.[19]

In fairness, it must be said that Lusk was not the only guide or packer known to be overly fond of the bottle, as almost to a man their feats could rival those of the most notorious imbibers. The King Edward Hotel in Banff quickly became known as the "packer's bar" and many a night while in off the trail was spent within its confines. To his credit, Lusk's knowledge of horses gained in Texas was second to none. Wilson realized this and gave him the position of a head guide upon hiring him.

Finding two individuals of the calibre of Stephens and Lusk allowed Tom to assign them to take out a party on their own the first year they were in his employ. Spurred by the success of their 1895 expedition to Assiniboine, Barrett and Wilcox decided to explore the country north of Bow Pass in 1896. The lure of the area was provided by the continuing mystery surrounding the two legendary sentinels of the historic fur trade route over Athabasca Pass, Mounts Hooker and Brown. Described by Scottish botanist David Douglas during his traverse of the pass in 1827 as being not less than 16,000 or 17,000 feet above sea level, the two giants had long been regarded as the highest known peaks in Canada. University of Toronto geologist Dr. A. P. Coleman had succeeded in reaching the location of the supposed monarchs in 1893 and on climbing Mt. Brown reported it to be only some 9,000 feet in altitude. Nevertheless, there were some skeptics, Wilcox among them, who believed that Coleman had climbed the wrong mountain and that the question deserved some further examination.

Coleman had begun his journey from his brother Lucius's ranch near Morley, travelling by way of the Front Ranges and then entering the mountains at the lower end of the Red Deer River Valley. Wilcox felt that this was the correct route to follow, but not so Wilson. He insisted that an easier and more scenic route could be found by way of the Bow River, Mistaya River, North Fork of the Saskatchewan and then over a pass which should connect with a tributary of the Athabasca River and ultimately with the Whirlpool River flowing from Athabasca Pass. Realizing that this as yet unknown country would need some difficult trail blazing and would be hard on the animals, he decided that Stephens and Lusk would be the most suitable for the job.

The outfit, which included five saddle and ten pack horses and provisions for sixty days, was plagued by two of a pack train's worst enemies, muskeg and forest fires, as it made its way up the Bow. Eventually, the North Saskatchewan was crossed and they began following old Indian trails up the North Fork. Barrett proved everything a guide could hope for in a dude as, according to Wilcox, "he would join up with Fred Stephens after seven or eight hours on the trail and explore the new region ahead for half a dozen miles and return to camp with full knowledge of every ford and burnt timber patch in that distance."[20] The pass to the Athabasca (Wilcox Pass), the key to the trip, was discovered by Wilcox but it was found to be long, tedious and extremely wet in some spots. Finding a suitable route leading off the pass to the Sunwapta River, a tributary of the Athabasca, was not a simple matter, but Stephens finally found a safe path. In the meantime, Barrett had proven overzealous and had gone off on his own and become lost in the burnt timber of the Brazeau River country. Three days later he casually walked into camp around eleven o'clock in the evening without so much as a word of explanation. While he awaited his companion's return, Wilcox, whose photography was later acknowledged as the finest done in the early days of exploration, had contented himself with taking exposures of the exciting new country which lay stretched out ahead of them.

Unfortunately for the intrepid explorers, after discovering the correct route they were unable to reach their destination. Advancing down the Sunwapta and then up the west fork of the Athabasca for eight days, they reached Fortress Lake, where a lack of time and provisions allowed them to go no further. Barrett and Wilcox did, however, climb a peak north of the lake from which they thought they could spy Mount Hooker, satisfying themselves that it was not over 10,500 feet high. After exploring Fortress Lake on a raft built with the skillful axe of Stephens, the pack train was turned back in the direction of Lake Louise. The return trip proved to be more of a forced march as two-thirds of the provisions had already been consumed, but Barrett and one of the men did make one side excursion to explore the Molar Pass region. Forging on ahead, the rest of the party quickly reached Lake Louise where some very disquieting news of a recent incident on Mount Lefroy awaited them.

Chapter III
Muskeg, Burnt Timber and
Bad Language

E arly in 1896 Wilson had been contacted by Abbot, Fay and Thompson who, along with another Appalachian Club member, George T. Little, wished to attempt Mount Lefroy, which had defeated them after their return from the climb of Mount Hector in 1895. Following an expected first ascent, they wished to outfit with Tom for a trip up the Bow River so that they might tackle Mount Balfour, a snowy peak to the west they had caught sight of from the summit of Hector. Tom agreed and arranged to rendezvous with the foursome at the Lake Louise Chalet on the morning of August 4th.

When he reached the chalet with Willoughby Astley, who had accompanied him from Laggan, Tom was greeted by three distraught, rain-soaked climbers. Fay, Thompson and Little hurriedly recounted how, at Abbot's insistence, they had begun their ascent the previous day through "The Death Trap," a narrow snow couloir between Mounts Victora and Lefroy. Once it was surmounted Abbot had proclaimed that there was a clear route to the summit, but the party had then encountered an immense, seventy-five foot bastion guarding the final pitch. Abbot, who was leading, had unroped in an attempt to find a way around the obstacle, and while making his way up a gully had apparently slipped. His horrified companions had watched helplessly as he fell backwards and tumbled several hundred feet before coming to rest. After making their way to his limp form the three had attempted to lower him gently down the mountain, but it soon became apparent that life was extinct. Realizing that any attempt to bring the body down further without assistance was fruitless, they had decided to try make it to the chalet for help. Benighted on the pass that would henceforth bear Abbot's name, they did not arrive at the chalet until the following morning in a driving rain.

Immediately volunteering their services for an attempt to recover Abbot's body, Wilson and Astley were on their way with Fay, Thompson and Little by 10 a.m. The pass was reached by 2:30 p.m. but snow squalls enveloped them and made further progress difficult, making it 4:00 p.m. before the work of bringing the body down was begun. Only able to reach the Victoria Glacier by nightfall, the recovery attempt was temporarily abandoned. The following day a party of six CPR labourers completed the task, and the corpse was conveyed to Banff for the official inquest. The jury found the death accidental and assigned no blame to Abbot's friends, thereby bringing an end to the events surrounding the first climbing fatality in the Canadian Rockies. It also marked an early end to Tom's mountaineering business for 1896 as, understandably, the proposed trip to Balfour was immediately cancelled.

For the remainder of the season, with the brief exception of a visit with Wilcox to Lake O'Hara, he had to rely on hunters to pay his bills. This type of clientele had been an important consideration from the beginning, with popularity being divided between spring bear hunts and fall expeditions in quest of trophy bighorn sheep and mountain goats. As such hunting trips were not as well recorded as mountaineering and exploring trips, it is difficult to know exactly who Tom's hunting customers were at this time. However, two names that constantly re-appear, General Fred Pearson and a Mr. Dickerson, were probably typical of the wealthy outdoorsmen in search of fish and game in the years prior to the turn-of-the-century. Pearson was a retired U. S. Army officer while Dickerson was a millionaire New York stockbroker. When they first arrived to participate in a hunting trip, they assumed that their part was to relax in camp until the guide had spotted a suitable trophy for them to pursue. But they were soon informed that, despite their wealth and social position, Tom's men were not their lackeys and that they were expected to take part in the hunting as well as the shooting. Once the air was cleared they greatly enjoyed the sport offered by big game hunting in the Rockies and felt that the fishing was the best they had encountered anywhere. During one memorable evening of angling in the Bow River below Bow Lake they succeeded in landing eleven trout weighing a total of eighty-two pounds, falling short of a world's record for the weight of that number caught at one time by a mere half pound.

While such parties helped Tom make it through the remainder of the 1896 season, his thoughts were plagued over the winter of 1896-97 by how the accident on Lefroy would affect his mountaineering business. As it turned out, he needn't have worried. In writing about the accident for *Appalachia*, Professor Fay stated "it occurs at the very dawn of a new era of genuine alpine climbing, for the extension of which among our young countrymen Abbot was so earnest an advocate,"[1] and concluded that it should not affect that trend. Indeed, it seemed to have just the opposite effect for rather than discouraging new expeditions it became a factor in attracting both new and old climbing enthusiasts alike to the Rockies. Tom's fears were, therefore, quickly allayed and, in fact, it soon became apparent that he would need to expand his services in the period ahead.

Those services had undergone some changes in the short time since 1888 when most of his clients were Banff Springs Hotel guests taking one week or ten day hunting, fishing and sightseeing trips. By the late-nineties he was outfitting major mountaineering, exploring and hunting trips often in the field for up to two months. This not only demanded increases in manpower, livestock and outfitting equipment but also changes in the type and amount of supplies that longer trips demanded. In the late-eighties and early-nineties foodstuffs had been of the most basic variety, consisting of flour, salt pork, tea, coffee and "the omnipresent bean." But as the time away from the sumptuous menus of the CPR hotels increased, the clientele became more particular in their diet. Witness, for example, the requests the Fay party made for their proposed trip to Mount Balfour:

As to food: — we want plenty of jam and marmalade (but very little strawberry jam, as Mr. Thompson can't eat it). No butter; no sweet crackers; **plenty of lemons;** *little potted meat, and that either chicken or lamb's tongues, preferably the former, and certainly not ham or corned beef or beef tongues; more coffee than tea; and a number of cans of soup – canned ox-tail or tomato being the best. We will provide our own chocolate and raisins, as we can do it more cheaply and get somewhat better quality, and will charge up to you whatever proportion of the price seems fair. We will also bring our own protection against mosquitoes.[2]*

All of this was to be provided along with the men, horses and rest of the outfit for $3.50 per day each. Tom acquired most of these goods from one of the general stores of Banff, that of pioneer merchant Dave White being the usual source. In fact, the large quantities of these supplies and other equipment bought over the course of a season were an important factor in supporting the fledgling economy of Banff.

Another change brought about by the increased length of trips was an expansion of Wilson's bases of operation. At the outset, all outings had originated in Banff, usually at the Banff Springs Hotel or his Buffalo Street corral. But as the distance covered and the time on the trail increased, most parties preferred to meet the pack train somewhere en route. Some parties gained the railway's permission to ride on the freights running between Banff, Laggan and Field, enabling them to start out several days behind the outfit and still catch it before it left the railroad right-of-way. As time went on some chose to stay in the Lake Louise Chalet or Mount Stephen House at Field and begin their journeys from these points. To tailor his operations to meet these changing preferences, Tom stationed guides, packers, cooks and livestock at these locations for the summer season in order to simplify preparations and cut down on wear and tear on both man and beast.

The longer duration of these trips also put more pressure on the relationship between the guide and the dudes. Short tempers and personality conflicts were bound to arise, particularly when clients decided that they knew better than the guide what route should be followed or where a camp should be placed. But it was the unwritten rule of the trail that the guide's word was law, making confrontations a not infrequent occurrence. A good example occurred when Fred Stephens had a German army officer out with him. After breakfast the first morning on the trail the officer, map and ice-axe in hand, took up a position on a nearby rock and began to inform the men of the day's route as if delivering orders for one of his campaigns. Somewhat taken aback, the men at first stood dumbfounded while the harangue continued. Finally Fred interrupted, asking the "god damned silly fool" if he was finished and advising that if he wasn't he was going to personally knock him off the rock on which he was preaching. He then berated the now amazed German, informing him that he and his men weren't soldiers, that he was perfectly capable of guiding the party without interference and that he didn't want to hear any more of his "sauerkraut."[3] Presumably, this settled the issue once and for all.

One final development, a consequence of expeditions into largely untrodden regions, was the difficulty Tom's men experienced with the trails. While the shorter trips of early days had followed well-defined trails in the neighbourhood of the railroad, the longer trips often followed faint Indian or game trails which crossed numerous high passes and wild rivers. But the most severe obstacles proved to be the many forest fires, burnt-over areas (brûlés) and muskegs encountered.

Forest fires were often left to burn unchecked in the days before the creation of an adequate warden service, resulting in large tracts of timber being completely razed. Wilcox reported in 1891 that "a very large percentage of the forests, from Bow Pass to Banff were desolated by fire" and that when he later visited them "the borders of Moraine Lake and Consolation Valley were a waste of bare poles and fireweed."[4] Ignited by lightning, sparks thrown off by coal and wood burning locomotives and the carelessness of man, these fires usually meant that the regular trail had to be abandoned and a tedious, out-of-the-way detour taken with consequent loss of precious time and energy. Equally frustrating was the occasional forced passage of a recently burned area, which called for chopping the charred and fallen trees blocking the trail.

The muskeg problem was related to the fact that most of the

old Indian and game trails followed river bottoms where the ooz-
ing muck was most likely to occur. An animal caught in muskeg
meant some time-consuming and back-breaking labour for a packer, since in most cases it had to be unpacked and then pushed,
pulled, lifted or otherwise cajoled back onto solid ground.
Perhaps the most extensive muskegs were to be found on the trail
along the upper Bow River to its source in Bow Lake. Some of the
worst patches were below the slopes of Mount Hector and around
the shores of Bow Lake itself, where pack trains often took to the
shallow water to avoid getting hopelessly mired. Even considering these hindrances, the old trails were often found to be prefer-
able to the clearing of new ones. Not only would this have meant
more work than most outfits were prepared to expend, but new
trails would have bypassed the traditional camping grounds with
their good pasturage, wood, water and neatly stacked teepee
poles, each a normal day's trek from the previous camp. Still, the
desire of an increasing number of parties to penetrate into country
cursed with forest fires, brûlés and bogs makes one observer's
description of being constantly surrounded by "muskeg, burnt
timber and bad language" quite believable.

The first order of Wilson's business for the 1897 season was
providing the means for the Appalachian Club members to complete their interrupted quest of 1896. Philip Abbot's father was
anxious to have the feasibility of his son's route up Lefroy proven
and had appealed to Fay to organize another attempt. He agreed
to resurrect the plan of 1896, which would call for a move up the
Bow for an attempt on Balfour after the expected revenge on
Lefroy. He decided to make it an international party by inviting
the Alpine Club (London) to send representatives. Accepting the
invitation were Professor Harold B. Dixon, who had climbed with
Abbot in the Alps, and Dr. J. Norman Collie, recognized as one of
Britain's leading climbers and soon to establish an equally celebrated reputation in Canada.

Collie was a professor of organic chemistry who taught at various English colleges and later held the prestigious post of director
of the chemical laboratories at University College, University of

London. He had grown up near Aberdeen, where he spent much of his free time in solitary rambles through the hills, and at Bristol, where he often practiced climbing on the sheer cliffs. His appetite whetted, he had continued to participate in mountaineering ventures in the British Isles and Alps during the years of his education and early career. Drawn further afield, in 1896 he had accompanied two well-known British alpinists, A. F. Mummery and Geoffrey Hastings, on an ill-fated expedition to the Himalayas. The party succeeded in reaching 20,000 feet on the gigantic Nanga Parbat, but then tragedy struck when Mummery perished in an attempt to cross Diama Pass. This heartfelt loss led Collie to forsake the Himalayas and turn his gaze toward some other area which would offer new and unconquered peaks. Professor Fay's invitation could not have come at a more opportune time.

The party assembled at Lake Louise on August 3rd to attempt Lefroy had the international character that Fay sought. In addition to Dixon and Collie it included Fay, A. Michael, Reverend Charles L. Noyes, Herschel C. Parker, J. R. Vanderlip and Charles S. Thompson, all from the Appalachian Club, and the Swiss climbing guide Peter Sarbach. Sarbach, brought from his native Saint Niklaus by Collie, had accompanied Abbot in the Alps and was the first Swiss guide to appear in the Rockies. After an early morning row across the lake and an ascent through The Death Trap, the entourage reached the 9,800 foot level and split into three separately roped groups. From there they proceeded with care but no real difficulty to the summit, which was reached at 11:00 a.m. Two days later the first ascent of Mount Victoria was completed by Fay, Michael, Collie and Sarbach. They then awaited the arrival of a third Alpine Club member, George P. Baker, before setting out for the attempt on Balfour.

Following Baker's arrival on August 7th, the outfit, with Bill Peyto as guide, began its trek up the Bow in quest of Balfour. Collie, Baker and Dixon started out after the main party and being new at travel in the wilderness were introduced to "what was for convenience of speech, called 'the trail'." Following Peyto's blazes they first had to deal with fallen timber "piled like spillikins one above the other" and finally emerged, only to get hopelessly stuck in the endless swamps. Here the horses sank up to their bellies, one getting so deep in a hole "that only with difficulty was he prevented from vanishing altogether," and for a time it appeared that they might have to spend the night in this beleagured position. Fortunately, Bill had become worried about his patrons' tardiness and returned to find them with the aid of his dog. Leaving the horses under its watchful eye, he led them to the warming fire of his camp. The following day the going proved easier, and Bow Lake, their proposed base camp, was reached. However, they were to be disappointed in their attempt on Balfour as en route "Thompson sought to investigate the lower layers of the ice-sheet that covers Mount Gordon, by falling headfirst down a deep crevasse." Collie, being the only unmarried member of the party, made a daring rescue by being lowered down the crevasse on a rope. With some effort he was able liberate his shivering friend from an icy tomb. Because of this mishap the party had to content itself with the ascent of a lesser peak, Mount Gordon, and from its summit spied a large mountain to the north supposed to be Mount Murchison. As Dixon and Michael had to return to Banff immediately, Collie and Baker decided to return with them and then re-outfit for an attempt on what was actually Mount Forbes.

Following a consultation with Wilson about the area of their interest, Collie, Baker and Sarbach began their journey from Laggan on August 7th. Peyto was again their guide, assisted by two relatively new employees, packer L. Richardson and cook Charlie Black. The trip, which was to result in the first exploration of the Mount Forbes area and a partial ascent of Mount Freshfield, was to give Collie cause to reconsider his initial impression of guides. On the first day out the weather was oppressively hot and the mosquitoes swarmed in huge clouds, causing Peyto to call a halt early in the afternoon. Collie, like many fellow travellers new to the ways of the trail, disagreed and told Bill that such an early stop was unnecessary. It was patiently explained that he had no idea how far a pack horse could travel in a day and that pushing them too hard early in a trip would only cause sore backs and lameness and result in longer delays later on. Not wanting to cause an argument, Collie acquiesced but still harboured some resentment at being, in effect, told off. However, these feelings soon dissipated as the trip unfolded and he saw the correctness of Peyto's decision:

That Peyto was right was abundantly proved in the sequel; for, owing to the excessively hot weather, we soon had more than one pony with a sore back and ill. This remedied itself, however, for later the weather got cooler and the packs lighter. Moreover, it was no vain boast of Peyto's that he was there to look after the horses; many a time after arriving in camp after a long day's journey, when something to eat and drink was one's first thought, Peyto could be seen driving the sore-backed ponies down to the stream where he carefully washed them and smeared the raw places with bacon-grease to keep off the flies.[6]

Collies' estimation of his guide was further amplified by the way he handled the situations and obstacles met on the trail. Flooding rivers were one of the worst hazards and when the boiling waters of the Mistaya had to be crossed he marvelled at the way Bill, constantly in danger of being swept away, probed one spot after another until a suitable ford was discovered.

Peyto's mettle was further tested on the trip homeward. It was decided to return via Howse Pass, which probably hadn't been traversed since Wilson's trip with Calverley and Brearley in 1888, and the heavy timber and prickly devil's club of the western slope made the going extremely tough. When the downed timber and forest fires finally made the Blaeberry impassable, he successfully led the pack train over Amiskwi Pass. This route was not known to have been previously traversed on horseback and was particularly trying at the time because of a recent heavy snowfall. From this pass Bill led his now weary party down the Amiskwi River to the Kicking Horse and eventually to Field, where the expedition was successfully terminated.

Repairing to Mount Stephen House, Collie and Baker learned of the return of Dr. Jean Habel, a recent guest, from an interesting

65

exploratory trip of his own. Habel, a Berlin-born teacher of mathematics already in his sixties, was a member of the German-Austrian Alpine Club and had first visited the Rockies in 1896. At that time, he was travelling by train to Field and observed a snowy peak at the head of the Yoho Valley. As the mountain alternately disappeared and reappeared as the train moved along, he named it Hidden Peak (later Mount Habel and now Mount de Poilus) and resolved to return and attempt to reach it the following year. At least that was Habel's explanation for the trip. Wilson had a contrary opinion, claiming that the trip was his idea and that he had been the first one to explore the Yoho Valley on his prospecting trip of 1884. Perhaps on no other issue concerning the early history of the Rockies was he more adamant. In a short summary of the work he had carried out for the CPR in his early days, he wrote the following concerning Emerald Lake and the Yoho:

In 1895 I tried to get some members of the Appalachian Club to explore and write it up — In 1896 I cut and cleared out the old Indian Trail from Field to the crossing of Emerald Creek, and from there cut a trail to the Lake, and along the North side to the Gravel Flats at the East-end — Then in July 1897 I got Jean Habel to go into the Yoho, photograph it and write it up.[7]

His case was further stated in a series of letters written to Commissioner of Dominion Parks J. B. Harkin in the 1920s:

In 1897 in order to get the CPR interested in this region, I got a German Professor to go in and take photos and write it up in the magazines — I gave him three men. . . and seven head of horses, Provisions, Tents etc. all for $7.00 per day and it cost me $11.50 per day cash and then the dam German took all the credit![8]

Tom was known to tell his share of tall tales but his repeated and vociferous statements on this issue lead to the suspicion that he had been done out of some of the credit due him.

Whatever the truth concerning Habel's exploration of the

Yoho, it added materially to the knowledge of the west slope of the Waputiks. It also added a few experiences to the campfire repertoires of the men who Wilson assigned to the trip; guide Ralph Edwards, packer Fred Stephens and cook Frank Wellman. The latter, a broad-shouldered youth with curly red hair, described as being "little more than a schoolboy" was just that, being only fourteen at the time. Francis Lorn Wellman had been born at Kingston, Ontario in 1883 and had just recently arrived with his widowed mother at Anthracite, the mining community a few miles east of Banff, where she ran a hotel. Of sufficient stature to contribute to his own livelihood, he had convinced Tom to hire him for the summer and this was undoubtedly his first trail trip. Even at that he was at no real disadvantage as neither of his elder compatriots had ever been through the country on the west slope of the Divide where increased moisture made conditions much different from those to which they were accustomed.

Departing Emerald Lake on July 16th in the steady rain that was to plague them most of the trip, the party made its way through the North Fork (Yoho) Valley and on July 22nd reached Takakkaw Falls in less than ideal conditions. On the descent from the pass the men had to drive the horses through a carpet of moss so thick that the heavily-laden pack horses sank completely up to their hocks and were in danger of breaking a leg. But Edwards and Stephens soon found their problems were just beginning. On reaching the valley floor the vegetation was so lush that neither Indian nor game trail could be discerned, and they were forced to hack through the thick undergrowth all the way to their destination. Another complicating factor was the steep sides of the valley which often necessitated riding along narrow benches up to a hundred feet above the river. These were particularly dangerous for the pack horses when one decided to pass another. Most cayuses, once their order on the trail was established, resented any attempts by those further back to pass them. One of Edwards' horses committed just such a breach of etiquette and was promptly kicked and bitten until it lost its balance and plunged over the edge. Incredibly, the animal was not injured as about half way down the thirty foot embankment it landed astride a spruce tree growing at a right angle and hung there balancing precariously. Edwards was thereby confronted with an unenviable situation:

Now I was like the man who had the bull by the tail — he had him, but didn't know what to do with him. I concluded that the first thing to do was to get the pack off. This, after a great deal of difficulty, I was able to do . . . . At last an idea struck me. I tied the lash rope around the hocks of his hind legs and, bracing myself against a stout tree, I heaved with all my might. Gradually he slid forward a little at a time on the tree trunk until at last he overbalanced and went crashing to the bottom where he immediately picked himself up and nonchalantly began cropping what grass there was.[9]

While potentially serious, the fall of the pack horse was superseded by one of a different sort that could have proven fatal. After reaching the terminus of the Wapta Icefield, Habel felt that a tour over its surface to examine a possible route to the summit of Mount Balfour would be in order. He convinced Edwards and Stephens to accompany him and while crossing a seemingly solid snow bridge Fred suddenly dropped from sight into a yawning crevasse. Fortunately, the precaution of roping together had been taken allowing Habel and Edwards to brace themselves and prevent him from falling very far in. By heaving in unison they were able to drag the chilled and shaken packer back to the surface, more convinced than ever of the "damn foolishness" of mountaineering. Shortly thereafter, Habel was able to convince himself of the futility of approaching Balfour from the west side and the outfit was immediately headed back towards Field, this time following the Yoho to its junction with the Kicking Horse.

The continued success of Mount Balfour in avoiding the pick of a mountaineer's ice-axe on its snowy mantle led several adventurers back to Wilson's door in 1898, among them Professor Fay and R. F. Curtis. Discouraged by his own party's failure to reach the peak from Bow Lake and Habel's report of the drawbacks of an approach from the Yoho Valley, Fay decided on a new route of attack. This would involve a hike by foot up the small valley east from the Yoho bringing him to the foot of the icefield on Balfour's southern side. As a porter and third man on the rope, Tom provided a young Banff school teacher named Robert E. "Bob" Campbell.

Born in 1871 in Lanark County, Ontario, the youngest of thirteen children, Campbell had been raised on a farm on the Nottawasaga River close to Wilson's home of Barrie. After attending school near the farm, he went on to study at the Barrie Collegiate Institute, where he graduated as a teacher, and later at the Northern Business College of Owen Sound, where he studied law. Coming west in 1893 with the intention of working in a law office, he found the prospects so poor that he ended up teaching near Moose Jaw, where his brother Dan was living. The school district soon fell on hard times and his position was eliminated, forcing him to take a substitute position in Regina while also doing the books for a gentleman's furnishing store. Not surprisingly, when an invitation had arrived from Banff to take on a teacher's position there he jumped at the opportunity. Wilson had recently been elected chairman of the Banff School Board and in an attempt to find a new teacher had written to the superintendent of education in Regina, who recommended Campbell. He arrived in Banff on New Year's Day, 1896 and took up residence in the Sanitarium Hotel, flush with a $500 a year contract and eager to learn something of the mountains. Because he was familiar with horses from his farm background and available for the summer, the young teacher was an ideal candidate for a trail hand, and Tom began to employ him in that capacity in the summer of 1897.

On August 2nd the two alpinists and their neophyte porter set out on a handcar, which took them from Hector Station to the mouth of Sherbrooke Creek. From there they hiked upstream, past Sherbrooke Lake and around the base of Mount Niles before camp was made. Still four miles distant from their goal, they made an early start on an exciting day the next morning:

Once under way, we plodded hopefully on over the miles of névé along the

69

Divide. At length the snow became so soft that my stout companion [Curtis] was sinking almost to his waist. Declaring himself out of it, he urged Campbell and myself to keep on for the now imminent prize. We two were soon on the northern arête and were crossing a well marked notch, when in climbing its farther wall, my ice-axe slipped from my hold and fell a few yards, yet was easily recovered. At this moment "Bob" called my serious attention to the fact that he had a wife and children at Banff, and I looked at my watch. It was 5:30, the very hour, and the day was August 3rd.[10]

Although Fay felt that what lay ahead was no more difficult than that already accomplished, the portent of the anniversary of Abbot's death and Campbell's loss of heart called for a retreat. It was accomplished without incident, and Bob was able to redeem himself somewhat two days later when he accompanied Fay on the first ascent of Mount Niles.

Soon afterward, Fay and Curtis made their way to Lake Louise to make an attempt at the first traverse of Abbot Pass to Lake O'Hara. To assist them they hired a stocky, rather bowlegged "lively youth" named Jim Brewster, who was a pony boy and guide at the chalet. The Americans found the trip, especially the stretch down from Abbot Pass to Lake O'Hara, to be without scenic equal in the Canadian Rockies. They also found that young Brewster's gymnastic agility made him a valuable companion on the trail. He was able to make his way with ease over the fallen timber and when a small tree was the only bridge spanning a raging torrent he "ran across like a squirrel." But he was not without his drawbacks, as when camp was made he immediately "slept the sleep of the just and the young" while his clients performed the chore of gathering enough wood to keep the night campfire burning.[11] Later, when writing to Thompson about the trip, Fay offered his opinion about Brewster's future possibilities as a guide:

Would make a capital guide with proper training. A little too fresh just now and fond of telling big stories. We learned within two days, to our amazement, that he had just saved Curtis's life on the way up to the Pass!

70

C's feet went out from under him on a steep snow slope and he slipped fully a yard. No crevasses near.[12]

Despite the success of this traverse, Fay was soon disappointed to learn that a group of his fellow Appalachian Club members had accomplished the feat that had so recently eluded him — the first ascent of Mount Balfour. Reverend Harry P. Nichols, Reverend Charles L. Noyes, Charles S. Thompson and George M. Weed had accompanied Fay and Curtis on the train from the east to Laggan. There they had outfitted with Wilson, and on July 30th began making their way up the Pipestone River with Ralph Edwards as guide. As they were on a tight schedule, Tom had suggested they try the Pipestone route as a means of saving time and had provided them with a sketch map. Through the excellent work of Edwards, who took them over the first recorded crossing of Dolomite Pass, they succeeded in reaching Bow Lake in record time. A few exploratory climbs were made on the Bow Glacier and around Peyto Lake before moving on to Hector Lake for the main assault on Balfour itself. According to Noyes, the climb on August 11th "tried tact, agility, and care, but was not difficult or dangerous" and the long sought summit was reached by four o'clock in the afternoon.[13]

While Wilson was providing the means to allow the Appalachian Club members to test their skills on Balfour, he was likewise aiding J. Norman Collie in his attempt to reach the far-famed Mounts Hooker and Brown. Believing that he had seen them from the slopes of Mount Freshfield the previous season, Collie was determined to return in 1898 and lay to rest the question of their size once and for all. Collie had been impressed by his outfitter the previous summer and the two struck up a friendship that was to withstand the test of time, involving an exchange of correspondence until Tom's death over thirty years later. In the course of planning for the 1898 trip Collie had consulted all available literature and had written to him several times to plumb his memory for further information In appreciation, he sent Tom one of his most valuable finds, a copy of the government "blue book" that recounted the events of the Palliser expedition through the Rockies some forty years previously. This became the nucleus for a fine historical library that Wilson was to assemble in the years ahead. Although not immediately able to reciprocate, Tom remembered the favour and other gestures of friendship and in 1931, when Collie was retired on an inadequate pension, gained permission from the CPR for him to ride free of charge to visit the Alpine Club of Canada annual mountaineering camp. Of course, this was still in the distant future in 1898, but because the two had hit it off so well it was understood that when Collie returned that year with two English climbing companions, Hugh E. M. Stutfield and Hermann Woolley, he should once more outfit with Tom.

Having been introduced to the value of a good guide the preceding summer, Collie was pleased to find on reaching Laggan that his party had again been assigned to the care of the versatile Bill Peyto. Completing the outfit were packers Nigel Vavasour and Roy Douglas, cook Bill Byers, thirteen horses and three dogs. This entourage set out up the Pipestone a few days behind the Appalachian Club party and as they proceeded Collie, mounted on his perennial favourite "The Grey," had the opportunity to observe and reflect on the hazards the men continually faced while journeying through the rugged landscape. He concluded, "Death . . . confronted the backwoods traveller in quite a remarkable variety of shapes; and even if we did not break our necks on the mountains, we gathered it would be hard lines if some member of the outfit did not die of sunstroke, get burned in bed, starved, slain by falling trees, or drowned while fording rivers."[14]

The accuracy of his observation was borne out by some of the events of the trip. After crossing the Siffleur River the outfit encountered a bad patch of burnt timber and muskeg where the remaining few standing trees proved to be a constant hazard. With every wayward breeze "there arose a great creaking and groaning among them, like the wailing of lost souls in some arboreal Hades" forewarning their toppling over, often narrowly missing horse and rider. The falling timber soon gave way to the standing variety, and the three mountaineers were forced to impatiently wait for hours while the men laboriously chopped their way through the thick undergrowth. Whiling away the time, they idly mused on the thick haze of smoke drifting in from the north where the country was said to be ablaze through the carelessness of the "wretched folk" making their way to the Klondike. When the trail was finally cleared the party was able to continue across the Kootenay Plains to the banks of the North Saskatchewan River under the shadow of the towering cliffs of Mount Wilson, named by Collie for his outfitter. With the river in full flood, Peyto had the misfortune of having four of his horses plunge into its treacherous currents, wetting a good deal of the vital supplies and requiring a dangerous rescue. Next, the fast flowing Mistaya had to be forded with Bill taking a very philosophical view of its dangers. He felt that it could be crossed quite simply, and if anyone was upset they should be able to struggle ashore somehow, unless, of course, they struck their head on a rock whereupon "one would die easily."

The way up the North Fork Valley proved even more arduous as the heavy timber allowed only three or four miles of progress each day. Finally an impenetrable muskeg of several miles extent barred the way, as the river was also running high Bill contended that no sane person would attempt to go further. But Collie was not prepared to be denied his objective after coming so far and plied his guide with the only means available: "This called for heroic measures, so I ignored Peyto's picturesque language and suggested whisky. This saved the situation for when it was carefully argued a little later that the river must be crossed at any cost, Peyto at once agreed, and finally we all got across somehow."[15] Similar difficulties were each in turn overcome and Collie was eventually to be rewarded for his persistence. Eighteen days of travel brought them to the base of a mountain, estimated to be 12,000 feet in altitude, which they named Athabasca Peak. On August 18th, while Peyto, Baker and Vavasour went off in quest of much needed game to fill the larder, Collie and Woolley ascended it and were greeted with the amazing view of "a vast icefield probably never before seen by human eyes and surrounded by entirely unknown, unnamed and unclimbed peaks." One of the two particularly magnificent summits, which reminded them of "lonely sea-stacks in mid-ocean" they took to be Mount Hooker while to the north-east of it lay a slightly flatter peak they felt sure was Mount Brown.[16] Although Collie was soon to discover that he was mistaken, he and Woolley had unwittingly made a discovery of far greater significance — the Columbia Icefield marking the hydrographic apex of the North American continent.

Bolstered by their initial success, the climbers next made the ascent of Snow Dome. Afterward Peyto moved part of the outfit farther north so that an attempt on what were thought to be Hooker and Brown, but which would subsequently be named Mounts Columbia and Alberta, could be tried. Both proved inaccessible, however, and the three alpinists had to be content with the ascent of the less lofty Diadem Peak. This accomplished, the dwindling larder demanded their return home. Vavasour and Stutfield had succeeded in killing three sheep while Collie and Wolley were on the heights, but these were now almost completely consumed. Peyto was thereby forced to hunt ahead of the pack train as it made its way back towards Laggan, ranging as far ahead as the Brazeau River. Recent forest fires had made the hunting fruitless, and before reaching a cache they had left on the Mistaya all seven men were reduced to eating "biltong," a form of dried meat. It was so unappetizing in appearance that "when the first morsel was put before us on the plate we thought that that mad wag, Byers, was serving the outfit the uppers of Peyto's boots, which had recently shown signs of disintegration."[17]

The cache at the mouth of the Mistaya allowed the party to regain Laggan with body and soul still together and after a hot bath and a few square meals Collie was able to reflect on the trip with satisfaction. One of his strongest memories was the camaraderie which had developed between the trailman and the mountaineer as they shared the experiences of the mountain wilderness. Nowhere was this fellowship more evident than at the nightly gathering around the campfire after the trials and tribulations of the day were past. Here the client and the employee met on equal terms and engaged in the mutually enjoyable pastime of "swap-

LAGGAN
TO THE
COLUMBIA ICEFIELD

ping yarns." The dudes took the opportunity to tell the assembly of their experiences in distant and exotic countries where they had scaled the giants of the Himalayas, Caucuses and Alps. In response, the guides and packer regaled the listeners with stories of wild Indians, dangerous bear hunts and fabulous gold strikes, or introduced them to the exploits of that most famous of all mountain creatures the Sidehill Gouger. According to legend, this elusive beast had been blessed with one leg considerably longer than the other to enable it to more easily make its way around the steep mountainsides!

The campfire pow-wow also allowed Collie and his compatriots to gain an understanding of the simple philosophy of the trailmen, gained through long association with life in close contact

75

with nature. One noteworthy example, which Collie well remembered, occurred at one of the camps on the North Fork when the
conversation turned to the interpretation of certain verses of
Genesis:

> . . . *Byers took the opportunity to pronounce a glowing eulogy upon the
> scheme of Creation, which in a passage of singular eloquence he described
> as "a mighty fine outfit." Some rash person venturing to controvert his
> views, our cook promptly overwhelmed him with a torrent of backwoods
> satire and invective; and the would-be objector, crushed in argument, took
> refuge in an outburst of somewhat pointless profanity. Then the tobacco
> was passed round, and the discussion ended — as such discussions usu-
> ally do — in smoke.*[18]

Collie's compassion for the feelings and character of his men
would soon draw him into one of the closest relationships of his
life. Returning to the Rockies in 1900 after a season in the Alps, he
intended on climbing some of the newly discovered peaks of the
Columbia Icefield in the company of Stutfield and Sydney Spencer.
Peyto was away fighting in the Boer War and therefore Wilson
assigned Fred Stephens as guide. Collie took an immediate liking
to him, pronouncing him to be "one of the best fellows it has been
our good fortune to meet," and thereafter would consider going
out on the trail with no-one else.

Collie felt that his objectives, Mounts Bryce and Alberta, might
be more easily reached by an approach launched from the west
side of the Divide. He was wrong. Although his 1898 outing had
tested the patience and endurance of man and beast, it did not
hold a candle to this trip. After considering an attempt by way of
the Wood River, the Bush River, which it was felt would bring
them closer to the foot of their objectives, was chosen. Realizing
that it would take some chopping to forge their way up it, Tom
assigned another excellent axeman, Charlie Bassett, to assist the
famed Stephens. Rounding out the crew were cook Charlie Black
and packer Alistair MacAlpine, a young lad newly arrived from
Belfast. Bad luck plagued the expedition from the outset.

Immediately after hitting the trail, Bassett's horse fell on him, necessitating his return to Banff for medical attention. Replacing him was Harry Lang, who, although and excellent packer, was no match for Bassett with an axe. Once the Bush River was reached the water was so high and the undergrowth so dense that Collie wrote in his diary, "the chopping of the axe and the drip of the water from the leaves are the only sounds unless some unprintable language is suddenly hurled on some wretched pack animal."[19] He had conservatively estimated that progress might be restricted to three miles a day, but soon even this proved unattainable. The rain poured down in torrents, the mosquitoes hummed in thick clouds and on some evenings the camp would still be in sight of that left in the morning.

Stephens felt, without question, these were the worst conditions that he had ever encountered and later, in a letter to Wilcox, gave a rather interesting description of them:

Better late than Never so as i Promised you; would Rite and tell you something of our Bush River trip i will just give you a Pointer to Pass it by, we left Donald and followed an trail whitch Led through a Dence forest to the mouth of Bush River we apparently followed the Columbia but was out of sight of it most of the time; never saw sutch undergrowth mud and wet, with mosquitoes that would stop a syclone; the poor Englishmen looked like Plum Puddings walking around with faces swolled up to twice their Natural size well we wanted to get to the head of the bush River But found it in high water to be impossible to follow up the Bank, we took the trail back 6 miles then climbed up over a mountain with the outfit and struck the River 7 or 8 miles up it was raining 7 days out of 6, to make it more pleasant, the Pack horses got covered with Brittish columbia mold, the oat meal soured, the hard tack swelled up so we had to Pack our saddle horses the wood would not burn and a few more things went Rong we finally got up the River far enough so it commenced to get deep and the valley was narrow and filled with Burnt fallen timber we nearly drowned Harry Long because he could not ride a raft of water soaked logs we found it impossible to follow up the valley to the foot of Mt. Bryce and Columbia so we took to the hills and camped 7000 feet above sea Level and here it snowed for 4 days and the wind blowed so we had to tie down the Pack Saddles to keep them in camp. i suppose this would be Delightfull to you But somehow it didn't catch me. this was as far as we got although i could go much farther but the weather was so cloudy that it was useless to go farther. here we turned and came back to Donald. i think we were about Due west of the west branch whitch comes into the west fork of the Saskatchewan. Well Walter this is a Poor Pen, Poor Paper and the Boy is jerking thing around so i will wind this interesting slip to a close; have no Doubt you will find this a very interesting country to go to as the mountains are very high and craggy the whole country is verry Rough and the weather in July will freeze a kyote so i am sure you would call it Grand.[20]

Actually Collie had overestimated how far north the head of the Bush River was and instead of ending up at the foot of Mount Bryce, found himself much further south and at the foot of Bush Peak instead. However, the expedition was not a complete failure as he was able to fill in many blank spaces on his sketch map of the Rockies.

With the numerous expeditions of both American and British parties to the area north of the CPR line after 1896, it became obvious to Wilson that the impetus had shifted away from the once popular country south of Banff. But this region still had a few loyal devotees who called upon his services, and he encouraged them in his belief that it contained some of the finest country in the mountains. Among the enthusiasts was Wilcox, who remained enchanted with the many hidden valleys and lakes of the Lake Louise region and with the possibility of conquering the as yet unclimbed Mount Assiniboine. The year 1899 proved to be his most active, beginning with a trip to Assiniboine in July with two fellow alpinists, American Henry G. Bryant and Englishman Louis J. Steele.

Outfitting with Tom as usual, Wilcox's party was escorted by Bob Campbell as guide and set out over a new route suggested by their outfitter. It was a variation on the Simpson Pass trail wherein they would follow a branch of Healy Creek to the summit of the

Divide and then continue on to Assiniboine over open meadows providing easy travelling and good pasture for the horses. Because of their unfamiliarity with this new path, Campbell and Wilcox were forced to rely on a Topographic Survey map and soon became lost. Only by dogged determination and some excellent trail finding by Campbell was the Simpson River finally reached and with it the now familiar way to their objective. Unfortunately, Wilcox lost a knapsack containing his personal effects and while he and Campbell returned along the trail in search of it, Bryant and Steele attempted an ascent of the peak. They managed to reach the 10,000 foot level before being turned back by a thunderstorm, which initiated a long period of inclement weather. The situation required an abandonment of further assaults and a premature return to civilization by way of the Spray River.

Undaunted by his own failure to even gain an attempt on Assiniboine, Wilcox immediately re-outfitted in Banff for further explorations of the Lake Louise region. Wilson provided him with a rather capable young man named Ross Peecock who had recently entered his employ. Peecock, the son of an English rancher who at one time had some business interests in Banff, came to notice as a result of a ranching venture of his own. Along with fellow Englishman Nigel Vavasour, he had hoped to raise cattle in the Banff vicinity in order to supply the beef requirements of the CPR. The site chosen for the venture had been the old CPR commissary camp at Hillsdale, where the open nature of the country was thought to provide a good chance for success. Although the pair had begun their project in one of the best Indian summers on record, they soon fell victim to the heavy snows of November when more than four feet fell in one six day period. With insufficient supplies of hay, the young ranchers had seen the writing on the wall and had opted to slaughter their forty head of cattle in order to at least break even on their investment. Having no more ambitions to continue in such a risky business, both Peecock and Vavasour had decided to throw in their lot with Wilson in 1897 and had quickly proven themselves to be very capable additions to his crew.

Wilcox and Peecock started out from Lake Louise on August 13th with the intention of penetrating to Desolation Valley (Valley of the Ten Peaks) where, in the course of their 1894 work, Wilcox and Allen had caught a glimpse of an interesting lake from the slopes of Mount Temple. After a vigorous hike and two days of enforced idleness due to a severe snow storm, the lake was reached and named Moraine Lake after what appeared to be a glacial deposit damming its lower end. From their camp on its shore, the entire region was explored, and on the 19th a stream from the south-east was explored to its source in another interesting valley. At Ross's suggestion it was named Consolation Valley to distinguish it from the recently visited Desolation Valley. Not content with these interesting discoveries, Wilcox insisted on pushing on to investigate the Vermilion Pass area, but all progress soon came to a halt when the four horses wandered off and could not be relocated. Peecock was thereby forced to make his way to Banff by foot and four days later returned with fresh mounts and Tom Lusk to assist in the search. As luck would have it, the four missing animals had re-appeared in camp that morning. Nonetheless, the lonely Wilcox was so overjoyed to see human faces that he prepared a special meal featuring "a corn-starch blanc mange flavoured with Scotch whiskey," probably much to the delight of the connoisseur of spirits Lusk. Adding the new horses to their string, Wilcox and Peecock continued on their wanderings the next day and visited Boom Lake, Vermilion Pass and Prospector's Valley in the course of their return to Banff.

The Wilcox party's failure to hang Assiniboine's scalp on their belts led to another assault on the elusive peak the next year. This time the hopefuls were a couple of amateurish Chicago brothers, English and Willoughby Walling. Their equally unsuccessful attempt added little new except it was the first time Swiss guides were used on Assiniboine and it provided the debut on an extended mountaineering expedition for an interesting young trail cook named Jimmy Simpson.

Justin James McCartney Simpson was born on August 8, 1877 at Stamford, Lincolnshire, and it was there that he received his early education. His father was a noted authority on Roman coins, and the family had a coat-of-arms which Jimmy was later reluctant to show in Canada, believing that "most people would think was an advertisement for Beecham's Pills." Being somewhat of a rascally lad, he got into all kinds of mischief, including poaching on the Marquis of Exeter's estate, and after disgracing the family in church was labelled a black sheep and sent to Canada to go farming in March, 1896. But after spending one night on a farm near Winnipeg he decided that rural life wasn't for him and removed himself to the city, where he quickly drank up his supply of English sovereigns. Penniless but happy-go-lucky, he stowed away on a west-bound train, getting as far as Castle Mountain before the conductor got wise and kicked him off. With no means of support or means of travelling further, he hired on with the CPR and went to work with "tools I had never seen before, i. e. pick and shovel."

Laid off by the railway at the end of the summer, he departed for San Francisco with fifty dollars in his pocket. He soon found himself broke and joined a band of a thousand hobos marching on Washington under the leadership of a General Kelly and California author Jack London. Failing to discover the purpose of the march, he left the group near Albuquerque and worked for the Santa Fe Railway until he returned to the coast at Los Angeles. From there he shipped out on a Victoria, B. C. schooner and put in three months sealing off the California and British Columbia coasts. After being paid off in Victoria he experienced one of the greatest difficulties in life, "how a newly landed sailor learns to pass the first saloon." Once again out of pocket he determined to return to Banff in 1897, where an incident he witnessed led to an important decision:

One summer morning I was strolling down the main street when I saw a group of horses being tied up at the hitching rail outside Dave White's store. They were pack ponies from Tom Wilson's corral. . . . The packers were supposed to be getting them ready to take a party of tourists in to Mt. Assiniboine. After tying up the ponies the packers went off for a

81

drink, leaving the tourists sitting hopefully on the hitching rail. Time passed and the packers still weren't back. At last, around 4 o'clock, they returned, loaded themselves, and began struggling to load the horses with sacks of flour and sugar, every rope looking like six. An old Scotsman, who was watching them fumble, lost patience, whisked off his hat and hit the nearest pack pony over the head, shouting "Get to h--- out of here!" The horses reared and then dashed across the road, taking the hitching rail and the tourists with them and busting the flour sacks all over the packers. The ponies fetched up in the minister's garden, where they ate up all his geraniums. I decided then and there that Banff was the place for me.[21]

Jimmy had been offered a job by Wilson during his previous visit and was soon at work picking up the tricks of the trade from Tom Lusk and his idol Bill Peyto. But as was the case with most green hands, he was first assigned to the beginner's position in the outfit — trail cook. His first real baptism by fire in this job came in 1898 when he accompanied guide Bob Campbell to Emerald Lake to cook for a group of fourteen Philadelphians camped there. Philadelphians were among the most numerous of the early American visitors to the Canadian mountains and in the party were William, George and Mary Vaux, who had been carrying out glacial studies in the Glacier House region, and Dr. and Mrs. Charles Schäffer, who had been doing botanical studies in the same region. Their acquaintance would lead to many important connections for his future career.

For further training in 1898 Jimmy was given the task of cooking for a party from Richmond, Virginia under the care of guide Ralph Edwards. The clients were a girl and her young, tubercular brother who visited Badger Pass, the head of the Cascade Valley and Sawback Lake before returning to Banff by way of Forty Mile Creek and Edith Pass. The boy died shortly after returning to the States, and Jimmy was so unsure of his skills at the time that he claimed he never knew whether it was from the tuberculosis or the effects of his cooking! The year 1899 was spent mostly in cooking for hunting parties north of Banff during which his artistry improved to the point that he was picked to accompany the

Walling party to Assiniboine in 1900.

As Jimmy remembered it, this trip proved to be somewhat of a fiasco. The brothers and the climbing guides, in an attempt to save time, took one horse and made for Banff by way of the Spray River while the rest of the pack train headed back through Whiteman's Pass. Due to the heavy timber on the Spray, the mountaineers found the going rather more than they had bargained for and were forced to kill the horse to keep from starving to death. Little did they realize that they were within fifty yards of a lumber road and only a short hop from the Banff Springs Hotel. The Swiss guides, fed up with their patrons' incompetence, abandoned them at this spot and pushed on ahead to the hotel that evening but did not report that the brothers were lost until the next morning!

Because of their troubles on the Assiniboine expedition, Wilson agreed to send the Wallings on a free week's recovery trip to the Lake Louise area. Along with the services of Tom Lusk as guide and Simpson as cook, he provided a generous supply of blackberry brandy, known to be the brothers' favourite. But in so doing he forgot to reckon with Lusk's famous thirst. While Jimmy had the pair out hunting on the first day of the excursion, Tom got into the brandy and one thing soon led to another. When they returned to camp the thirsty hunters found only several empty brandy bottles and one "well-baked" guide.

Simpson was not the only trail hand hired on by Wilson at this time who was later to make a name for himself as an outfitter and guide in his own right. The expansion of Tom's bases of operation required the employment of considerably more men, and among those he hired were a few who really excelled. One of these was a young Ontarian named Jack Otto who would later go on to successes the equal of his confrere Simpson. Born into a family of six boys and three girls at Haliburton, Ontario, very early in life he went to work in the local lumber camps. As well, he worked in the mines and spent his winters trapping, finding the latter particularly to his liking. As a result, when he arrived at Golden some time in the late-nineties he set up one of the longest traplines in the district and achieved quite a reputation, bringing him to Wilson's attention. Tom convinced him to join his crew at Field, where, like Simpson, his first assignment was to the position of trail cook.

Although Otto was usually a very quiet individual and not one to complain, while out with one particular party he found that their remarks about his cooking were just too much to endure. Informing the party's leader that he quit, he only agreed to reconsider when the leader told the others that if there were any more complaints they would have to cook for themselves. After that he received only compliments but to find out what lengths they would go to in their good behaviour he devised a fiendish test:

> . . . I came into camp early, got supper and baked a pan of biscuits. When the meal started the soup was perfect, the roast was good, the food was fit for any king etc. etc. Meanwhile I opened up 2 or 3 biscuits and filled them with salt. The first man bit into one and said "Food for the Gods," the second agreed and said "Nectarine for the angels." The third man bit into the salt. He stood up, spluttered, spat, waved his arms wildly and with red face pounded the table and roared "Just as I like 'em."[22]

When they learned of the trick, the dudes accepted it with good grace and Jack, soon famous for his sense of humour, became one of the most popular members of Tom's staff.

Tom Wilson, the Oracle at Banff

A typical CPR pack train

*Tom Wilson (in light stetson at centre rear) looks on as Donald
Smith drives home the last spike, Nov. 7, 1885*

Tom Wilson and his family, 1896
Left to right — Eddie, Tom, Ada, Rene, John, Bessie, Minnie

Packing up in Wilson's corral. Tom Wilson at the right

Bill Peyto bringing in the lynx to the Banff Zoo

Party on the way to recover Philip Abbot's body, Aug. 4, 1896
Left to right — T. Wilson, G. T. Little, W. Astley, C. E. Fay

Mount Lefroy first ascent party, Aug. 7, 1897 including C. E. Fay
(second left), H. B. Dixon (seated), J.N. Collie (third right), C. S.
Thompson (second right) and P. Sarbach (right)

*Fred Stephens and Tom Lusk packing up on the
Columbia Icefield trip, 1896*

A guide clearing trail through burnt timber

Jimmy Simpson

Chapter IV
The Long Trail

A s the number of parties he outfitted grew, Wilson found that problems like those with the Walling brothers occasionally occurred. Not everyone could be expected to find the life of the trail, with its frequent hardships and discomforts, to their liking, with the result that many did not return for a second trip. On the other hand, those who found it offered a meaningful and exciting diversion to normal life were equally common, resulting in Tom having all the business he could handle by the turn-of-the century. More challenging was how to make it profitable.

The most important source of customers continued to be the CPR. His relationship with the company had amplified through the nineties as it continued to develop its tourism program and increasing numbers of visitors arrived in Banff and the Rockies. The CPR and the government had cooperated in the development of Banff and its hot sulphur springs, but the opening up of the country away from the line had been left almost entirely in the hands of the railway. Consequently, a steady program of building new bridle paths, trails and carriage drives had been undertaken, all of which were of benefit to Tom's operations. Equally gratifying was the decision to supply Swiss climbing guides for mountaineering parties. The lack of such guides, who were common in Europe, had been one of the drawbacks of the region as far as mountaineers were concerned and, largely stemming from the Abbot tragedy, this was remedied in 1899. That year Edouard Feuz and Christian Häsler were recruited from Interlaken, Switzerland and brought to Glacier House, the first of numerous guides who would eventually be stationed there and at Lake Louise. While trail guides and climbing guides, with their different cultural backgrounds and responsibilities, would not always see eye-to-eye, their skills would complement each other's admirably.

Tom was able to reciprocate for these beneficial actions by continuing to provide excellent attention and service to the parties sent his way and by performing several important public relations functions for the CPR. One of his major contributions got them out of a difficult spot in the summer of 1894 and it went on to become an important part of their annual tourist program. In June of that year high water on the Bow River washed out several miles of track causing a large number of tourists to be stranded at the Banff Springs Hotel. Asked by manager Mathews for his ideas about how to keep them occupied, Tom suggested that the Stoney Indians be approached and asked to participate in a series of athletic contests for prizes put up by the railway. Personally travelling to the Stoney reserve at Morley as the company's emissary, he succeeded in convincing the natives of the benefits of his plan and brought back a large contingent to a camp near Banff's animal paddock. The next day the Stoney, decked out in their full regalia, paraded through town to the Banff Springs to make the delighted guests aware of their presence. Then everyone proceeded back to the camp where the men staged horse races, bucking and roping contests and bow and arrow demonstrations while the women competed against each other in teepee pitching, horse packing and other accomplishments of the trail. The success of this impromptu exhibition led to a request by the CPR for it to be repeated, and Banff Indian Days thereafter became an important Banff attraction, with other local businessmen, such as Dave White and Norman Luxton, assisting Tom with its organization.

Other public relations activities carried out for the CPR included the telegraphing of matters of local interest to the passenger traffic manager to be used in advertising campaigns and the securing of specimens of native animals requested of the CPR by scientific and wildlife institutions. In 1901, the American Museum of Natural History offered him a price of $30 to $50 for caribou hides, and the next year the International Forest, Fish and Game

Association of Chicago promised $250 a pair for mountain sheep and goats. But perhaps Tom's most important function in this regard was the handling of many of the VIPs who visited the mountains under the railway's auspices. His early work clearing trails into Lake Louise for the visits of the British Association and the accompaniment of Madames Ross and Brothers fell into this category, as did a similar trail blazing to Moraine Lake in 1900 to allow the visit of Agnes Laut, Canada's foremost author-historian. However, it was to be the provision of his services to Edward Whymper, the day's most celebrated mountaineer, during his widely heralded visit in 1901 that was to be the best remembered.

Whymper, the London-born son of the noted wood carver and engraver Josiah Wood Whymper, was regarded as the foremost product of mountaineering's Golden Age during the mid-nineteenth century. First visiting the Alps in 1860, he had become infatuated with the as yet unclimbed Matterhorn and set his sights on being the one to destroy its almost mythical invincibility. Seven unsuccessful attempts were mounted between 1861 and 1865 until finally in the latter year he had succeeded in leading a party of seven to the conquest. But the achievement had been tragically marred when a rope broke on the descent, and for the rest of his life he was haunted by the vision of four of his companions sliding off the edge of a cliff, arms outstretched, to their deaths below. By the time he visited the Rockies, the spark of youth that had driven him to great accomplishments was no longer evident, and he was rumoured to be an alcoholic and past his mountaineering prime. Yet he was still an imposing figure and a somewhat awestruck reporter for the Calgary *Daily Herald* described him in admiring terms on making his acquaintance: "He is an Englishman 62 years old, very active and aggressive, smooth-faced, of medium height, and showing traces of a pretty hard life away from the luxuries of civilization. It is only necessary to see him and hear him talk to be convinced that he possesses that British bulldog tenacity which stops at no obstacle and that he belongs to the strong type of humanity that does things."[1]

Bulldog tenacity must have been a prominent aspect of his personality, for it was also later commented on by Jimmy Simpson, who spent a day with him in a pastime enjoyed equally by both:

Whymper was peculiar, possibly because he had been lionized too much, but he was so determined an individual and such a strong character that he resembled a bulldog very much like the cartoons of that dog standing astride the Union Jack ready to devour anyone who touched it.

He got me very drunk at the old Field Hotel after the camp was over and confided in me that he had a very clever brother who drank himself to death and said he, "Yes Simpson, very clever and I often used to say to him 'George, why don't you take it in moderation the same as I do'." You know what moderation he used. . . .[2]

Whymper's visit to the mountains in 1901 resulted from a cross-Canada rail trip the previous year, after which he had convinced the CPR to accept a proposal that would see him climb and explore in the Rockies at their expense. He would be provided all his own transportation and lodging costs as well as those for his entourage of four Swiss guides. In return, he would attempt to advertise the Rockies through newspaper reports and written accounts in English publications. Wilson's job was to see to it that he was provided with the best men available to ensure the smooth carrying out of the summer's campaign.

On his arrival at Banff in early June, Whymper requested that he be provided with Bill Peyto, recently returned from the Boer War, based on the recommendation of a comrade-in-arms met on the train. In some respects, the request was an unfortunate one. Bill was no longer in Tom's employ, as he was attempting to establish his own outfit, and his temperament was such that it was unlikely that he would be able to deal with Whymper's imperious attitude for any length of time. Nevertheless, Tom's instructions were to give the great man what he wanted and he had no difficulty convincing Peyto, anxious to test his independence, to take him on. Assisted by Jack Sinclair, his Australian-born friend and partner in a copper mining venture, Bill met Whymper, his four Swiss guides and his photographer, W. G. Francklyn, at Castle

Mountain en route for the Vermilion Pass on June 18th. A base camp was quickly established in the Vermilion River Valley and from it a number of worthy peaks were climbed and several side valleys explored during the latter part of the month. Despite the rather adverse weather conditions, Whymper's famous temper seemed particularly benign at this early stage in the season, and although he found cause to complain of the numerous faults of the Swiss conceded that Peyto "properly executed his commission."

These amicable relations were not to remain in evidence for long, as on a further excursion to the Yoho Valley in July the situation deteriorated rapidly. Matters were exacerbated by continuing foul weather, by numerous misunderstandings between Whymper and the Swiss, who felt they were being treated as porters rather than climbing guides, and by a strange malady which laid Bill low. Whymper was led to record in his diary that "instead of being roused by my example (I am always at work), the more I do the less they seem inclined to do."[3] Finally, Bill lost his temper when scolded for coming back to camp too early from trail clearing and for attempting to get into one of the cook boxes that his client didn't want opened. A shouting match erupted and a few days later, after moving the camp from Yoho Pass to the upper Yoho Valley, Bill summarily returned to Banff with the excuse that two sick horses needed replacing.

Left somewhat in the lurch, Whymper went down to Field and, fortunately, found Wilson there. Tom took immediate steps to rectify Peyto's temporary desertion by providing Tom Martin, one of his men stationed at Field, to help find a better route than via Emerald Lake between the upper valley and Field. He also introduced him to a fellow English mountaineer, Reverend James Outram, who was looking for climbing companions. Outram was invited to join the party which, under Martin's direction, set out on August 5th to find the valley that Whymper believed would hold the key to the direct route. They were unsuccessful, but on August 8th Wilson himself joined them and was able to lead Whymper and one of the Swiss over a previously untried pass (Kiwetinok Pass), through the Amiskwi Valley and out to the town. Whymper pronounced the day "the hitherto best accomplished" and admitted "our success was very much due to Wilson."[4] Although business demanded Tom's return to Banff, Whymper wished to have his personal attention whenever possible and quickly sent him a note both requesting this and paying him a high compliment:

I shall be very glad if you can find it possible to join us in the Yoho Valley at any time. We shall not be difficult to find. I have no very appropriate name to suggest for the valley we discovered yesterday on account of its natural features and if you have no objections I will propose that it will be called Wilson's Valley. . . .[5]

Unable to elicit Wilson's immediate return, Whymper soon wanted him more than ever as relations with Peyto continued to deteriorate. On reaching his camp in the upper Yoho he found that Peyto and Sinclair had returned from Banff, and he promptly ordered them to find a route between the upper and main Yoho Valleys. Again he found reason to disagree with their performance, and for the next two week's Bill's temper again verged on the boiling point. The last straw came at Field on August 24th when he requested his pay and Whymper disagreed with the amount owing. After Bill threatened legal action, an agreement was reached and Bill happily took his leave. This left Whymper, who had been planning a trip to the Ice River Valley, once more without a trail guide and horse transport. Again, Wilson came to the rescue. Although he could not accompany Whymper personally for the entire time, he provided two of his best men, Bob Campbell and Tom Martin, to be at his service.

An initial reconnaissance of the Ice River was made with the assistance of Campbell, and for a few days in early September they were joined by Wilson himself, who pointed out some interesting mineral deposits. Later Whymper and Campbell were joined by Martin for a more complete investigation of the area, and during this period an incident occurred that showed that Whymper's crustiness was sometimes only a façade. Martin, a tall, thin American who one acquaintance described as "that dry, humorous old stick," was resting while his patron paced up and down the trail, as was his custom when thinking things out. On this particular stretch of trail there was a fallen log which he had to step over on each of his passings to and fro. Eventually it got on his nerves and he called, "Martin! come here and cut this log." The peacefully reclining guide gazed at the obstruction reflectively for a few moments and then replied, "Wall! Mr. Whymper, I've been up and down this valley many times and every time that log has been there, and I'm thinking Mr. Whymper, that if you want that log cut you'll have to cut it yourself." The flabbergasted Whymper retorted, "Martin! you're fired" and haughtily stalked off to his tent. Martin was by this time used to being fired for such presumed insolence and when a short time later he heard another shout, "Martin! come here," he casually wandered over to the tent. There stood Whymper with a bottle in one hand and a mug in the other and in exactly the same tone he ordered, "Martin! have a mug of beer."[6] Whymper's patching up of his relationship with Martin was further cemented later in the trip when he named a creek in the upper Ice River Valley for him.

The Ice River explorations concluded Whymper's work for 1901, but he was to return for further exploits. Wilson handled the outfitting for the trips of 1903 and 1904 but they proved much less tumultuous and demanding than the 1901 outings. In 1903 he was called upon to supply a man for a rather unusual expedition, accompanying Whymper on a walk over the railway line from the Gap to Revelstoke. In 1904 Tom again provided his personal services, escorting Whymper as far afield as the Crowsnest Pass in the extreme southwestern part of Alberta. On this occasion he and two Swiss guides accomplished the first ascent of Crowsnest Mountain while Whymper remained "indisposed" on terra firma.

With the passage of the years and time for reflection on the services supplied to Whymper and his other associations with the CPR, Tom came to the conclusion that his connection with the company was not always as beneficial as it had earlier seemed. Particularly frustrating was the fact that he had never been fully reimbursed for many of the jobs carried out on their behalf. But at the conclusion of the 1901 season these hindsights were still in the distant future, and he was well satisfied with the relationship. To this point it had been an informal one, but by the turn-of-the-century the railway's management was becoming increasingly adamant about having securely contracted services available to it. Consequently, in 1902 Tom was offered concessions on part of the company's livery and outfitting business in return for signing an agreement specifying certain obligations on his part. Somewhat surprisingly, he chose Field and Laggan as the locations for his concessions rather than Banff. While it is possible that Banff was not offered to him, it is more likely that the more lucrative business was to be found in the "long trail" rather than in livery work and touring sightseers on bridle paths in proximity to the hotels. As mentioned, it had been the growing popularity of the country north of the CPR main line that had led him to establish at Field and Lake Louise in the first place, and he continued to believe in the area's future. This was particularly true with respect to hunting which continued to provide a good portion of his business. It was probably not coincidental that the year he contracted was the same which saw the former 250 square mile Rocky Mountains Park and fifty-one square mile Lake Louise Reservation, made in 1891, included in the new 4,900 square mile Rocky Mountains Park. Now the North Saskatchewan River had to be crossed before any legal hunting could begin.

In any event, the concessions expanded the type of services that Tom would offer. In the agreements he guaranteed "to accommodate and supply the requirements of the Company and its guests in connection with the transfer and conveyance of baggage and passengers and furnishing and supplying of horses, conveyances, drivers and attendants at the said stations and in connection with their said Hotel at Field and their said Chalet at Emerald Lake and also between Laggan and their said Chalet at Lake Louise upon the terms and conditions hereinafter contained." Among these conditions were maintenance of "a sufficient number of Democrat wagons, buggies, pack saddles and work horses;" agreement to "meet the regular trains and special trains to convey the passengers to the three hotels;" employment of "only such men in the conduct of such business as shall be sober, competent men of good character and shall in the performance of their duties conduct themselves courteously;" and finally agreement to "carry Company employees and provisions and equipment free of charge." In return, the railway agreed to carry feed and supplies for the maintenance of the stables without charge and to collect the following fares on his behalf: "Conveyance from Field to Emerald Lake and return (1 or 2 persons), $4.00 — for each additional person, $2.00. Conveyance from Laggan to Chalet at Lake Louise (single fare) for each passenger including hand luggage, 50c — for each piece of baggage additional, 50c. Hire for each saddle horse or pack horse per day or part, $2.00. Hire for each Packer or man per day or part, $2.00."[7]

These contracts required some changes in Tom's operations. Since pack horses, saddle horses and outfitting equipment were his stock-in-trade, he had to begin his livery operations with only one wagon, but he soon was able to rectify the situation by acquiring the necessary conveyances, mostly from the CPR itself. It also was apparent that the work load the agreements were going to create was too much for one man to handle on his own, leading Tom to seek a partner. His eye fell on Bob Campbell who had already purchased a small share of the business in 1898 and with his financial experience had begun to work as Tom's bookkeeper. By the fall of 1901 he had retired from his teaching position, and early in the spring of 1902 a deal was concluded forming a partnership under the banner of Wilson and Campbell. To ensure the smooth performance of their new enterprise it was agreed that Wilson would oversee the operations at Laggan and Lake Louise while Campbell handled those at Field and Emerald Lake. A contemporary description of the set-up at Field mentioned "a little shop on the north of the river where curios are for sale including sheep's heads, bark canoes, sweet grass blankets etc." as well as "extensive and expensive equipment in horse saddles, tents, buggies, democrats, pack saddles etc."[8]

While Wilson's contract with the CPR effectively put the business at Field and Laggan in his and Campbell's hands, there remained a wide open field for competition at Banff. Until the turn-of-the-century Tom's supremacy in the whole Banff-Lake Louise-Field region had remained virtually unchallenged, but by 1902 this situation was quickly changing. Not surprisingly, with one exception all the competitors had at some time worked for him. They were, in fact, some of his best men, including Fred Stephens, Jimmy Simpson and Bill Peyto. The exception had begun as a partnership of two young brothers whose initial shoe-string operation was to eventually develop into the largest trans-portation enterprise in the entire Canadian Rockies and was to extend as far afield as Hawaii. They were Jim Brewster, Curtis's and Fay's agile young guide of 1898, and his elder brother Bill.

The sons of John and Bella Brewster, William A. and James I. Brewster were born at Kingston, Ontario on July 15, 1880 and February 10, 1882 respectively. Of Irish descent, their father had apprenticed as a blacksmith but rarely practised the trade, prefer-ring veterinary work instead. Sometime in 1882 he fell victim to the lure of the west and headed to Winnipeg where, among other jobs, he worked as one of the first drivers on the newly created street railway. With the exception of part of 1883, when he went to Medicine Hat as foreman of a crew to install boilers in a river boat, he remained in Winnipeg with his family, swelled by the addition of two more boys, Fred and George, until 1886. That year his brother William, who was in Banff working on the construction of the first permanent buildings at the Cave and Basin, advised him that there was a need for a dairy in the community to serve the needs of the town and the railway's dining cars. Since the eco-nomic outlook of Winnipeg appeared unfavourable, John decided to take a chance and test his luck as a dairyman, arriving in Banff on October 6, 1886 and acquiring a lot near the corner of Banff Avenue and Moose Street.

For a year-and-a-half he spent his time acquiring cows and constructing a log house on his property. On March 17, 1888, St. Patrick's Day, the family arrived to take up residence in their new home, and soon their numbers were swelled again with the birth of two more sons, Jack and Forrest (Pat), and a daughter, Pearl. Meanwhile, with the addition of the Banff Springs Hotel as a customer, the dairy had begun to prove more successful than the elder Brewster had dared hope, and the need to expand soon led to a move to a new location across the CPR tracks on Whiskey Creek. By 1892 his dairy herd had increased to the point that he found it necessary to register a brand (an algebra x), and by 1898 he was paying as much as $100 per annum to the federal government for rent of pasture lands at Vermilion Lakes and Hillsdale.

Shortly after arriving in Banff, Bill and Jim began attending the town's first school classes, which were held in part of Superintendent Stewart's office. Then in 1892 they were sent to Saint John's College in Winnipeg, although their more formalized education ended rather abruptly in 1893 when the school was closed by an epidemic of scarlet fever. Thereafter, for the few remaining years of their education, they attended the newly built school in Banff. But they did not appear in class very often, either assisting at the dairy or spending their time out hunting and fishing with William Twin, a Stoney who had befriended the family. Deliveries for the dairy to the Banff Springs Hotel brought them to the attention of manager W. L. Mathews, and their knowledge of the mountains so impressed him that, despite the fact they were mere boys, he began to ask them to guide the odd fishing party out from the hotel. After these initial trips they sometimes spent their summers working as guides for the CPR, as witnessed by Jim's activities at the Lake Louise Chalet in 1898.

In the winter months Bill Brewster began to tend bar for his uncle Jim at the Russell House Hotel in Golden, an occupation that was not without its hazards. In the course of one of the frequent bar room brawls he found himself acting as the floor for a particularly large lumberjack dancing a jig in his spiked boots. He was to bear scars as a constant reminder of the incident for the rest of his days. The job helped to keep him occupied until 1898 when he got restless and decided to take a string of horses north to sell to the thousands of foot-weary souls heading for the Klondike. He got as far as the headwaters of the Liard River before deciding to call it quits. Happily, he was able to trade the horses for some furs which fetched good prices when he reached Edmonton in October.

After playing hockey for Edmonton's Thistle Club during the winter of 1898-99, Bill found his wanderlust at least temporarily satisfied and returned to Banff. There he and Jim decided that with their boyhood knowledge and experience of the trail it would be to their advantage to go into the outfitting and guiding business, and their father agreed to stake them. During the summer of 1899 they acquired some pack and saddle horses from the Stoney and built a pack shed at the dairy to serve as a headquarters. In May, 1900 they launched their enterprise under the guise of "W. & J. Brewster, Guides and Packers" with an advertisement in the recently launched *National Park Gazette* that announced "Complete Camping and Packing Outfits And Experienced Guides Furnished to Any Part Of The Mountains On Short Notice At Reasonable Rates." Initially, the "experienced guides" were themselves, periodically assisted by William Twin, resulting in their first customers continuing to be almost exclusively short trip sightseers and fishermen from the Banff Springs Hotel. As a result, other sources of income were needed to stay afloat, and Bill hired on as the park's first fire guardian in 1901. The job paid $50 a month for patrolling the railroad right-of-way to extinguish fires ignited by wayward sparks from CPR locomotives.

Early in 1902, Bill and Jim agreed to take part in a new venture that was to be critical in their future success. This endeavour was their appearance at the annual New York Sportsman's Show in Madison Square Garden at the invitation of the CPR. Only with the continued assistance of their father, who helped to defray expenses, were they able to accept the offer, but they soon found that any costs incurred were well worthwhile. Their authentic depiction of trail life in the Canadian Rockies, complete with William Twin as the centre of attention, proved a tremendous drawing card. What started as a one time effort soon developed into an annual event supplying the Brewsters with many new and wealthy customers. The financial assurances that these clients provided allowed them to expand their operations, and by the end of 1903 they had amassed a string of seventy-five pack horses and were employing a considerable number of men.

Forming the nucleus of their guides and packers were those who had previous experience on the trail in the vicinity. When looking for manpower Bill and Jim wanted to obtain the best available and they were found in Wilson's corps of well-trained men. Several of their early employees came from this source, including Tom Lusk, Frank Wellman, Fred Tabuteau, Bert Sibbald and Bob Logan, the latter two from ranches in the foothills east of the mountains. Added to them were the younger Brewster sons — Fred, George, Jack and Pat — who aided their brothers whenever possible, and several inexperienced but capable men who would eventually establish excellent reputations for themselves. Among the most noteworthy were Bill Potts and George Harrison.

Bill Potts, born at Plattsburg, New York about 1885, moved west when a lad to live with his grandparents Mr. and Mrs. James Potts, an elderly Scots couple who had homesteaded near Wilson in the Morley district. His father, William J. Potts, was an early partner in the Alberta Hotel at Banff, and young Bill attended school in the town over the winter of 1901-02. After an abortive attempt to reach the Klondike and a period spent cow-punching at Morley, he moved to Banff permanently in 1903 and hired on with the Brewsters, whose acquaintance he had made during his school days. Harrison was also American, a native of Sibley, Iowa where he was born in 1887, and spent part of his youth in Billings, Montana before coming to Canada at age thirteen. He first went to work on a cattle ranch in the Cochrane district, but eventually found a job with the Brewsters at a horse ranch they were establishing on the Red Deer River. Because of his excellent knowledge of horses, he was quickly invited to come to Banff to serve on their trail outfit, and in 1903 spent his first summer in that capacity.

Some of W. & J. Brewster's early work had been contract packing, which entailed bidding on contracts to haul equipment and supplies for mining exploration taking place in the Bow and

Cascade valleys. In 1901 they had won the contract for an exploration of what was known as the Jubilee property near the headwaters of the Cascade River. The success of this effort had brought them a further contract packing job in 1902 when they supplied transport to a body of fourteen "prospectors" near the mouth of the Cascade. Rumours as to what they were seeking were rampant in Banff, but, as in the case of all such work for resource developers, the brothers were close-mouthed. Ultimately it came out that the interested party was the Natural Resources Department of the CPR and that they were prospecting for coal, the beginning of development on what became the area's largest resource extraction operation, the Bankhead Mines. Already in the CPR's good graces as a result of their relationship with Mathews and the Sportsman's Show appearance, this service drew them even more closely to the company and resulted in the offer of a more formal relationship. The outfitting concession at the Banff Springs Hotel had not been awarded when Wilson had contracted for similar concessions at Lake Louise and Field and in the spring of 1904 the sole right to take parties out from the hotel was granted to the brothers, apparently in return for ten percent of all monies earned. The granting of this privilege resulted in the re-organization and refinancing of the company. In May, 1904 after taking in two American partners, Philip A. Moore and Frederick B. Hussey, it began advertising itself as "Brewster Brothers, Guides and Packers to the Canadian Pacific Railway Co."

Moore and Hussey were classmates at Princeton University in the class of 1902. Moore had been born at Bayonne, New Jersey in 1879 into a family heir to the Old Crow Whisky Distilleries fortune. Hussey was a native of Pittsburg, where his family were principals in Hussey, Howe and Company, the country's pioneer manufacturer of crucible steel. At school the two were drawn into a close friendship by their shared love for athletics, both becoming members of several university teams, and the outdoors. Moore in particular excelled as an athlete, tying for the United States intercollegiate championship in pole vaulting in 1901 and winning the gymnastics championship on the parallel bars in 1902.

During the 1902 term the pair's interest in the outdoors led them to the Sportsman's Show in New York where they met the Brewster brothers and talked with them about the excellent hunting to be had in the Rockies. Deciding that they must go and see for themselves, they were able to convince their respective parents to make such a trip a reward for successful graduation. Fortunately, both were able to pass their examinations and that fall, under Jim Brewster's personal guidance, were treated to one of the most exciting experiences of their young lives. The close friendship with their guide which resulted from this outing brought the two back for a further trip the following year, at which time they began to formulate plans to go into business with the Brewsters if the occasion arose. The impending CPR concession provided just such an opportunity and the pair invested some $25,000 in the new venture.

In order to celebrate their new partnership, a particularly ambitious trip was planned for their outing of 1904. Beginning early in July, an advance party with eighteen pack horses under the direction of Bill Potts was sent north through Wilcox Pass and down the Sunwapta and Athabasca rivers as far as Athabasca Falls. Here Potts awaited the remainder of the group, which included not only Moore and Hussey but also Halsey Williams, a Princeton classmate, and Dr. Stearns, a well-known manufacturer of patent medicines from Detroit. Guiding them was Jim Brewster, assisted by packers George Harrison, Fred Tabuteau and Bob Logan and cook Sid Collins. On rendezvousing with Potts, the entourage continued down the Athabasca to the vicinity of the mouth of the Miette River where a permanent hunting camp was set up. For the next two months, this became a headquarters for many comings and goings, including one trip by Brewster and Hussey back to Banff and on to the Ice River where the company had another large party out for a six week trip. Near the end of September, Bill Brewster and Bert Sibbald arrived at the camp to help Potts bring Dr. Stearns and his trophies back to Banff. The rest of the party went the opposite direction led by Jim Brewster, crossing the Yellowhead Pass to the headwaters of the Canoe River and down it to Boat Encampment, then up the Columbia to Donald and finally back to Banff by railroad. Although little was thought of it at the time, this circuitous journey proved to be very historic for it marked the first recorded occasion on which a party starting from Banff had reached the Yellowhead.

Moore and Hussey returned to the States at the conclusion of this exhausting summer, but when they arrived back the following spring it was with the intention of staying. Along with Bill Brewster they became involved in the construction of a large residence across Banff Avenue from John Brewster's original lease. Known as the Brewster Bungalow, it soon became notorious as a bachelor's haven hosting many a wild and woolly party. Despite his original intention of making Banff his permanent residence, Hussey did not remain an occupant for long, preferring to spend most of his time in the U. S. and becoming more-or-less a silent partner in Brewster Brothers. Not so Moore, who stayed on and became involved in all facets of the company's interests. In fact, his close association with the Brewster family became even more firmly cemented in January, 1907 when he married Pearl Brewster.

Meanwhile, Brewster Brothers had taken immediate steps to diversify itself, the preliminary one being an investment of $5,000 in 1904 in a livery service, originally known as Banff Livery but later as Brewster Brothers Livery. The same year the erection of a large general store next to the King Edward Hotel on Banff Avenue was initiated. Another interesting project was the building of a combined boarding house-bakery on a lot behind the same hotel. Dubbed "The Birdcage," it became the abode of Brewster guides and packers when they were off the trail, and if its walls could have spoken they would have been able to tell many a tale about all night card games, drinking bouts and sundry other carouses. But perhaps the most impressive enterprise was the building of a large entertainment hall to serve the needs of the town's growing population. The Brewster Opera House opened on June 1, 1905 on Bear Street, but in 1913 it was moved to a new location on Caribou Street and renamed Brewster Hall.

Investment funds for its numerous projects were so extensive that when a new and tantalizing proposition was presented to the company the partners were at first unable to accept. When granting the outfitting concession to the Brewsters in 1904, the railway's officials had decided to retain the rights to the livery service. However, by the spring of 1905 the new CPR Hotel Department decided that it wished to have securely contracted services available in all phases of its operations. Brewster Brothers were the logical successors but their shortage of cash meant that they did not have sufficient capital to purchase the CPR's equipment. Eventually, management proved so anxious to unload the burden that in June, 1905 they agreed to lend the company the necessary funds with liberal terms of repayment. Among the equipment turned over was the hotel's famous four-in-hand tally-ho, which had made its maiden appearance between the Banff Springs and the station the previous year. It was immediately put to work, for not only did the deal include the sole right to solicit conveyance at the Banff Springs Hotel but also on the Banff station platform.

With their new and time-consuming interests to look after, Bill and Jim had little time to devote to the personal guiding of the parties which they outfitted. Therefore, they were constantly on the outlook to find new and able trailmen. Many colourful characters thereby found their way into the ranks of the company's corps of guides and packers, some of whom remained for only a short time and others who found the life to their liking and stayed on. Two of the latter, who became recognized as a pair of the most interesting individuals ever to trail the Rockies, were Herbert Alonzo "Soapy" Smith and Nello "Tex" Vernon-Wood.

Named after the famous character of Yukon fame, Soapy was born in Vermont and first came to Canada in 1904. After working briefly for pioneer rancher Frank Ricks near Morley, he and his half brother Fred Scott established their own ranch in the Jumping Pound district. Quickly tiring of spending his whole life on the range, he came to Banff in the summer of 1905 and was hired on as a harness maker by Brewster Brothers. Although accomplished in his trade, he was always anxious for the opportunity to get out on the trail and Bill Brewster eventually relented, appointing him to the position of trail cook. This was the inauguration of a twenty-four year career as cook, packer, guide and outfitter combined with his winter occupation of ranching. With wire-rimmed glasses and a visage somewhat like "a combination between a walrus and Teddy Roosevelt," as one dude put it, Soapy was a rather droll individual who rarely cracked a smile. Yet his reputation as a humourist and practical joker was unsurpassed in the annals of the Canadian Rockies. His talent for adding a light note to even the most glum of situations was witnessed on one occasion by a group of fellow trailmen who visited him at his ranch one wintry Christmas eve. The rather downcast assembly was sitting around the fireplace drinking and swapping lies while a blizzard raged outside when Soapy suddenly got up and announced he was going out to clean the barn. Although somewhat surprised that he should chose that particular moment to perform the chore, they said nothing as he disappeared into the swirling snow. A short time later he returned and sitting down to resume his drink remarked offhandedly, "Well, if Jesus Christ wants to be born tonight the stable's ready." The resulting guffaws undoubtedly helped to lift the visitors' spirits markedly.

Cut from much the same mould as Smith, Tex Wood came with his mother from Haddon Hall, England about 1900 and settled at Medicine Hat. He then went to work on a ranch near Gleichen where, during the 1906 round-up, a horse fell on him badly injuring his leg. A recuperation in the famous Banff hot springs was suggested and with only three dollars in his pocket he set out for the mountains. The second day in town he disposed of his money in the King Edward bar where fortune led him into an acquaintance with the smooth-talking Jim Brewster. It proved a fairly simple matter for Jim to convince him to go exactly where he wasn't supposed to be — back on a horse. Shortly after joining the Brewster outfit it became obvious that a handle like Nello Vernon-Wood was going to cause him no end of grief working with their rough-an-ready bunch, and he was soon telling his dudes that his name was simply Wood. However, when he returned to Banff wearing a pair of Texas bat-wing chaps after a trip south of the line, fellow guide Jim McLeod tagged him with "Tex." His career with the Brewsters lasted eight years, mostly at Lake Louise, before he joined the warden service and later went into the outfitting business for himself. At Louise he spent his summer living in a teepee and on more than one occasion had his uninitiated eastern guests adamantly demanding that their gear be moved outside if he was going to insist on incinerating himself by lighting a campfire inside. These and numerous other anecdotes about his "Pilgrims," as Tex referred to the dudes, provided a wealth of material for the highly amusing articles he began writing for American sporting magazines in the thirties. The most successful of these were a series known as "Pipestone Letters" which started appearing in *Hunting and Fishing* in June, 1935.

Prior to the awarding of the CPR concession to Brewster Brothers, their main competitor for the trail business at the Banff Springs Hotel was Bill Peyto. He had remained Wilson's most knowledgeable and popular guide until 1900 when he left to serve in the Boer War. This came about through some unusual circumstances. Bill and Jack Sinclair were sitting around in Bill's cabin one evening drinking and discussing the war when it was decided that as both were loyal subjects of the British Empire, one should volunteer while the other stayed home to work their copper claims. To determine the lucky participant a coin was tossed and Bill being the winner he immediately enlisted in Lord Strathcona's Horse under the command General Sam Steele.

Peyto's experiences on the veldt fighting the wily Boer were later to make excellent fodder for the nightly tale swapping around the campfire. One of the most popular stories, as first related by Steele himself, was about Bill's assignment to draw fire:

Somewhere Bill 'salvaged' an umbrella. He tied it to his saddle and carried it wherever he went. What for? Well, we'd be riding over the veldt and come to a kopje. Bill would dismount and open up the 'brolly' [and] parade up and down just within long rifle range. If someone took a pot at him the inference was that the boer were concealed in the hills.[10]

Bill's bravery in these hazardous circumstances resulted in two horses being shot out from under him and soon led to a promotion to corporal. But it was to be short-lived. To celebrate his success he felt a spot of liquor was called for and decided to 'borrow' an officer's cape coat containing several bottles. General Steele promptly learned of the incident and immediately ordered the return of the coat and its contents. Back it came but considerably lightened of its contents and before long Corporal Peyto was stripped of his new rank and two months pay.

Upon his return to a hero's welcome in Banff in 1901, Bill decided to go out on his own in the outfitting business. Some equipment and horses were borrowed from Wilson for his initial outing, which was the aforementioned trip with Whymper. By 1902 he had constructed a corral on his lot along the Bow River as well as expanding his land holdings near Cochrane for winter pasturage. But putting his business on a firm footing was not the only noteworthy event of that year, as on January 9th the taciturn and elusive bachelor was married. His bride was Emily Wood, a sister of fellow guide Jim Wood, from Eburne, B. C. where her father was a merchant and later mayor. The marriage, which would end tragically with Emily's premature death in 1906, resulted in the birth of one son, Robin. The boy so caught his father's fancy that Bill had an advertising calendar made in 1906 featuring Robin's picture while he relegated himself to a smaller photograph in the corner.

When starting out in 1901, Bill was fortunate in being able to capitalize on the contacts and excellent reputation which he had established during his years with Wilson. For example, in his advertisements he cited as references "Members of the American and English Alpine Clubs." Also, his acquaintance with the powers in the CPR allowed him to advertise as "Guide for the CPR hotel" until the Brewster concession put an end to that opportunity. These devices ultimately led to the attraction of many new customers, but at the outset his foremost parties were composed of those he had already taken out on the trail and had impressed with his abilities. Such was the case with his first "long trail" expedition as an independent outfitter, that of James Outram in 1902.

Outram's and Peyto's first trip together had been a whirlwind affair the previous fall after they completed their respective sojourns with Whymper. The former Vicar of St. James, Ipswich, Outram had first come to Canada for his health in 1900. Later he would become involved in a land company, the Northern and Vermilion Development Company, which had considerable interests in northern Alberta but which, like so many similar ventures, would eventually go bankrupt after the First World War. In the meantime, he would inherit a baronetcy and retire to Calgary from where he could continue to make frequent visits to his beloved mountains. During a 1900 trip with his brother, Outram had accomplished several ascents in the Lake Louise and Field regions and had also caught a glimpse of Mount Assiniboine from the summit of Cascade Mountain. This peak was his main objective for the 1901 season but he held little hope of achieving it because his financial position would not allow the expense of outfitting an attempt on his own. However, while exploring with Whymper, word came of the failure of Wilcox and Bryant on the peak and as it was being discussed around the campfire Peyto unabashedly asserted that from his considerable knowledge of the peak it should present no serious difficulty for the experienced mountaineer. Furthermore, he stated that if the occasion should ever arise he would guarantee to get a party from Banff to Assiniboine in two days and back in less, thereby making the trip of little expense. Outram indicated that in these circumstances he was prepared to go, and Bill's abrupt termination with Whymper had presented the opportunity.

Bill was to prove as good as his word. Meeting Outram and his two Swiss guides at Banff, he set out on August 31st with a four horse pack train assisted by Jack Sinclair. Following the trail pioneered by Campbell and Wilcox in 1899, he delivered his party to the base of Assiniboine on September 1st, and the next day accompanied them to a high altitude on the southwest side before leaving them to their own devices while he prospected. Due to poor visibility, the climbers reached only a secondary summit on the first attempt, but on September 3rd almost exactly the same route was followed to the summit. Returning to base camp from where Peyto and Sinclair had seen them reach their goal through a telescope, the summiteers were greeted with congratulatory shouts and "strains of martial music from the latter's violin," a famous instrument Jack had constructed from a Stilton cheese box scrounged from Dave White's store. They then hurried quickly back to Banff, re-entering the town only five days and five hours after departure with Outram anxious to tell the world of his grand conquest.

Success in tackling Assiniboine in 1901 was responsible for leading Outram's gaze in the direction of the exciting peaks north of the North Saskatchewan for a 1902 adventure. As his financial position had improved, the planned trip was going to be a lengthy one and Peyto was at first unsure as to who to send out with it. Sinclair had departed for the gold fields of South Africa, and since Bill had to give his business constant attention he could not spare too much time away from Banff. Luckily he was able to find two of Wilson' former men at loose ends and convinced them to take on the job. The two were Fred Ballard and Jimmy Simpson.

Ballard had much the same background as Fred Stephens, coming to Banff around 1900 with his brother Jack from the Michigan woods where he had literally been raised with an axe in his hands. Working with Wilson for a short time, his first trip had been in 1901 when he served as cook on Habel's second expedition in the Rockies. This was an attempt by the zealous professor to reach Athabasca Pass and to study the region between the Bush and Wood rivers, but had mainly turned out to be an exploration of the Fortress Lake area. The party had been placed in charge of Dan Campbell, Bob Campbell's brother, assisted by Joe Barker and Ballard. Habel and Ballard did not see eye to eye and had locked horns frequently while on the trail, especially since Ballard always referred to Germans as Dutchmen. When Habel reminded him that "Shermans are not Dutchmen" Fred's standard response was that they were all "squareheads" anyway, and the perturbed professor could do nothing but throw his hands up in disgust and mutter, "ach, such arrogance." While making a detailed examination of the Fortress Lake area, Habel had been constantly searching for the blazes of the A. P. Coleman party, which had explored the same vicinity in 1892. Shortly after returning from the trip, Habel died unexpectedly and upon being informed of it Ballard was heard to say, "Good, he can see the blazes now."[11]

The Outram party which set out from Laggan on July 8, 1902 included fourteen horses to carry the abundant provisions to prevent the experiencing of "privations more or less severe" that had to date been the lot of those venturing north. Because of the need for his presence at Banff, Peyto accompanied them only as far as the Saskatchewan before turning over responsibility to Simpson and Ballard. Thereafter, the two were to prove equal to the tasks facing them north of the river where, as usual, the trail needed constant clearing. On the few afternoons that such was not the case or Outram and his Swiss guide Christian Kaufmann were on the heights, they busied themselves building rough cabins which they expected to use while trapping the next winter. Outram's primary objective was to climb the peaks and map the Divide between the Freshfield Group on the south and the Columbia Icefield on the north. He decided to begin with Mount Columbia, one of the most striking peaks in the Rockies. Simpson requested permission to accompany he and Kaufmann on the first ascent on July 19th but, to his chagrin, was abruptly turned down. However, he gained a modicum of revenge a few days later when Outram asked for his help in carrying some heavy survey equipment to the top of Mount Lyell and he flatly refused. Eventually Jimmy was to have his day on Columbia for twenty-one years later he took part in the second ascent with Dr. J. Monroe Thorington of Philadelphia.

After the ascents of Columbia and Lyell were completed, Outram had the pack train move on to the Mount Forbes region where, by prearrangement, he was to take part in some climbing with Collie's party. After his disastrous adventure on the Bush River in 1900, Collie had spent the 1901 season climbing in Norway and the Lofoten Islands. But at Stutfield's instigation it was decided to return to the Rockies in 1902 and lay siege to much the same group of mountains as Outram. Although the reverend

114

had written to Collie in March hinting at a combination of forces for the season, the professor was at first reluctant to agree. As Collie put it, he preferred that "the people who first started the mountaineering out in the Rockies get some of the scalps," and that as an "interloper" Outram should be excluded. By June, though, he had come to the realization that a temporary joint effort might be beneficial and laid the appropriate plans to bring it about.

For purposes of a guide, Collie confided to his companions "I must have Fred," and wrote to Wilson to make the arrangements. But he was to quickly learn that his old outfitter could not comply as Stephens, like Peyto, had decided to go his own way in the outfitting game. Apparently the two had had some sort of falling out as Fred later wrote Collie that "Tom is no longer a friend" and this had led to his decision to strike out on his own. Fred was married by this time with a small son and was living near Lacombe, Alberta. There he would make his headquarters for the next few years, recruiting most of the men needed for his outfit from among the many new settlers appearing in the district. When eventually contacted personally by Collie, he decided to employ Dave Tewksbury and Clarence Murray, two recent American arrivals, and Jack Robson, his close friend from Banff.

Meeting Collie, Stutfield, Woolley and the American George M. Weed at Laggan on July 23rd, Fred was astounded to see what his clients expected him to pack. Because of the disappearance of some of their baggage, the Englishmen had been forced to borrow what they could in Banff, including a large mattress. "What's this blamed truck?" questioned the disbelieving guide while Robson inquired if they should await the wardrobe and the rest of the bedroom suite before proceeding. Upon being provided with an explanation, Fred agreed to attempt to pack the monstrosity, which with considerable sweat and vituperation he succeeded in doing. However, it would remain the butt of many jibes and the source of constant irritation as the cayuse assigned to pack it would vent its displeasure by depositing in unceremoniously in the middle of the trail at every opportunity. On their way northward they tested their skills by conquering Mount Murchison, which had defeated

them in 1898, while the as yet green packers took wonder and
delight in the unfamiliar mountain scenery. En route, a visit was
made to Simpson's and Ballard's trapping cabin on the Mistaya,
giving Collie cause to cogitate on the "grit and endurance" that a
man needed to deal with such wild country during the frigid winter trapping season.

Joining Outram at the junction of the streams emanating from
Mount Forbes and the Freshfield Glacier on July 31st, Collie's
party was surprised and somewhat chagrined to learn of his recent
successes on Columbia and Lyell. But despite the undercurrent of
resentment, the combined forces spent what all admitted was a
glorious eleven days together. Mount Freshfield was ascended on
August 4th, and after three days of trail cutting by Simpson,
Ballard and Stephens to get to the base of Mount Forbes, the magnificent 11,852 foot peak guarding the headwaters of the Howse
River was captured. At that point, the two groups went their own
separate ways. Outram returned to the West Branch (Alexandra)
River and made the first ascents of Mounts Bryce and Alexandra
before completing the first traverse of Mount Wilson on the journey back to Laggan. The Collie party moved at a more leisurely
pace, ascending Howse Peak and then continuing on to Glacier
Lake in order to explore the nearby Lyell Glacier. Since the undergrowth around the lake made passage almost impossible, Fred
was once again called upon to demonstrate his skill with an axe in
the building of a raft. According to Collie, the finished product
and its navigational conduct proved to be quite a sight:

*It was a large and very fine specimen of naval architecture made of good
sized logs lashed together with cinches, and wooden cross-pieces and
branches laid thereon to raise our goodly pile of baggage above the water.
She was named "The Glacier Belle", but we had no liquor to waste on her
christening. The baggage was brought down on the horses, and piled up
and lashed securely on the raised portions of the raft, the edifice being fitly
crowned by the colossal form of the mattress amid jeers from the packers.
Punting poles were fashioned out of pine saplings; Fred sang out, "All
Aboard" and with everybody pushing and shoving with poles and chat-*

tering a strange medley of railway and nautical jargon, we committed ourselves to the deep.[12]

As it transpired, the examination of the Lyell Glacier had to be curtailed because of a raging forest fire that suspiciously seemed to originate in one of Outram's former camps. The return trip to Laggan was therefore soon begun and was completed in five days, with a brief stop to complete the first ascent of Mount Noyes.

All in all, the Outram and Collie expeditions made 1902 the most productive year ever in the Canadian Rockies from a mountaineering standpoint. Outram alone was involved in first ascents of ten major peaks while Collie's party participated in five, allowing him to substantially complete his map of the southern portion of the Rockies. The successes of the respective parties also reflected well on both Peyto and Stephens in their quest to establish reputations as outfitters. It also set the stage for their colleague Jimmy Simpson to do likewise.

In 1898 Jimmy had passed his twenty-first birthday and "immediately cabled our English lawyers . . . to get the legacy coming to me on that date from some relative I never knew who, in a moment of weakness, left it thus."[13] Over time, he began to buy some horses and saddlery with a view toward eventually going out on his own, but in the meantime remained in Wilson's employ, probably until the end of 1901. But the trip for Peyto in 1902 undoubtedly provide a realization that he could now outfit and guide such a party himself. Unlike Peyto and Stephens, though, he did not want to spread himself too thin merely for the sake of independence and, accordingly, first sought a suitable partner. One was found in the person of George Taylor, a Yorkshireman who had been a rancher prior to becoming chief packer for A. O. Wheeler's Selkirk Range topographic survey in 1902.

As Taylor had been able to secure the CPR concession at Glacier House, he preferred to work out of that location while Simpson found the surroundings of Banff more to his liking. An arrangement was therefore reached in the spring of 1904 allowing Taylor to handle Glacier while Jimmy took on the Banff end of the business. Soon they had two excellent Boer War veterans working for them; Ernie Brearley, a former stockbrokers' clerk from Yorkshire, and Sydney Baker, an apprentice surveyor from Suffolk. Some of Simpson's and Taylor's work continued to be provided by topographic surveys, but a few private clients also began to come their way. The most notable were Professor W. H. Schulyer of Ypsilanti, Michigan and Mary de la Beach-Nichol of England. Schulyer was taken out from Glacier House by Taylor and Brearley to make scientific observations on the Asulkan and Illecillewaet Glaciers while Mrs. Beach-Nichol was guided from Banff by Simpson and Baker to engage in entomology in the Yoho Valley.

Although the 1904 season proved to be successful, Taylor decided that ranching and not outfitting was his forte. Deciding to dispose of his interest in the business, he found an eager purchaser in the person of his affable and well-educated employee Syd Baker early in 1905. Thereafter, Simpson and Baker continued in partnership for three years until Syd bought out Jim's interest in the Glacier operation. For a number of years, Baker continued to provide horses and guides to those interested in visiting the popular tourist spots of the region, including the Illecillewaet Glacier, Avalanche and Glacier crests and the spectacular Nakimu Caves in the Cougar Valley. To supplement this business he established a curio and photographic tent near Glacier House run by his wife, which became a favourite for both guests and train passengers to browse in. Unfortunately, his mind was affected by the altitude, and after a period of rather strange behaviour he sold his concession to Jim Brewster in 1915. He then moved his family to Vancouver, where he became established in the photographic business and ultimately developed a highly successful bookstore. As for Simpson, the break-up of the partnership left him completely independent and free to make his own mark as an outfitter and guide, something he was able to do with legendary success over the following four decades.

Chapter V
Changing Circumstances

*T*he increasing number of guiding and outfitting interests appearing along the line of the CPR through the Canadian Rockies in the years after the turn-of-the-century was bound to have some effects. A positive one was that the growing influx of tourists in the area were provided with the means to pursue their particular interests, be they climbing, hunting, fishing, scientific investigation, exploration or merely sightseeing. Satisfied customers ideally would translate into financial success for the outfitters and their employees as well as for other tourist-oriented enterpises as well. However, things were not necessarily as they seemed, for detracting from these benefits were two considerations — the implications that the seasonal nature of the occupation had for those involved in it and the possibility that increased competition might eventually force some outfitters out of the profession.

The seasonal nature of work on the trail made it imperative for those involved to find alternative ways to keep body and soul together over the winter months. Beginning in April with the first spring bear hunt, the season built to its peak in July and August with fishing, climbing, exploring and scientific parties and culminated with the final sheep or goat hunt in October. At that time it was the custom for the men coming in off the trail to gather at Banff for the annual Packer's Ball. Initiated in 1902, this shindig soon became the social event of the year for the Banff populace, featuring dancing till dawn and "huge punch and claret bowls [which] were kept well replenished." "Huge" was right, for some participants at these functions later remembered the receptacles to be brim full washtubs placed at convenient locations on the stage of the Brewster Opera House. While in town, many of those in whose honour the event was held bunked in at The Birdcage, regularly adding another chapter to its already notorious reputation.

While enjoyed by all, the Packer's Ball marked the last date that most outfitters were able to keep their guides, packers and cooks on the payroll. Indeed, even they themselves had to face the prospect of having no income from their business for a minimum of six months and had to look elsewhere for employment. In some respects, it was the men who worked for Brewster Brothers who were the most fortunate because of the company's quickly expanding interests. Two of these, in particular, lent themselves to the possibility of winter work — looking after their growing herd of livestock on its winter range and working on the ice harvest.

Because of their rapid success, Brewster Brothers' stock had increased quickly, numbering some 250 head in 1905 compared with only seventy-five in 1903. Even at the earlier date the challenge of finding suitable winter pasturage had been a difficult one, but had been at least temporarily solved by keeping the stock on a sheltered and productive range along the upper reaches of the Red Deer River. In 1904 a formal application for a grazing lease on one township of this land was made to the superintendent of the park, but was turned down. The following year upon reapplication the request was approved at a cost of $100 per annum, and the subsequently famous Yaha Tinda (Mountain Prairie) Ranch officially came into existence. By 1907 a few buildings had been erected and it became customary for two or three men to spend the winter months seeing to the horses' welfare and protecting them from marauding wolves. Despite it being a rather lonely occupation, there were those who welcomed the opportunity to have a secure job over the difficult winter stretch.

Lasting some six weeks to two months, the ice harvest did not keep men employed for as long a period, but it gave work to many more of them. The harvest resulted from a contract whereby Brewster Brothers undertook to supply the refrigeration needs of the CPR in western Canada with ice cut from the Bow River. It began about the middle of January when the ice had reached a thickness of about two feet and often required as many as fifty men and twenty teams of horses to carry it out. The labour involved cutting the 700 to 800 pound blocks and hauling them to waiting boxcars for shipment to ice storage houses. In a good year, the contract might call for the filling of up to 700 boxcars and was an employer of a large amount of otherwise idle manpower.

Apart from those lucky enough to find work in the Brewster enterprises, most trailmen seeking winter work found it in either the mining or logging industries, activities that were an early feature of the Rocky Mountains Park economy. Perhaps the least favoured occupation was that of miner for those used to living in the outdoors, but because of the relatively high wages and the proximity of the mines to Banff several men were attracted to it. As early as the mid-eighties coal mines had gone into production a few miles east of Banff at Anthracite, and in 1904 the CPR established more extensive operations at Bankhead on the Cascade River. But mining proved to be a hazardous occupation, even for those conditioned to the hardships of the trail. For example, in the fall of 1904 it was reported that Jim Wood, fresh from a season of guiding, had badly crushed his foot on his first shift at Bankhead. A few years later, the popular Joe Barker was killed there when some mining timbers he was unloading fell from a railway car knocking his head against the rails.

Logging was carried out mainly in the numerous timber berths leased out by the federal government along the Bow River and its tributaries, the Eau Claire and Bow River Lumber Company having the largest interests. This company engaged in major cutting at several sites on the Spray River, and the trailmen's experience with horses made them ideal for skidding out the logs with two and four horse teams. Others preferred to cut timber for themselves. In the spring of 1900 the citizens of Banff watched as Jimmy Simpson and Ross Peecock drove their logs down the river after a fruitful winter's cutting in the upper Bow Valley. A few years later, Tom Martin and Jack Otto began to take out ties near Field for the use of the CPR in railbed maintenance.

Favoured by some over actually working at logging was the

scouting and estimating of timber limits for large lumber interests. Timber cruising, as it was known, attracted many trailmen at one time or another, but one of the most noteworthy exploits carried out by any of them occurred when Jimmy Simpson took a trip to the Fortress Lake area in the interests of a Revelstoke firm. Starting out from Banff with a pack train in the fall of 1907, he found the North Saskatchewan in full flood from recent rains and, unable to get his horses safely across, decided to continue the journey on foot. After rafting the torrent he completed the amazing feat of traversing the seventy-five miles to the lake in two-and-a-half days and staked out eleven sections of timber before a party coming up the Wood River from Golden could beat him to it. When he completed the task he immediately started back for the Saskatchewan, hoping to be home before the snow flew. However, his tight schedule had allowed little time for hunting to keep the larder full and by the time he reached Wilcox Pass the hunger pangs were becoming acute. As the region contained an abundance of grouse he easily managed to kill five and proceeded to devour them all at one sitting. After a brief halt for rest and digestion, he continued without stopping to Kootenay Plains, where he believed his pack horses would have by this time made their way. As luck would have it, the lumber company failed to properly register the sections and Jimmy's payment, which was to be a commission on the sale of the timber, never materialized.

Despite the popularity of mining or some aspect of the logging industry as a means of taking up the winter slack, the most popular off-season activities were prospecting and trapping. Given their individualism, it is not surprising that these men of the trail were attracted to more singular endeavours which allowed them to work for themselves. Prospecting, of course, was not entirely limited to the winter season. Sometimes interesting formations were discovered on summer trips but were not revisited until the late fall when time allowed for more thorough examination and possible claim staking. After this, the winter months were usually spent in the onerous chore of proving up the claim. Trapping, on the other hand, was strictly limited to the coldest part of the year when fur-bearing animals were in their prime and rapid travel over the trapline was made possible by the use of snowshoes.

Tom Wilson, one of the more avid prospectors, had begun his prospecting during 1884 in the regions of Mount Stephen, the Yoho Valley and Quartz Creek. Upon entering full-time into outfitting he had much less time to devote to it, although he continued to dabble whenever a particularly interesting opportunity presented itself. His favourite locale was the Ice River Valley where, about 1897, he found traces of two minerals which he was unable to identify. Providing samples to Collie and Dr. Dawson for analysis, he soon learned that they were varieties of sodalite and garnet. But being unable to find financial support to develop mines for the minerals, he did not bother to register any claims. Eventually, though, interest in the soldalite did come from an unlikely source, Edward Whymper. In the course of his visits to the Ice River in 1901 he examined Tom's discoveries and took back samples to England with him. Finding that there was sufficient ore to make mining feasible, he directed Wilson to stake a claim in 1903. Over the next few years Whymper orchestrated an elaborate investment campaign through his wide connections in Europe and had several orders in hand early in 1905 when he sent for the first shipment. Inexplicably, it did not arrive and Whymper expressed his anger in a letter to Tom:

I think you know that I am a little sore about the way in which this matter has gone along. You staked a claim, and I understood that it was to be our joint property. A considerable amount was got out, at my expense. I sent for it, and did not get it and was rather led to suppose that it had been annexed by someone else, who had taken possession of our claim. I want my stuff, and want possession of the claim. . . .[1]

Although it is unclear what actually happened, it is likely that when the time came to ship the sodalite the expense was found to be greater than its market value. Whatever the explanation, no further reference to it was made in Whymper's correspondence with Wilson and they remained on good terms.

Diamond Hitch

Bill Peyto, another inveterate prospector, was little more successful than Wilson. Bill's interest in minerals pre-dated his arrival in Banff, and it is possible that he spent the few years before he went to work for Tom in search of the elusive motherlode in the Rockies. Although not formally trained in geology, his enthusiasm for it led him to become self-trained, and he amassed a considerable library on the subject. On many occasions when out with a party he would forsake invitations to scale the heights in favour of prospecting. His main interest lay in the country up Healy Creek, where he staked several copper claims, one in conjunction with Jack Sinclair, and near the head of Red Earth Creek, where some interesting talc deposits were discovered. Rough cabins were constructed in both locales, and at the end of the season he would leave Banff to spend most of the winter working the claims. His "Bookrest" copper claim near Simpson Pass never amounted to much but the "Red Mountain" talc claim at Talc Lake offered possibilities provided a market could be secured. Unfortunately, he was prevented from putting a mine into production by the federal government's contention that the claim lay within the park boundaries and subject to stricter regulations regarding mining after 1911. Bill disagreed, believing that the claim lay just outside the boundary and was thereby exempt from park regulations. The continuing disagreement over this issue left Bill extremely bitter, but eventually he leased the claim to the National Talc Company and a mine was developed. Although they spent some $18,000 on building tote roads and cabins, no talc was actually mined and Bill entered into a new agreement with Western Talc Holdings. This company put in five drill holes in 1931 but due to a lack of financing soon ceased operations.

Despite years of high hopes, Bill never received a cent from his claims. Happily, though, some aspects of his prospecting did bear fruit. While searching for minerals he often ran across Indian arrowheads which he enthusiastically collected. They were later to form one of the most important and extensive collections ever made in the Canadian Rockies. His interest in geology also extended to the field of paleontology, and fossil remains were likewise collected whenever the opportunity arose. A particularly interesting specimen was found near the mouth of Johnston Creek, an almost perfectly preserved, rhomboid-shaped unknown species of fish (*Platysomus canadensis*) which would eventually reside in the National Museum at Ottawa.

While prospecting rarely offered much return for the amount of time and effort spent, such was not the case with trapping. There were still a few locales in the mountains where populations of fur-bearing animals made running a trapline worthwhile. One of these areas was the vast extent of territory between Bow Lake and the Alexandra River where Jimmy Simpson spent many of his winters. Attracted by the abundant marten, or Canadian sable, as well as lynx, muskrat, fox and bear, Jimmy and his trapping partner Fred Ballard began to build a series of trapping cabins in 1901, with their main headquarters in a well-constructed cabin near the mouth of the Mistaya. Collie described it upon running across it during his trip of 1902: "The interior, which smelt very fusty and damp, was filled with skins, horns, traps of all kinds and sizes — conspicuous among them being two bear traps, cruel looking instruments like gigantic rabbit-traps, and requiring a force of nearly 400 lbs. to open the jaws when closed — tools of various sorts, and other trappers' implements."[2] Some time later another traveller making his way down the Mistaya also visited this cabin and found a poem pencilled by Simpson on a slab of wood attached to the door:

These few lines are dedicated to the low lived sucker who is in the habit of breaking in here.
If you look for excitement, be ye here
When the owner hereof is standing near.
Proceed at the game of breaking in,
But mutter farewell to all your kin.
You son of a gun (?), you've not the nerve
To let the owner of this observe
The way in which the deed is done
Or, Jesus Christ, we'd have some fun.[3]

125

As Collie had noted, trapping in this rugged landscape required "grit and endurance," but it also had its lighter side. The trapline was invariably a lengthy one requiring several days travel on snowshoes in extremes of weather to cover its extent. Famous for the speed and distance he could make in the difficult conditions, Jimmy soon earned the name "Nashan-esen" (wolverine-go-quick) from the Stoney. His partner Ballard, being short of leg and always choosing a wide pair of snowshoes, was not quite so adept. As a consequence of his physical limitations and poor choice of equipment, he was forever stepping on one foot with the other making what he termed "a buffalo waller" in the snow. His troubles also extended to other types of footwear. On warm days when there was little snow the snowshoes were discarded in favour of oil-tanned shoepacks which, according to Simpson, were "slippery as a cable of banana skins over a cavern in Hell." On one occasion, descending a steep grade from Mount Sarbach, Jimmy slid down on both feet creating a track followed by Fred coming behind. Half-way down the latter's instep caught in a pine pole and he fell head first into a pile of logs. The air turned blue with bad language, and Jimmy thought it best to hurry on ahead to the cabin and await his partner's appearance. Soon Fred came storming in, threw his shoepacks in a corner, jammed a cartridge in his rifle and pointing it at his footwear yelled "Move one, just once, you sons of bitches." Roaring with laughter, Jimmy ducked outside to prevent getting caught in a barrage, but Fred soon cooled down and decided to let his shoepacks live to slip another day.[4]

As spring approached, the partners sometimes ran short of supplies, something Jimmy put down to Fred's voracious appetite. Early in 1903 with no flour left to make the staple bannock, it was decided one of them would have to snowshoe into Laggan to restock the larder. Because Jimmy could made it quicker and knew his partner's penchant for carrying food in his stomach rather than on his back, he volunteered to go. The journey took several days and on his way back he laid over at a little cabin north of Bow Pass in order to hunt goat. While sitting at the cabin's doorway that evening he heard a crashing in the woods and grabbed his rifle, expecting to see an early spring bear. But soon the night air carried the unmistakable sound of a human voice bellowing "Jesus Christ, lend me your wings." It was Ballard who, feeling the familiar grumbling in his stomach, had set out on broken snowshoes from the Mistaya cabin to find Jimmy and, more importantly, the food. Floundering through the snow he finally reached the cabin completely exhausted, but was able to summon up enough strength to lay siege to the new grub pile. Without a word of greeting he emptied the contents of the pack and went to work on them until Jimmy had to stop him or make preparations to return to Laggan for more.[5]

A good winter's trapping in the Rockies could see a capable man clear about $800 for his efforts, but as time went on and furs depleted that became the exception rather than the rule. This situation and the extreme loneliness of the life led Ballard to abandon it in favour of the townsman's lot. His last season with Jimmy was 1903 after which he trapped one more winter with his brother Jack at Fortress Lake and then opened a small upholstery and carpentry shop in Banff. After his departure, Simpson carried on the trapline even though such an enterprise was fraught with danger. A man alone in the wilderness had to rely solely on his own knowledge and instincts for survival and could not afford to make mistakes. As Jimmy himself once put it, if one should seriously injure himself many miles from help in deep snow and sub-zero temperatures there was only one recourse, "Load your rifle and look down the barrel to see if it is clean." Indeed, a certain element of such fatalism was an integral part of every trailman's psyche, for they realized that in both their summer and winter activities death was a constant possibility.

Although the issue of finding winter employment was a major one, it was just part of life for those who chose to live in the mountains. Such also became the case with respect to the decision to follow the profession of an outfitter and guide, for as time went on the possibility increased that there would be an overabundance of services available. If visitors continued to arrive in increasing numbers there would be enough business for all, but the tourist trade was subject to fluctuations, caused by world economic conditions, weather and a variety of other factors over which trailmen had no control. Similarly, skill on the trail did not necessarily translate to an ability to balance the books, and even such seemingly secure operators as Brewster Brothers found there were times when they didn't know where their next dollar was coming from. Surprisingly, though, the first to feel the squeeze of competition and the pinch of finances enough to abandon the outfitter's life was Tom Wilson.

When returning from his 1902 expedition, James Outram noted several of Wilson's parties heading north and commented that if his good fortune continued he would soon be a wealthy man. Unfortunately, his observation could not have been further from the truth. Although Tom seemingly had all the work he could handle, he had an easy-going nature and often didn't press too hard for the collection of unpaid bills. Despite the wealth of many of his customers, some were notoriously tardy in the payment of their debts while others drove tremendously hard bargains in negotiating the costs of a trip. Sometimes in his early years, not knowing what the future held, he was forced to book a party at very little profit simply to ensure that he could meet the high costs of keeping sufficient numbers of men and horses available in the event of a really good season. The CPR concession should have removed some of these problems, but even the railway itself was not noted for being particularly prompt in paying its bills. For example, in January, 1903 Bob Campbell informed him that they still had not been paid for several CPR parties from the previous year and were having problems meeting their accounts.

Tom had first contemplated retirement from the trail as early as 1898. Upon hearing the rumour, the mountaineering fraternity had been appalled and Professor Fay quickly sent off a missive appealing for him to reconsider:

. . . I earnestly hope that such is not the case for at first glance (and even on thinking it over) I find it hard to conceive of the region as a field for mountaineering and exploration without you. All this side of tourist

interest is so closely connected with yourself in my mind, that I find myself at a loss to see how you could possibly be spared . . . . Who could replace you?[6]

Campbell's purchase of a small share in his business had probably saved the day, and the following few years proved to be the most lucrative Tom ever experienced. By 1904, though, some of his perennial problems were being exacerbated by the appearance of widespread competition. On returning from his trip with Whymper to the Crowsnest Pass, he announced his intention to sell out and this time no appeal for reconsideration came from any quarter. The logical buyer for his interest was Bob Campbell, and a deal was reached which saw him receive full ownership of the business but Tom keep many of his horses and some of his equipment. The livestock soon found a home at his ranch on the Kootenay Plains.

Situated on the upper reaches of the North Saskatchewan River between the mouths of the Siffleur and Cline rivers, the Kootenay Plains were formed by a series of shingle terraces varying from one to four miles in width and were almost completely ringed by mountains. Having received their name from the Kootenay Indians, who in early times had annually crossed Howse Pass from the interior plateau of British Columbia in quest of the plentiful wood buffalo of the region, they eventually became a favourite hunting territory of the Stoney Indians. Game was attracted by the thick bunch grass, the plains being a natural short grass prairie, and by the remarkable winter weather conditions which left the ground virtually free of snow. Such conditions made the plains attractive as a site for winter pasturage and ultimately attracted Tom's attention for that reason. Although he undoubtedly discovered them early in his mountain rambles, it was not until the winter of 1902-03 that he had some Stoney construct a rough cabin and corrals near the mouth of White Rabbit Creek, where he wintered about forty head of horses. He found the location to his liking, and his attraction to the area probably played a role in his decision to abandon outfitting. Certainly some of the funds received for his business were put into a stock of trade goods, including rifles, ammunition, flour, tobacco and even a few cattle, which were traded for furs with the natives.

For the next few years Tom spent about ten months of the year trading from his cabin and caring for his increasing herd of horses. The practice only came to an end in the winter of 1908 when he almost fell victim to the harsh environment which, despite his long experience, he regarded too lightly. The incident occurred near Christmas when the desire to spend the festive season with his family at Banff led him to set off on snowshoes in less than ideal conditions. Beset by a blizzard and plummeting temperatures, he had the misfortune of breaking a snowshoe, and for several days he struggled through waist-deep snow down the Pipestone in a desperate attempt to reach the railroad. Nearing his destination, fate once more struck him a cruel blow when he broke through an ice bridge and fell into the river's numbing water. Normally Tom would have built a fire to dry himself out in such circumstances, but exposure had dulled his mind and he stumbled onward in frozen clothes. Several hours later he had all but resigned himself to his fate when he heard the welcome sound of the whistle from the daily passenger train pulling into Laggan. As close as he was, he barely made it to the station and had to immediately be transported to the hospital at Banff. Examination showed that Tom's extremities were severely frostbitten, and eventually four of his toes and a part of each foot had to be amputated. With typical dry humour, he later remarked that at least the doctor had enough sense to take the same amount from each foot so that he wouldn't become unbalanced. But even with an optimistic outlook, his convalescence proved to be a lengthy one, and it was not until the summer of 1910 that he was once more fit for travel on the trail.

Before this painful and almost tragic event there were some interesting developments on the Kootenay Plains. In the spring of 1905, Elliott Barnes put in an appearance at a location across the river from Wilson's range. Barnes was somewhat of a "rolling stone" originally hailing from Bismarck, North Dakota and was in his early thirties when he arrived from Red Deer with a string of horses. Following Wilson's example, he built a cabin and corrals and turned out his horses on what became known as the Kadoona Tinda (Windy Plains) Ranch. Early in July, 1905 his wife and two young sons arrived to join him at Banff and he began a small, short lived outfitting operation in partnership with Reggie Holmes, an Englishman recently arrived in the vicinity. In addition to his trail stock, Barnes also attempted to raise Clydesdale heavy horses on his ranch, but he quickly realized that they did not take to the surroundings like cayuses. This setback and his peripatetic nature led him to sell out to Wilson for $450 in August, 1908. Meanwhile, Tom had begun an attempt to turn his own original squatter's rights into a formal lease. Corresponding with Minister of the Interior Frank Oliver, he was informed that since the area had not yet been officially surveyed no lease could be granted. Almost as an afterthought, Oliver added "hopefully your interests will not be materially affected whether you are covered by lease or not." [7] Such were Tom's hopes as well, but time was to prove them very vain ones indeed.

Wilson's departure from outfitting in 1904 was a significant development in the history of the Canadian Rockies. His concentration on the "long trail" meant that he had personally provided the means whereby almost every important climbing, exploring or hunting party had penetrated the unknown reaches of the mountains away from the CPR line and he had become a virtual encyclopedia on the area. Additionally, with the exception of Brewster Brothers, every individual employed in the outfitting business in a major way had got their start and learned the trade working for him. The question now was whether changing circumstances would lead others to emulate him and abandon the trail as well. Certainly some of his fellow outfitters must have contemplated the thought in the following few years with the increasingly tight grip of the CPR concessionaires on the cream of the tourist crop. But everyone seemed to be able to keep their head above water and, indeed, a few new faces even appeared in the profession. Then, in 1906, a new factor came into play that would provide a significant boost to the non-CPR people — the Alpine Club of Canada.

Diamond Hitch

The Alpine Club was the brainchild of an aggressive and extremely active Irishman named Arthur O. Wheeler who was ultimately to hold a large place in the annals of the Canadian Rockies. He was a dominion land surveyor who had served his apprenticeship surveying Indian reservations and CPR townsites at various locations in western Canada prior to 1885. After serving in the Surveyor's Intelligence Corps during the Riel Rebellion, he went into private practice for a few years, but by 1893 was back with the Surveys Branch employed mainly on irrigation work. However, earlier in his career he had been trained by Surveyor-General Edouard Deville in photogrammetry, the method of camera-assisted surveying then being utilized for mountain surveys along the line of the CPR, and it was here that his true interest lay. In 1901 he was scheduled to participate in these surveys in the Rockies but due to the impending explorations of Whymper in the region the government decided to shift the survey to the Selkirk Range. Wheeler was placed in charge of these surveys for 1901 and 1902 and by necessity soon became adept at climbing the many and varied peaks of the range. The challenge of these climbs and the inspiration of the scenic views obtained during them convinced him that he wished to spend as much of his life as possible in the mountains. Happily, after the completion of his Selkirks work, the results of which were later published in his book *The Selkirk Range*, he was assigned to recommence the survey in the Rockies.

Wheeler's enthusiasm for climbing soon led to his acquaintance with some of the area's foremost mountaineers, in particular Professor Fay. He was in the process of resurrecting Philip Abbot's idea of creating an American Alpine Club, and Wheeler discussed with him the possibility of forming a Canadian club at the same time. Fay supported the concept, but Wheeler met with "scepticism and indifference" from all but a few Canadians he contacted. The professor offered an alternative — the inclusion of a Canadian section in the proposed American club — and in attempting to gain support for this idea Wheeler sent letters to many of the country's leading newspapers. Among them was the *Manitoba Free*

Press and immediately he received a copy of the paper containing an article, signed by one "M. T.," taking him to task for being so unpatriotic as to even suggest the idea. Intrigued by this response, Wheeler wrote to M. T. and found, to his amazement, that it was a woman columnist for the paper, Mrs. Elizabeth Parker of Winnipeg, a one time resident of Banff and a lover of the mountains. Soon the two had joined forces and were able to convince the paper's editor to open its columns for the promotion of a strictly Canadian club.

Support gradually came from a number of other newspapers and, among others, from the CPR and the Banff outfitters, both whom could see the potential benefits that such an organization might have for their particular interests. Gaining confidence, Wheeler made a bold suggestion to a meeting of CPR executives being held at Mount Stephen House in February, 1906. Approaching William Whyte, second-vice president, he requested twenty railroad passes to Winnipeg to enable delegates to take part in the formation of a Canadian club. To his surprise, Whyte readily agreed, and Wheeler was soon at work on deciding on the list of delegates to be invited. In doing so, he placed a high priority on outfitters as he foresaw that the main focus of the club would be an annual mountaineering camp in the Rockies and that their cooperation in making livestock and packing services available would be vital. Consequently, the list of invitees included: Syd Baker of Simpson and Baker; Bill Brewster of Brewster Brothers; Bob Campbell and his brother Dan, who had joined him in his business; Tom Wilson; and Tom Martin, who had gone into partnership with Jack Otto at Field, Glacier and Leanchoil.

All these individuals were actively engaged in outfitting with the exception of Wilson, who was asked because of his considerable herd of horses which might be placed at the club's disposal, his wide knowledge of the mountains and not least of all because of his reputation as the foremost guide in the Rockies. Wheeler was quick to capitalize on this reputation, arranging a newspaper interview in which Tom could extol the virtues of the landscape and the concept of an entirely Canadian mountaineering club:

That Canadian mountains surpass in beauty the wider famed beauty spots of Italy, Switzerland and the Himalayas is the opinion held by Tom Wilson, for years a guide in the Canadian Rockies, who has come to Winnipeg to tell of the wonders of the mountains he loves to the delegates to the alpine club.

It makes the blood of the old guide boil to realize that English and wealthy Canadians are touring the Alps and the mountains of other countries while the mountains of home are neglected. . . . "It's a sad fact that the beauties of the Canadian Rockies are being discovered and toured by other than the Canadian," said Mr. Wilson. "Tourists from France, Italy and Switzerland have been touring the Canadian mountains while Canadians have been oblivious to the scenery lying in the recesses and valleys of their own mountains. It is for the purpose of securing the interest of the Canadian people in their own beautiful scenic spots that many other men besides myself have come to attend the meeting of the Alpine Club.[8]

Above all, though, Tom deserved a part in the creation of the club because he had been one of the original enthusiasts for Wheeler's idea and had done all he could to foster it. In a letter to Mrs. Wilson at the time of Tom's death, the surveyor freely acknowledged this fact, stating that "Personally, I feel that it was in a large measure due to Tom's support that I was able to found the Alpine Club of Canada and I always think of him in that regard."[9]

The founding meeting commenced at the YMCA building in Winnipeg on March 27, 1906, with all twenty delegates in attendance. Committees, appointed to draw up a constitution and to provide for an election of officers, reported the next day, and the club was formally organized. Wilson was elected to the three man Advisory Committee, and a further committee comprised of surveyors A. O. Wheeler, H. G. Wheeler, M. P. Bridgland and all the outfitters present was appointed to complete arrangements for the first annual camp. The site decided upon for it was a little lake on the summit of Yoho Pass, first visited by the Habel party on their way from Emerald Lake into the Yoho Valley in 1897. The spot was an excellent one from the point-of-view of initiating those unfamiliar with the arts of climbing, the comparatively easy Mounts President, Vice-President, Collie and Burgess being close at hand. But from the packing angle it was not nearly so ideal as it required a trip of nearly twenty miles from the nearest railway depot and an ascent to an altitude of almost 6,000 feet at the top of the pass. The prospect was therefore not greeted with a great deal of enthusiasm by the outfitters, particularly so since they were not to be paid for their services. The extremely limited funds of the club at its inception left no room for payment of horse transport, and Wheeler was fortunate that the outfitters agreed to volunteer their services at the founding meeting.

Given the circumstances, it is not surprising that as the time for the camp approached there began to be a few who had second thoughts. Foremost were Brewster Brothers. Bill Brewster agreed to supply ten horses with saddles at the Winnipeg meeting, but by the end of May he had withdrawn from both his commitment and the club itself. Reasons for the decision are not known with certainty but may well have resulted from a personality conflict with the often difficult Wheeler. In any case, the withdrawal left him ten horses short and he turned to Wilson to fill the gap, offering him a few added incentives:

Can you arrange to supply ten more than you were booked for. Think we had you down for 8 but I think you will see by referring to the letter I sent you on the subject we will be in a position to pay for these at so much per day. Packing and Riding saddles will be required with them.

I wonder if you heard that you would be in charge of the packing between Mr. Stephen Ho. and camp. Tom Martin is in charge beyond the camp.[10]

Tom complied with the request for additional horses and saddles but could not take charge of the packing. The stock and the trading post at Kootenay Plains demanded his full attention during the summer and he made no appearance at the first annual camp. Fortunately, Wheeler was able to convince Elliott Barnes to take his place.

The long anticipated event was scheduled to get underway on July 8, 1906 with a rendezvous of the participants at Mount Stephen House in preparation for the trek to the campsite. Some days previously the outfitters and their men began the task of packing in the tents, provisions and equipment necessary to provide for the needs of an expected 112 attendees. Most of the essentials had been donated — the canvas dining canopy from the CPR, the tents from the Royal North West Mounted Police and Campbell and Baker, and the bunting from Superintendent Howard Douglas. In addition, the CPR had also donated the services of two Swiss guides, Edward Feuz jr. and Gottfried Feuz, and the cooks from its now flourishing Yoho Valley camp. After completing the erection of the camp the men returned to Field with the horses to bring in the neophyte alpinists, and upon arriving at the hotel were greeted by an amazing sight. The circular advertising the camp had specifically outlined the criteria for dress:

Those climbing require heavily soled leather boots, well set with Hungarian nails. Knickerbockers, puttees, sweater and knockabout hat furnish the most serviceable costume. No lady climbing, who wears skirts, will be allowed to take a place on a rope, as they are a distinct source of danger to the entire party. Knickerbockers or bloomers with puttees or gaiters and sweater will be found serviceable and safe.[11]

Apparently most of those in attendance had failed to read the literature. One observer noted that while the costumes were not nearly so stylish as those worn in the Easter Day parade at Atlantic City, they possessed infinitely more variety. Many of the ladies had long skirts and straw hats decorated with flowers, while some of the men wore Derby hats and carried umbrellas. Tom Martin, never one to let such a choice opportunity to slip by without comment, remarked to Wheeler in his humorous drawl, "Say Boss! Git yer eye on them thar outfits what's comin: They're fierce!"[12]

Despite the almost total lack of preparedness and experience of those attending, the week long camp proved surprisingly successful. A total of eight peaks were scaled, the qualifying climb for active membership being Mount Vice-President, and several side trips were made, including a two day circuit of the Yoho Valley and an expedition to initiate measurement of the Yoho Glacier. The Yoho Valley excursion was particularly well enjoyed, and the outfitters added to the occasion with their colourful tales around the campfire: "I would like the space to tell of that night in the Yoho around our campfire, of the tales told by Jack Otto — honest Jack Otto — of the bear stories that fell from his lips till the sight or sound of a fat old porcupine made us believe that we were face to face with a grizzly!"[13]

Everyone at the camp realized that its success was almost entirely attributable to the capabilities of "the men in buckskin." Without their freely offered services and their skill and determination it would not have been possible, a fact commented upon by Wheeler in his rather flowery address to the assembled congregation:

That the first camp has been a possibility is almost entirely due to the loyal patriotism and keen love of the mountains of a number of the prominent outfitters. If you do not know what an outfitter is I can only advise you to make their acquaintance right now. They will tell you more you ought to know in five minutes that otherwise you would learn in a life time. They have placed their resources at the disposal of the camp free of charge and are giving their personal assistance to show us the glories of this mountain world and the wonder of it, in order that you may spread the fame of them the length and breadth of Canada, and make known to our fellow citizens the superb birthright of which we are in possession. I think it proper that you should know the names of the gentlemen to whom we are so greatly indebted, as I feel that all would possibly like to confess their thanks. They are: Mr. R. E. Campbell of Laggan and Field; Mr. Tom Martin and Jack Otto of Field and Leanchoil; Mr. S. H. Baker of Glacier; Mr. E. C. Barnes of Banff.[14]

As it turned out, the club was also able to express its appreciation in a more tangible way as the larger than expected attendance put the budget in the black. Between them, the outfitters received a "bonus" of $239. In spite of these meagre returns, the outfitters realized the potential of the situation if further gatherings were held in the future. They were correct, for there were benefits for them in the form of private parties after the main camp and the annual camp itself would soon become a much more lucrative proposition. The 1907 gathering was held in the Paradise Valley where the little horse transport required was provided exclusively by Elliott Barnes, but the 1908 camp at Rogers Pass was an entirely different proposition. Although the campsite was located close to the railroad, the area offered much of interest for those willing to sign up for one the several two-day excursions offered. These included trips to the Asulkan Valley, where an auxiliary camp was established, the Illecillewaet and the Deutschman (Nakimu) Caves in the Cougar Valley. As all these excursions required both horses and guides, resulting in an excellent pay day for the outfitters involved. From a total budget of $2,368 for the camp, $400 was paid for the use of horses, $273 for wages and $138 for a bonus.

The main beneficiaries were Simpson and Baker and Otto Brothers, a new partnership between Jack Otto and his brothers Bruce and Closson. They had arrived from Ontario about 1904 and like their sibling had gone to work for Wilson. In fact, Bruce Otto had been involved in a rather interesting scheme of Tom's At the instigation of Whymper and several other clients, Tom had experimented with the idea of offering boat trips down the North Saskatchewan River from Kootenay Plains to Edmonton. In July, 1904, after the peak of the run-off had subsided, he and Bruce had constructed a canvas boat and made the maiden voyage, experiencing difficulty handling the light craft in the strong current. Realizing that a canvas boat was unsuitable and that a heavier boat would be too expensive to ship back upstream by rail, Wilson thereafter abandoned the idea. Bruce went on to work for the company that his brother Jack was involved in with Tom Martin until it disbanded in 1907 and the new Otto Brothers organization was formed.

It is likely that Simpson and Baker and Otto Brothers were chosen to handle the outfitting for the 1908 camp because of the proximity of their bases of operation at Glacier and due to Wheeler's familiarity with them from survey work. Simpson had spent some time with Wheeler or topographic work in 1904 and 1905 while the Ottos had been employed in the same capacity from 1906 onward. During this period Wheeler honoured them with the naming of Otto Pass and Creek, part of the watershed of the Amiskwi River. His rather difficult personality, which sometimes bordered on the dictatorial, made working with him problematic, but those who could handle it were usually well-rewarded. In his annual address at the 1908 camp he made reference to his desire that there be organized "a corps of reliable guides and outfitters, who shall be available in connection with the work of the Club." Because of their excellent service at the 1908 camp, discussions were held with Otto Brothers on this score and in 1909 they received the valuable appointment of "Official Outfitters to the Alpine Club of Canada." To Jimmy Simpson went the position of "Equerry," their assistant in charge of horses.

This combination handled the 1909 camp placed on a beautiful meadow near the shore of Lake O'Hara, a gathering which saw 190 participants in attendance. The large number present required a considerable number of men to deal with the transport, and for the first time the outfitters and packers were allotted a separate section of the campsite solely for their own use. Another innovation, also much appreciated, was the organization of a six-day expedition into the Yoho Valley after the completion of the camp proper. Thirty-three took part in the circuit of the valley with packers and horses accompanying them as far as Sherbrooke Lake and then rejoining them at the foot of the Yoho Glacier. The expedition appreciably increased the amount paid for horses and outfitting and helped to point out the wiseness of the Ottos' and Simpson's determination to remain on good terms with "the Old Man." Wheeler himself was highly pleased with the orderliness and dispatch shown by the outfitters in carrying out their duties and was firmly convinced that his decision to appoint an official outfitter was a good one. This was particularly so in light of what had been transpiring with respect to the CPR concessions.

Diamond Hitch

In 1908 Bob Campbell's contract with the company had expired and instead of renewing it he decided to move on to some other, possibly more lucrative, means of earning a livelihood. A purchaser for the concession was found in Brewster Brothers, a company constantly on the lookout to expand its already considerable interests. The bid was supported by the western officials of the CPR who had close contacts with the Brewsters and were not at all averse to seeing the firm secure a complete outfitting and livery monopoly at the mountain hotels. A deal struck during the winter of 1907-08 saw the contract pass into Brewster Brothers hands but Campbell retain control of most of his horses and equipment. These he kept until May, 1909, when, having no further use for them, he sold the lot to Jim Brewster as well. After selling out, Bob moved to Calgary and entered the grain and flour trade, eventually becoming a highly successful businessman. His contacts with friends and acquaintances in the mountains were kept up and by 1913 both the Liberals and Conservatives were approaching him to run in the provincial election for the Rocky Mountain constituency. He chose to run under the Conservative banner and won the seat by eighty-one votes, holding it for a number of years.

Although the Brewster interests did not achieve a complete monopoly at the CPR mountain hotels until 1915, when they bought out Syd Baker at Glacier, by 1909 it certainly seemed that they were about to. There were those who feared for the fate of the independent outfitters should such occur, the foremost of whom was Wheeler. Part of his consideration may have stemmed from the events of 1906 when Bill Brewster left him in the lurch for the first camp. In any event, he took the opportunity to speak out about the tendency for the railroad company to allow a monopoly situation to develop. This presented an interesting situation, for at the same he was forced to acknowledge the CPR's help and support of the Alpine Club. His annual address at the 1909 camp presents a good example:

I now wish to call attention to a matter connected with our alpine regions that bids fair to becoming a serious abuse. I feel that it is one against which the Alpine Club, in loyalty to its propaganda, is bound to throw all its weight to prevent so crying an evil. I refer to the determined attempt now being made to create a monopoly of the guide and outfitting business for the mountain centres along the line of the Canadian Pacific Railway. When the railway first opened up the alpine regions of the main range to the mountaineer, the nature lover, the art seeker and the incidental tourist, there was formed in connection with the business a corps of men who were accustomed to wrestle successfully with the forces of nature and who could safely lead the traveller through the mazes of the virgin forest, across the dangerous leaps of the rushing torrent and over the snow-clad passes. These were men who could do things, who knew how to make you as comfortable in a mountain camp as in a palatial hotel, and far happier.

The object of the present attempted monopoly is to drive these men out of the field by bringing to bear against them the weight of the Canadian Pacific Railway Company. Wilson has gone, Stephens has gone, Martin, Peyto and Campbell and others have gone, driven out by the usual methods of monopoly. And the guides of whom Canada's mountain regions were so proud are now only a name. What have we instead? A service of boy youths imported during the holiday season from schools and colleges in the East, on whom is clapped a brand new suit of buckskin and they are dubbed "guides". God save the mark! They remind me of babes in the woods, and the sooner the robins come and cover them up with leaves the better . . . . That minor officials are in sympathy is apparent, and the cry is "We must protect our livery privileges". That is alright so long as such privileges do not infringe the rights of Canadians. The Canadian people have given certain rights to the Canadian Pacific Railway Company . . . but it cannot be that any such privileges were given for the purpose of preventing competent and reliable men from plying a legitimate business in a legitimate way, and from reaping a fair share of the mountain business. . . .

I now wish to make acknowledgement of the valuable assistance given to us at the present camp by several departments of the C.P.R. — consisting of the loan of two guides for the camp, transportation facilities and sundry other privileges.[15]

As it turned out, Wheeler was to be hoist on his own petard.

The 1910 camp was planned for the Consolation Valley, and, in addition, it was decided to establish a permanent camp in the Yoho Valley on a trial basis. A double camp demanded additional men, horses and equipment along with careful planning to ensure success. Over the winter, Wheeler was able to convince the Ottos and Simpson to take on the added responsibilities and matters proceeded apace until the very eve of the event. Then the roof fell in. Without warning the Otto brothers decided to pull up stakes and re-establish themselves in the Jasper district where two rail lines were pushing westward promising new opportunities for outfitting interests. As usual, Jim Brewster was on the scene to purchase their business, and with the sale went the contract to handle the Alpine Club's 1910 camps. Wheeler thus found himself in the unenviable position of being forced to rely on the services of a company with whom he was completely at odds. Although Brewster reached an agreement with the Otto brothers to superintend the outfitting from the Consolation camp before they took their leave, Brewster Brothers handled the transportation into this camp and all services connected with the Yoho Valley camp. Wheeler found much to be desired in their performance, stating that at the Yoho camp the result was "a most indifferent service" and that at the Consolation camp "the service was bungled by incompetent subordinates, causing annoyance to many of our visitors."[16]

The experience of 1910 reinforced Wheeler's feelings about the necessity of using independent outfitters for Alpine Club activities. Although it was several years before another official outfitter was appointed, he continued to use one of the independent outfitters along the CPR line, mainly Jimmy Simpson, when a camp was held in the region. As a result, the club continued to remain an important factor in the financial security of the area's trailmen and became a precursor for the direction which the guiding and outfitting profession would take in the not too distant future.

Chapter VI
Artists, Hunters and the Ladies

T he Alpine Club of Canada's support of independent outfitters while an important factor in the stability of the profession along the line of the CPR was not the only one. Another was the simple fact that the number of potential clients was growing rapidly with the ever-increasing onslaught of tourists who were annually descending on Rocky Mountain Parks and were anxious to visit the back country. Although there were yearly fluctuations, the number of visitors increased at such a brisk rate that by 1913 the park's hotels were registering some 61,000 guests, double the number of 1906. But there was another consideration that accounted for there being room to maneuver in the face of the Brewsters' grip on the CPR concessions — developments that were taking place in the operations of that company itself.

In 1908, when Brewster Brothers added the concessions at Lake Louise and Field to the one they held at Banff, it appeared only a matter of time until the company would have a complete stranglehold on outfitting along the CPR through the mountains. Yet there were several factors at work which tended to make this situation unlikely to occur, including the very nature of the concessions themselves. They allowed the company the sole right to solicit conveyance of any kind, be it by horse or carriage, within the confines of the railway's hotels and on station platforms. Often the carriage trade proved the more lucrative and consequently it received the most attention. This was particularly true in wet years when the convertible tally-hos used for sightseeing continued to run at full capacity while the trail business languished because of poor weather. In the same vein, the nature of the company's other business interests affected their trail operations.

143

Although its historic roots were in outfitting, the expansion of its activities into other concerns, including a store, livery stable, blacksmith shop and opera house, meant that a lot of attention was devoted to them, sometimes at outfitting's expense. The company's reputation and success as outfitters was mainly attributable to the guiding talents of Jim and Bill Brewster, but after 1905 neither could afford much time to personally lead parties on the trail.

A related factor was some internal developments in the company's management. As mentioned, when formed in 1904 Brewster Brothers partnership had been composed of Bill and Jim Brewster, Fred Hussey and Phil Moore, and for a number of years this combination worked effectively. However, before too long it became apparent the its success hinged more on the colourful personality of Jim Brewster than on its other members. He was the dynamic promoter, flamboyant public relations man and maker of contacts, while Bill preferred to remain behind the scenes and attend to the more mundane details of the business. Hussey's involvement seems to have been motivated more by his friendship with Jim than any real interest in the operations, and the two were close companions, not only on the trail but also in the salons of high society in the eastern United States. Moore, after he became a Brewster in-law in 1907, tended to be much more his own man. Although these differences did not lead to any serious difficulties, by 1906 Jim was finding the conditions of partnership too constraining and he and Hussey decided to pull out. In April he and Hussey sold their interest in Brewster Brothers, Hussey receiving a promissory note for $25,000 and Jim a mortgage note for $10,000. Jim remained in Banff until the fall of 1907 and then moved to Victoria, where his father had opened a real estate office after selling the Brewster Dairy to Frank Wellman. Although he came back to Banff to spend the summer of 1908, it was not until 1909 that he returned permanently because of the continuing inability of the company to pay off his note. An agreement with his brother Bill, who by this time had acquired Moore's shares, was reached in June, 1909 in which he acquired all the shares in Brewster Brothers and then converted it into two new companies, Brewster Transfer

Company and Brewster Trading Company. He retained the majority of shares, with Fred Hussey taking a minority position and his brother Fred Brewster being awarded a single share.

Upon the break-up of Brewster Brothers, Moore entered into an agreement with Fred and Jack Brewster in a new company, Brewster and Moore, and departed to enter the freighting and outfitting business west of Red Deer. Bill Brewster set his sights to the south and, after settling his family in San Antonio, Texas, took part in an extended trip to Chile with his friend Lincoln Ellsworth Upon his return, he moved to Reno, Nevada and then to Lake Tahoe, remaining there until approached with an interesting proposition in 1912. Glacier National Park in Montana was being developed by the Great Northern Railway, and company president Louis Hill asked newspaperman Jack Farrell, an acquaintance of Bill's, if he knew anyone capable of handling tourist transport at the lodges the company was building. Farrell claimed he knew just the man, and by the end of the year Bill was back in business with a new organization, the Park Saddle Horse Company.

It is not surprising that the difficult period it went through prior to 1909 affected the Brewster operation's ability to function efficiently. Indeed, even after outfitting came under the aegis of Brewster Transfer Company, there continued to be challenges. Again, this was largely a reflection of Jim Brewster's personality. When he chose to concentrate his full energies on the business it flourished, but all too often he was distracted by his involvement in local activities, from assisting with the organization of Banff Indian Days to serving on the Board of Trade, and by his attempts to encourage tourism in the Canadian Rockies. Being by nature a promoter, he travelled extensively appearing at expositions, sportsman shows and outdoorsmen's clubs and, through his associations with Hussey, visiting the "right" people in social and financial circles. A consummate showman, he often took the opportunity to play the part of the "wild west" character on these occasions. For instance, during a visit to the Earl of Suffolk's estate at Malmsbury he participated in the traditional fox hunt, appearing mounted on his hunter attired in buckskin shirt and grizzly bear chaps. Such antics were usually well received, and his ability to attract new and wealthy tourists for both the CPR and his own company was considerable. However, at the same time, his frequent absences from the office meant that subordinates had to look after the company's affairs, and the steadying hand of Bill Brewster was sorely missed. This sitution was aggravated when the business took on two new aspects with the purchase of the Mount Royal Hotel from David McDougall in 1912 and the acquiring of a newspaper, *The Rocky Mountain Courier*, in 1916.

Equally challenging to the effectiveness of the company's outfitting branch was the manpower situation, especially after the takeover of the concessions at Field and Laggan. At least three guides had to be stationed at these locations for the busy summer season, and it was often necessary to have more at Banff. And, of course, they had to be supported by a like number of cooks and numerous packers. With so many positions to be filled and the penchant for trailmen to drift from one outfit to another, it was a constant trial to find competent men at all times. Because of this and Jim's acquaintance with many wealthy easterners, the company sometimes reverted to the hiring of students. These young greenhorns, often drawn from the student ranks of Princeton, frequently left something to be desired in the performance of their duties. Wheeler had described them as "babes in the woods," but others also voiced their displeasure. Another disgruntled patron, identifying himself only as "Disgusted," wrote on the matter to the editor of the Banff *Crag and Canyon*:

The world can stand still for no one, and yet the pace at which the old sphere has been running along the CPR line for the past year or two has been an eye-opener to one who has visited your little town and other stopping places along the road in the past. Tom Wilson, Bill Peyto and Bob Campbell were familiar to all who loved the cayuse's back and the smell of the campfire. Where are they today? Who knew so well how to throw the diamond hitch, fry a pan of bacon, make a bough bed, or tell fascinating yarns when the day's march or hunt was over? We find but a handful of the old men left, the men who have dug deep into the secrets of camp life

146

and with their strong personalities lured us from the stock markets, the exchanges, the rush of business life in the east to forget for a time our cares by living with men who knew how to live. . . . Wake up you people of Banff, wake up my old friend CPR.

We people of the east have known the very cream of camping in your country. You are giving us some very false coin in return for our loyalty. Bring to the fore the real, the reliable outfitter, and send back to town the youngster who in stage "shaps" pose as wild cowboys to the innocent and unsuspecting tourist.[1]

In fairness, it must be said that these complaints did not apply to Brewsters' regular men, who were as competent as any on the trail. Fortunately for the company, when the concessions were taken over they could rely on a nucleus of such stalwarts as George Harrison, Fred Tabuteau, Bill Potts, Soapy Smith, Tex Wood and Frank Wellman, who had been with them for several years. Added to them were men from a variety of backgrounds: James I. McLeod, a former guide for Campbell who became Brewsters' head man at Lake Louise and eventually the company's general manager; Reggie Holmes, who had been associated with Elliott Barnes' outfit; Ulysse "Frog" LaCasse, a native of Ontario who began as a baker in The Birdcage but soon possessed a reputation as the finest trail cook in the Rockies; and Stan J. "Windy" Carr, an English immigrant who worked on several prairie ranches before joining Brewster Transfer at Lake Louise in 1910. Others included Wes Latam, Art Jordan, Howard "Fat" Kane, Frank Beattie, Ben Woodworth, Jack Bevan, Ike Brooks, Ted Cook, Jack Warren, George Hankins, Ray Legace, Roy Brydon, Jack Thomas and "Lord Jim" Howard. All these men had skills that made them valuable in their own way, and many would provide material for the colourful stories that would make the Brewster guides and pack ers legends in their own time.

One of the most notorious Brewster guides stationed at Field was George Hankins. Known as "The Hooknosed Kid" because of a particularly obvious physical characteristic, he had a brother nicknamed "Big Foot" because of an equally noticeable appendage. A native of the Columbia River country, Hankins had fought in the Boer War and upon returning had gone to work for Wilson and Campbell, becoming one of their head guides. When Brewsters took over the concession at Field he had remained in their employ along with his friend Jack Giddie, whose name was usually transposed to "Giddy Jack." The pair had prominent reputations for living the high life when not on the trail, and in Hankins's case it carried over to times when he should have been working. In 1909, Tex Wood was assigned to meet Hankins in Golden, from where they were to take out a party bound for the Windermere district. Tex arrived at the designated meeting place only to find that his fellow employee had not yet appeared, and after a considerable wait began to inquire as to his whereabouts. Someone finally directed him to a house just west of town, and when he approached it he heard a terrific din coming from within. On entering he immediately realized that it was a "house of assignation" and quickly found the source of the racket. Agilely running up and down the keyboard of a piano in his boots and spurs, much to the delight of the "ladies," was "The Hooknosed Kid."

Another celebrated character who went on the trail for Brewsters was "Lord Jim" Howard, a classic case of a remittance man run amok. A younger brother of the Earl of Suffolk, the Honourable James Escourt Howard, Viscount Andover was one of those second and third sons who were paid a substantial stipend as the price of their absence from the home fires. He first appeared at Banff in 1908 when he was a guest at the Brewster Bungalow, probably as a result of his brother's friendship with Jim Brewster. For several years thereafter he was regularly forced to go to work as a cook or packer because of his penchant for spending his remittance at the Banff Springs Hotel in a grand spree. After one such wild and woolly bender he was assigned to cook for a wealthy Pittsburg steel magnate. While sitting around the evening campfire a few days out on the trail the client, obviously having heard of Lord Jim's recent escapades, asked the guide, "This Lord Jim I heard about in town, is he really an Earl's brother?" "I guess so," replied the guide. "Do you know him?" "Yeah, I know him."

"Extraordinary thing, imagine a real Earl's brother. I'd give a lot to meet him. Cook, do you know him?" After what seemed like a long pause while the cook stared woefully into the glowing coals, he replied, "Yeah, too goddam well."[2]

Several outfitters were to benefit from the developments on the Brewster outfitting scene in the years preceding the war but none more so than Jimmy Simpson, the individual who soon became their chief competitor. Interestingly, Simpson and Jim Brewster shared a number of similar traits, among them being keen intellect and wit, a colourful personality and a streak of wildness Both also had a strongly developed love of the wilderness and were especially fond of hunting. After 1905 Brewster had to restrict his hunting activities to one or two pleasure trips a year, but Simpson, with his smaller interests, was able to make hunting an integral part of them. Both men were also performers at heart and recognized that showmanship could be made to work to their advantage. Any number of ploys were used to impress the dudes, a particularly notable one being Simpson's practice of studying up on his customers' interests, be they medicine or the stock market, so that he could talk intelligently with them. As he put it, this would eliminate the necessity of them having to listen to "the first eighty-seven stanzas of the cowboy's lament" while out on the trail.

Other techniques to impress dudes were a highly developed abilities to prevaricate and play practical jokes, and the adoption of distinctive attire. Brewster's sartorial trademark was his grizzly bear chaps and buckskin shirt while for Simpson it was his Mounted Police pony stetson, drawn from a mysteriously endless supply. Brewster's interests in community activities and the encouragement of tourism were also duplicated by Simpson. He spent much of his time in the winter coaching local hockey teams and promoting the Banff Curling Club. Beginning in 1916 he also began to make frequent trips to the eastern Canada and the United States to advertise the attractions of the park and his own business. During these sojourns he would stay in the homes of some his wealthy and well-connected clients and would accompany them to the opera or to their clubs, where he often provided the entertainment for those interested in hearing about the wilds of the Canadian Rockies. Finally, as most trailmen, both Brewster and Simpson had a well-developed fondness for whiskey and rum, or "Nelson's blood" as Simpson called it, and they went on many a tear, sometimes together.

Apart from his previously mentioned ability to obtain the outfitting contracts for the Alpine Club camps, Simpson also had increasing success in attracting important private parties. One customer who provided him with many valuable future connections was "the butterfly lady." Mrs. Mary de la Beach-Nichol, daughter of a former chancellor of the exchequer of Great Britain, had taken up lepidoptery as a hobby after her family of six children had grown up, and her collection ranked her with other such noteworthy authorities as the Rothchilds. Being wealthy, she could afford to spend long periods of time each summer traipsing about the mountains searching for rare and interesting butterflies and moths, and after her initial successful expedition to the Yoho Valley under Jimmy's care in 1904, she decided to visit the Mount Assiniboine region. Other parties running across them must have been surprised to see an old lady clad in a weather-beaten black gown wearing a dilapidated Panama hat with a butterfly net in one hand and an ear trumpet in the other stalking her elusive prey around the shores of Lake Magog, her guide in hot pursuit carrying the collecting box.

Despite the effect such activities might have had on his reputation as a big game guide, Jimmy recognized a good thing when he saw it and agreed to accompany Mrs. Beach-Nichol again the next year. This time she desired that they go on an extended trip of three months and cover some new territory. The horses were shipped by rail to Salmon Arm, B. C., and from there Jimmy led them south around Okanagan Lake, across the Similkameen River on a barge and eventually down to Lake Chelan in Washington State. While searching for specimens, they ventured up the Ashnola River on the International Boundary and into rattlesnake country. Here Jimmy became quite concerned about his client's welfare since he felt that she would be unable to hear the snake's warning rattle due to her deafness. He soon found he need not be concerned as the intrepid lady began searching out the snakes, pinning them down with a forked stick, cutting off their heads and then skinning them out for a new collection. On returning from this remarkable outing "the butterfly lady" was able to pronounce it an unqualified success as she had captured and identified two previously unknown varieties of moths. This led to a third trip in 1907 when they spent most of the summer around Jimmy's favourite territory between Bow Lake and the Alexandra River.

Another contact made by Jimmy shortly after Mrs. Beach-Nichol's final trip was to be one of the most important of his subsequent life and would greatly influence the artistic history of the Canadian Rockies. While reading the periodical publication of the New York Zoological Society in the winter of 1909-10, his eye fell on a reproduction of a painting of a Dall sheep done by the German artist Carl Rungius, then living at Greenpoint, Long Island. The quality of the work so impressed him that Jimmy wrote to the artist care of the Society and invited him to come to the Rockies where he would personally guide him to the best bighorn sheep range available. As Rungius had already spent a considerable time in the field in Wyoming, New Brunswick and the Yukon, he was at first unenthusiastic and threw the letter away feeling that it was just another guide looking for another client. But as luck would have it, his wife Louise insisted that he retrieve it as she felt the offer was genuine, and after an exchange of correspondence a trip was organized for August, 1910. Staying at Simpson's own home, recently constructed along the river next to Bill Peyto's old cabin, Rungius quickly got to know his guide and soon they were off on visits to Consolation Valley and Ptarmigan Lake in order that some preliminary sketches could be done. Then, in early September with Ernie Brearley as an assistant, Jimmy took the artist up the North Fork of the Saskatchewan, over Wilcox and Nigel passes and into the Brazeau basin. Here Rungius spent some time sketching goats and was able to kill a small ram which, with the addition of a grizzly he bagged on Nigel Pass, provided excellent models for his canvases.

Rungius proved so enthusiastic about the results of his 1910 trip that it became the first of an annual visit to the Rockies. Quickly his reputation flowered to the extent that Jimmy was able to convince the CPR to issue him with a yearly pass to Banff as a publicity measure and he began to accomplish some art works for their advertising program. For several years he and Louise stayed at the Simpsons while in Banff, but in the winter of 1921-22 it was decided that a more permanent studio and home was needed. Jimmy acquired two lots on Cave Avenue and set to work to build what became known as "The Paintbox" based on blueprints provided by an architect friend of the artist's. Thereafter, it became usual for Jimmy to supply the outfit for his summer pack trips while Rungius paid for two men and bought the supplies. In return for the use of the outfit, the two made a "paintings for pack horses" arrangement whereby Jimmy was given a painting each year for making his outfit available free of charge. Eventually these formed not only a fine core for Jimmy's extensive art collection but also appreciated in value to the point that they were worth many times more than any payment that he had foregone.

Rungius's growing reputation soon led Simpson into relationships with other notable artists, including Archibald Thorburn, Louis Aggasiz Fuertes and Henry Emerson Tuttle, and by performing a variety of services for them he again added to his art collection. For Thorburn he collected bird skins which were sent to England and stuffed to use as models for bird paintings. Jimmy was suitably rewarded with a painting of some goldfinches, the models for which had been among the specimens he gathered. Fuertes requested the skinned out heads of game animals which had to be sawed into parts and sent to his studio in Ithaca, New York, work which was compensated for with a painting of a blue jay. Tuttle was taken out on an extended pack trip that he so enjoyed that he showed his appreciation by sending Jimmy a painting of a goshawk. Ultimately, all these men provided such an influence that they awakened in Jimmy a desire to do his own painting and in time he became an accomplished watercolourist.

A further important offshoot of Simpson's relationship with

Rungius was the connections it gave him with some of America's wealthiest big game hunters. Handling big game hunters was an integral part of every successful outfitter's business as in many seasons the income from tourists, mountaineers and fishermen was sufficient only to meet the year's expenses. In such circumstances, any profit would usually come from hunting trips at the end of the season. Fortunately for Jimmy, he had a passion for big game hunting, especially for bighorn sheep, the animal most prized by the majority of his clients. In 1903 Rungius had become a charter member of the Campfire Club of America, a social club composed of 150 of the United States' leading outdoorsmen. Always anxious to be placed in touch with guides capable of leading them to potential world record trophies, these men were soon enquiring as to whom it was that was handling his trips. This led to Jimmy's guiding of parties that were composed of those who would subsequently become his most loyal clients, including William N. "Billy" Beach and Joseph A. McAleenan, two of New York's foremost businessmen, and Dr. Harlow Brooks, a leading heart and lung specialist.

Jimmy's reputation as a sheep guide and his love of the occupation were perhaps best described by Robert Frothingham, an eminent American sportsman who often wrote for the outdoors magazine *Field and Stream*: "Simpson is, without doubt, the best hunter and most expert stalker of Bighorn Sheep in Western Canada. To quote his own words he would rather stalk sheep than occupy a front seat in the heavenly choir!"[3] Apart from Jimmy's stalking ability, his main attributes as a sheep hunting guide were unwavering patience and instinct, both of which were well-illustrated on Billy Beach's maiden attempt to procure a Canadian Rockies ram. For several years he had taken parties to different parts of the mountains in search of sheep with varying degrees of success, but it was not until about 1910 that he discovered the Brazeau River basin, henceforth his sheep hunting mecca. This was where he led Beach and his companion H. G. Morden, and soon after arriving he spotted some rams on a glacier. However, as it was late in the afternoon he decided it would be best to leave them undisturbed until the following day. Early next morning the rams were found in the same locale and the hunt begun in earnest:

Patience now came into the game, for we lay behind some rocks from eleven o'clock in the morning until five in the afternoon before they began to feed. At five-twenty we started the stalk and here was where Jim's ability as a ram hunter stood out. The wind was quite strong and though favorable there were so many draws on the moraine it was important to avoid places that might lead down towards the sheep. Jim worked carefully and deliberately, going well above and then gradually coming down until we were within about a hundred yard. The one decided on had a beautiful curl. . . and it took us but a short time until we were off to camp.[4]

Jimmy's patience in waiting six hours for the right moment and then a flawless stalk had resulted in a fine ram for Beach, and soon his instinct was to provide an equally good opportunity for Morden. While sitting in camp waiting for dinner, he became uneasy and rose from his seat, mentioning that he felt there were some sheep in the vicinity. Although the others scoffed at his suggestion, he nonetheless picked up his binoculars and began scanning the mountainside. Within a few minutes he was able to announce that there were eight good rams just behind camp. A flurry of activity ensued and in no time he and Morden started off after them. None met with their approval that evening, but the next day the same flock were tracked and an excellent trophy taken from the thirty-eight rams they spotted. Similar instances of premonition would stand Jimmy in good stead on many another hunt. In fact, in later life he claimed that he would sometimes dream there was game in a particular location and on investigating the next day would find it there.

One other interesting, although much less auspicious, aspect of Jimmy's big game hunting activities was his penchant for poaching if the opportunity arose. During the early years of the national parks' existence the regulations regarding game preservation were virtually impossible to enforce due to the absence of a well-

154

organized and staffed force of wardens. Taking game illegally was therefore a relatively safe and easy matter. Many of the trailmen in the Canadian Rockies took advantage of the situation at one time or another, although they rarely informed their clients that they were breaking the law. Eventually, though, the creation of an effective "game guardian" service coupled with the tightening up of regulations in 1909, including the licensing of guides and the registering of all hunting parties, began to bring the situation under control. Jimmy persisted in his old habits and was finally caught in the act of taking a sheep in the park. The outcome of the resulting court case was a $100 fine and the revocation of his guide's license for the remainder of the season. However, necessity being the mother of invention, he quickly found a way to get around the restriction. Having one of his men sign out the party as guide while he listed himself as cook, he would immediately take over responsibility for the party once out on the trail. Even considering the fine and the inconvenience, he was luckier than others who faced similar charges. Just prior to his own arrest a Brewster party had been convicted on the same charge and, in addition to fines levied on each member of the staff, the entire outfit, valued at some $1,000, had been confiscated.

Although poaching had its obvious drawbacks, the chance that Jimmy took on one occasion proved to be worth the risk. In fact the incident, which occurred in 1920, provided him with the sheep hunting moment of his life. While reconnoitering near the Divide in the Fortress Lake region at dusk on the evening of November 2nd, two days after the season had officially closed, he spotted a single ram but was unable to get a shot. The next day he stalked the animal and discovered that it had joined a group of fifteen others inside the park boundary. Acting on the premise that it was no worse to break two regulations than one, he decided to try take the animal because of its obvious trophy-size curl. But just as he was about to shoot, the ram hopped up on the back of another animal, as they were wont to do during the rut. Adjusting his aim, Jimmy squeezed off a shot, unluckily just as the ram was dismounting and watched disconsolately as it ran off with the rest of the flock.

But on the faint hope that he might get another opportunity, he began tracking them in the light sprinkling of snow that was on the ground. Before going far, he noticed that one set of tracks were blood-spattered and turned off from the rest. Following these to the crest of a small ridge he was amazed to see the ram standing under an outcropping of rock just below him, and he was easily able to finish it off with one shot. When he reached the animal it became apparent that his first shot had split its hoof and it had been attempting to hide. It was also obvious that he was a real grand-daddy, and when its head was later measured at Banff it was found to have a 49 1/2 inch curl, a world's record. Eventually Jimmy was able to sell it to an American collector for a good price and it went on permanent display in the New York Museum of Natural History. However, the money received was minor in comparison to the advertising value of a world record head and a representation of it soon adorned Jimmy's letterhead, attracting even more attention from the hunting fraternity.

Previous to 1910, Jimmy had guided most parties coming his way personally, aided by Ernie Brearley and occasionally some other temporary help. But the increasing business stemming from the relationship with Rungius and his friends soon meant that he had to increase his staff. The first two he chose to employ were local lads with good blood lines for trailmen — Joe Woodworth, the son of Ben Woodworth, who had been one of Wilson's first packers in the 1890s, and John Wilson, Tom's eldest son who had grown up in the business and had been assisting his father at the Kootenay Plains ranch since 1905. As time went on several more capable men were added to the roster as conditions warranted. Among them were Ulysse LaCasse, Jim Boyce, Max Brooks, Jack "Rosey" Powell, George "Mousie" Saddington, Verne Castella, John Musko, Percy "Beef" Woodworth, Jack Greaves, Ben Woodworth jr. and Jack Cooley. Likewise, it also became necessary to find additional pack animals, a problem that was solved by a deal worked out with Tom Wilson in 1911.

Wilson had been continuing to try convince the government to grant his leases on his Kootenay Plains ranches for a number of years, but without success. As well, the lengthy recuperation from his injuries sustained in the 1908 Christmas trip had required him to turn over responsibility for the ranches' stock to his son John. With the excellent grazing available on the plains, it had increased from the original thirty head of 1903 to one hundred and forty head by 1911. In October of that year his frustration had reached the point that he agreed to sell Simpson a one-half interest in the stock, buildings, improvements and leases, should they ever be obtained, for the sum of $4,000. The other half-interest was temporarily turned over to his son, who in December, 1911 entered into a partnership with Jimmy, known as Wilson and Simpson, to operate the ranches. Thus, after a strenuous spring of bronc busting in 1912, Jimmy had all the horseflesh he needed.

Although Simpson handled the majority of the parties not secured by Brewsters at this time, there were two other individuals who managed to successfully break into the outfitting business. They were William "Billy" Warren and Sidney J. Unwin, both English-born Boer War veterans, and their eventual success in establishing outfits of their own could be traced to a fortuitous relationship with a client whose reputation as a tourist-explorer of the fairer sex would be unparalleled in the annals of the Canadian Rockies. She was Mrs. Mary T. S. Schäffer, who would receive the Stoney name "Yahe-Weha" (Mountain Woman) for her accomplishments. Born Mary T. Sharples in 1869 at Westchester, Pennsylvania of moderately wealthy Quaker parents, she received her early education at local schools before going on to university to study art. There she befriended Mary Vaux, a girl with similar interests, and in 1888 she accompanied her on a summer vacation to Glacier House where her brothers, George and William Vaux, were engaged in a pioneer effort to measure and photograph the Illecillewaet Glacier. The next summer she again visited Glacier House, this time as the new bride of Dr. Charles Schäffer, a botanist connected with the Academy of Natural Science of Pennsylvania. Thereafter, until Dr. Schäffer's untimely death in 1903, the couple made an annual pilgrimage to the mountains so that he could engage in botanical work. After his death she collaborated with

Stewardson Brown, curator of the herbarium at the Academy, in compiling a book from her husband's data. She was responsible for the beautiful watercolours and photographs illustrating *Alpine Flora of the Canadian Rocky Mountains*, which was eventually published in 1907.

On her early visits to the mountains Mrs. Schäffer was not overly enamoured with "roughing it." Her most distinct recollection of camping on the shore of Lake Louise in 1893 was one of having "looked out on that magnificent scene with chattering teeth and shivering bodies." But thanks to the persistence of her companions and Tom Wilson, who was given the responsibility of showing her the sights, she gradually learned to accept the rugged landscape on its own terms and to enjoy travelling in it. At a later date, she acknowledged in a letter to Tom his part in her conversion: "I owe many a lovely bit of memory to Tom Wilson who simply dragged a poor little delicate tourist to points she would not have reached had you not insisted."[6] As her aversion turned to infatuation, she became interested in reports of the expeditions of Wilcox, Fay, Collie *et al* and along with a Quaker friend, Mollie Adams, soon wished to participate in such adventures herself. Sadly, she found that while it was acceptable for a lady to be a sightseer, it was not proper to take part in longer trail trips, that being the exclusive preserve of men:

We fretted for the strength of man, for the way was long and hard, and only the tried and stalwart might venture where cold and heat, starvation and privation stalked ever at the explorer's heels. In meek despair we bowed our head to the inevitable, to the cutting knowledge of the superiority of the endurance of man. . . . . They left us sitting on the railway track following them with hungry eyes as they plunged into the distant hills. . . . .[7]

So matters remained until the death of her husband brought with it the freedom to make her own decisions and the realization that she had as much right as any man to experience the dangers and hardships of the trail. In 1904, in company with Mollie

Adams, she convinced Wilson to set up a program of excursions which would gradually build up their ability to undergo the rigours of an expedition lasting an entire season. For the first three day jaunt into the Yoho Valley, Tom himself acted as the guide, but for the next trip he provided Billy Warren, a handsome young guide working for him at Field. Born at Harlow, Essex, on January 13, 1880, Warren had benefitted from an excellent education at Saint Mary's College. At the outbreak of the Boer War he had volunteered in the Imperial Yeomanry, and when the fighting ended he went to London to work as a clerk. Soon becoming discontented with city life, he decided to emigrate to Canada and arrived in Banff about 1903. Wilson offered him a job as a packer, and after one season he was found competent enough to graduate to guide, capable to leading shorter excursions while he gained experience. Such was the case of his first trip with Mrs. Schäffer and Miss Adams — a short excursion to Moraine Lake.

Upon returning for further "toughening up" expeditions in 1905 and 1906, the ladies were again assigned to Warren's care. The 1905 outing consisted of a week's stay in the Ptarmigan Valley, while that of 1906 was more extensive, covering an area as far north as Wilcox Pass and lasting some five weeks. By that time Mrs. Schäffer had become quite an admirer of Warren, for she found that while there were guides possessing more knowledge of "forest lore" and trails, she felt that "for kindness, good nature and good judgment under unexpected stress he had no superior." [8] When the time came the next year to take a trip that would last an entire season, it was understood that it would be under Warren's direction, and in order to facilitate matters she agreed to buy all the horses, saddlery, blankets and other tack necessary for him to outfit it himself. She also provided sufficient funds to hire another man who could act as a combination packer and cook, and Warren's choice fell on Sid Unwin, a fellow Englishman who had been establishing a favourable reputation as a tough and dependable woodsman in the few years since his arrival in the mountains.

Unwin, a young man of stocky build whose lantern-jawed countenance hinted at an inner strength and endurance, was the

nephew of T. Fisher Unwin, one of England's leading book pub-
lishers. Although details of his education are sketchy, it must have
been a good one for he was capable of making jokes in Latin. Like
Warren, he had been a volunteer for service in the Boer War and
had earned a decoration for bravery while serving with an artillery
battery. Returning from the war, he had gone to work in London
as a clerk before being lured to Canada by the prospect of adventure and a better future. Arriving in Banff in 1904, he had immediately joined Syd Baker on a snowshoe trip to his trapline on the
North Saskatchewan River. The next summer he had gone to work
for Simpson and Baker on the trail, and the following winter began
to run his own trapline up the Pipestone and down the Siffleur. It
proved to be an excellent means to familiarize himself with the
country and to toughen up to withstand its hardships. The winter
of 1906-07 proved to be particularly difficult, and on one occasion
the snow conditions were so bad on his fifty-five mile trek to the
Saskatchewan that it took him ten days to snowshoe the distance.
At the head of the Siffleur, he found himself so exhausted that he
fell asleep in front of his campfire and only awoke when his mack-
inaw pants and underwear caught fire and burned into his flesh.
In agony, he made the rest of the distance to the Wilson ranch without stopping and after perfunctorily answering Tom's queries and
having a bite to eat rolled into a bunk and slept for twenty-six
hours. A week later he joined Simpson at his cabin at the mouth of
the Mistaya with a piece of cloth from his underwear the size of a
hand still attached to the burn. Each day thereafter as the burn
slowly healed Jimmy cut away a small piece of the cloth with the
only painkiller being a swallow of rum.

Such was the measure of the man who joined Warren, Mrs.
Schäffer and Miss Adams at Laggan in late June, 1907. The proposed objective of the expedition was to investigate the sources of
the Saskatchewan and Athabasca rivers, but in the back of the
ladies' minds was the hope that they might be able to visit a lake
about which Simpson had told them. Called Chaba Imne (Beaver
Lake) by the Stoney, it was supposed to lie north of Brazeau Lake,
although the natives were somewhat reticent about its exact loca-

tion. Warren began by leading his charges on a trail they had travelled previously to Wilcox Pass and then down the Sunwapta to its junction with the Athabasca. From there, the branches of the Athabasca were followed, the west fork to Fortress Lake and the east fork to its source at Mount Columbia. Since it was by then well into August, they turned around and headed back through Wilcox Pass where, during a heavy snowstorm, they had a chance encounter with the A. P. Coleman party headed north for the Yellowhead Pass and Mount Robson. A few days later at "Graveyard Camp" at the mouth of the Alexandra River they met Simpson and Mrs. Beach-Nichol putting the finishing touches on their summers' collecting. Jimmy related what he knew about the mysterious lake, and before long the foursome were headed over Nigel Pass to Brazeau Lake. This they managed to reach without difficulty, but then their luck ran out as attempts to head further north were turned back by heavy snows obliterating the trails and all but blocking the passes.

Retreating to Pinto Lake and then down the Cline River to Kootenay Plains, their fortunes improved somewhat when they met a band of Stoney which included Sampson Beaver. Mrs. Schäffer had met Sampson the previous year and knew that he possessed as much knowledge about the surrounding country as anyone. Upon the completion of a dinner hosted by Elliott Barnes in his rough cabin, to which Sampson was shrewdly invited, she managed to get the exact location of the lake from him. In fact, he even agreed to draw a rough map showing her the route to get there. This was carefully stowed away for future reference, and the party soon continued on its way back to the railroad, following the route over Howse and Amiskwi passes out to Field.

Spurred by the new information they had acquired, the two ladies were determined to find the lake the next year. Arrangements were made with Warren to outfit and guide, and Unwin was again approached to be the assistant. Also recruited was Reggie Holmes, who was needed because the party was to be enlarged with Stewardson Brown, who planned to do some botanical collecting. Because of these additions, the pack string consisted of twenty-two horses, eleven being purchased from Bill Peyto's excellent stock. Armed with Sampson's map, this entourage set off from Warren's newly completed corrals near the Lake Louise Chalet on the morning of the 8th of June. This time there was little dilly-dallying along the way as the pack train was headed straight across the Saskatchewan, up the North Fork and through Nigel Pass to Brazeau Lake. Here the map came into play, providing directions around the lake and then over Poboktan Pass. Nevertheless, the trail soon became extremely faint and covered with burnt timber and mud slides, leading the guides to begin doubting the veracity of Sampson's directions. Turning up what they hoped was the right valley, it took two days of fighting snow and downed timber before they discovered a hopeful looking defile. Upon crossing it they continued to push on for the better part of another day, expecting to see the lake at every corner. As the dispirited party halted for lunch on the 7th of July, Unwin could no longer stand it and said he was going off to climb something high and not come back until he had discovered the lake:

. . . After lunch U. started out climbing to find the lake or bust, with compass, aneroid, maps, camera and field glasses, so that nothing should escape him. He left camp at about 3 p.m. and returned at 10:45, having, as he said "kept hopping all the time". He climbed about 2500 feet to the top of the ridge north of camp, dropped sown 2000 feet, then up again on what seemed to be a shoulder of Mt. _____ to 8750 feet — saw the lake! Went right down to it, 5600 feet, and around and home again over the lower wooded shoulders.[9]

Later the mountain would bear the name of Unwin as a fitting memorial to his efforts on that day and the trip as a whole. Likewise, another peak on the lake's shore would be named for Warren as a tribute to his part in the success.

Their hard-sought objective finally achieved, the ladies were treated to a raft tour of the lake over the succeeding few days. After this an attempt to explore its outlet to the Athabasca was frustrated by impassible timber, and it was decided they would have to retrace their steps back to Poboktan Creek, and then reach the Athabasca and Miette rivers and ultimately Tête Jaune Cache by the way of the now well-known route down the Sunwapta. When it was reached, Brown and Holmes took their leave while the rest of the party determinedly set their sights northwards. The elements were anything but propitious, moving Warren to remark after a day of constant drenchings that "in this country there are 24 kinds of weather for the 24 hours of the day — hot and cold and 22 kinds of rotten."[10]   However, they persisted and eventually reached the homestead of Lewis Swift, an American prospector who had married a Métis woman and had settled down to try farming and ranching at a location called "the Palisades." Gazed on with open-mouthed astonishment by his three children, the ladies learned that they were the first white women ever to appear in the valley. Departing from Swift's, they made a somewhat monotonous trip up the Miette to Tête Jaune Cache, where again they found that they were the first fair skinned females to visit that rough encampment. Finally, the shortening days told Warren that it was time to be thinking about home, and after a more-or-less routine trip arrived back in Laggan on September 20th.

The 1908 trip was a tremendous accomplishment for two ladies with backgrounds such as those of Mary Schäffer and Mollie Adams, and they were accorded much praise and recognition. But they realized that most of the credit was due to the two fine gentlemen who had made it possible. In later years, Mrs. Schäffer would state that it was "Mr. Warren's long outlook and Sid's determination" that had made the expedition such a success and would describe her own contributions as "like the tail to an active horse."[11] She would also acknowledge this in a book which she began to write upon her return to Philadelphia. Relying on Tom Wilson's knowledge and his excellent library, she corresponded with him on the history of the country that her trip had encompassed. He was able to provide many bits of background information largely from his copy of the Palliser Report, the most important being that the outlet from the lake had been referred to as the Bad or Maligne River by Dr. Hector in 1859. Maligne was therefore the name that the lake finally bore and as such it appeared in Mrs. Schäffer's book *Old Indian Trails of the Canadian Rockies* published in 1911.

After two years of working with Warren, Sid Unwin secured his own outfit in 1909, probably also with some assistance from Mrs.Schäffer. Even though his pack string was not large, he was able to guide some interesting parties in the next few years. Perhaps his most loyal client was Dr. B. W. Mitchell, a Philadelphia professor of classical and modern languages, whom he took on pleasure trips in 1910 and from 1912 to 1914. In a book which later recounted these journeys entitled *Trail Life in the Canadian Rockies*, Mitchell acknowledged his guide's abilities and deportment: "Here I desire to pay deserved and grateful tribute to that prince of guides, Sid Unwin. Unsurpassed in woodcraft and resourcefulness, unequalled in thoughtful kindness to his party, and with the charm of courteous manner that adds a touch of perfection to the little self-centred microcosm that a party in the wilderness constitutes, to him is owing through several seasons the personal safety, the perfect comfort, the entire pleasure of the expeditons."[12]

Mary Schäffer was also to have recourse to Unwin's services again when she took him along as an extra guide for the surveying of Maligne Lake in 1911. Meanwhile, in 1907, his sister Ethel had come out from England and had begun to help Mrs. Syd Baker set up a photo and souvenir tent to be run in conjunction with her husband's outfitting business at Glacier House. By 1912 Sid felt that his own operation could benefit from a similar enterprise and along with his sister and his brother Art established Unwin's Curios and Souvenirs. As well, he also began publishing a yearly edition of a *Guide to Banff* which listed all the points of interest in the park and advertised his ability to get tourists to them.

Billy Warren also continued to play an active role in outfitting for the next few years, running his pack train out of a headquarters established at Field. His most important patron continued to be Mrs. Schäffer who he annually took to some interesting place, often in the company of her sister-in-law Carrie Sharples and nephew Paul. Her relationship with her guide continued to develop and in June, 1915, in a romantic, almost fairy-tale ending to their adventures on the trail, they married and settled down in Banff.

Not all of those who attempted to make their livelihood by following the trail in the years prior to the First World War were as successful as Warren and Unwin. For example, two other well-known Banff residents, Joseph Boyce and W. G. Fyfe, outfitted for a season or two before finding the going too tough. Thereafter, both mainly turned their attention to the securing of government trail clearing contracts, which were becoming increasingly more common as the parks administration began to make more substantial efforts to open up the back country for tourists. In addition, Elliott Barnes, despite his close contact with the Alpine Club, found that after two years of trying his efforts were not meeting with the desired results. After disposing of his ranch to Wilson, he secured the position of manager of the Scott and Leeson Ranch near Morley and then in 1910 moved to a homestead in the Jumping Pound district. Finally, even such a hardy old-timer as Bill Peyto found that the trail no longer provided the life that it once had and he too disposed of his interests.

Peyto's departure from the ranks of Banff outfitters was as surprising as Wilson's had been several years previously. With the fine reputation he had built up, it seemed likely that the establishment of his own business would lead to a bright future. For a time these hopes seemed justified, as his outfitting of Outram in 1902 was followed by the servicing of several other important parties in the succeeding years. Among these was Gertrude Benham, a famous British woman climber who he and his assistant Jim Wood escorted to Mount Assiniboine in 1904, she being the third person and the first female to make its conquest. Others included Walter Wilcox in 1905 and a party composed of eight Bostonians led by J. F. Porter in 1906. However, that was the last year he outfitted any major parties, the immediate reason being the death of his wife Emily in September of that year. While he still advertised his services as an outfitter and guide in 1907, it was apparent his heart was no longer in it. About this time he admitted to climbing guide

165

Conrad Kain, who was visiting him at his mining claim on Red Earth Creek, that he would be "ten to fifteen years further from the grave" had his wife not died. By 1908 he had ceased to advertise and had disposed of most of his outfit.

After leaving outfitting, Bill spent most of his time prospecting and working his talc claim. When not engaged in these pursuits he lived a hermit-like existence in a home he had built on Banff Avenue, appropriately sporting a sign "Ain't it Hell" to sum up his view of life at the time. Happily, by 1910 his spirits had begun to pick up somewhat, and it was not long before he began to start guiding the odd party for Brewsters. Soon he was back to his old tricks, sparing no one, including his employers. On returning from one of his outings on their behalf he brought back a wolverine which he had wounded and then rendered unconscious with chloroform. Arriving at the Brewster livery, he dumped the ferocious animal out of the canvas sack he had been carrying it in only to find that it had succumbed during the journey. Noticing two of the Brewster brothers standing nearby he pushed back his hat, scratched his head and with a twinkle in his eye remarked: "Oh, I know what's the matter with that polecat. It couldn't take it living here amongst all these Liberals. He was too good a Conservative to hob nob with this gang."[13] Bill occasionally continued to go out with the Brewsters until 1913 when he was able to overcome his dislike for the government enough to join the warden service, thereafter becoming legendary in his patrols of the Healy Creek-Sunshine district to which he was assigned.

Departures from the outfitting business of older men like Peyto and the failure of newer ones to get established were not surprising given the nature of the occupation. Certainly the Brewsters grip on the cream of the tourist crop had much to do with this, but it was not the only factor. The country that had been visited by the Schäffer party on the Athabasca in their search for Maligne Lake was coming alive as a tourist destination and beginning to provide some real competition to the ascendancy of Banff. It was not surprising, therefore, that some of the former outfitters along the CPR would begin to find it attractive.

Diamond Hitch

Camp at the foot of Takakkaw Falls in the Yoho Valley

Hector Crawler and Tom Wilson at first Indian Days, 1894

Bob Campbell (on horseback at rear) at Lake Louise Chalet

A wag's memorial to
Edward Whymper

Fred Ballard

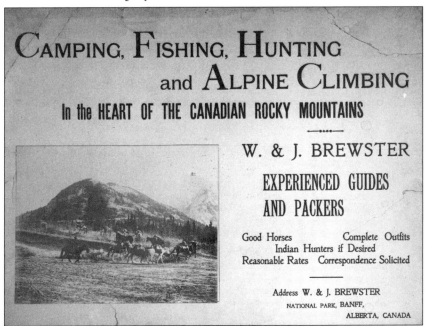

W. & J. Brewster advertising poster

Brewster party on trip to the Yellowhead, 1904. Standing — Bob Logan, Sid Collins, Phil Moore, George Harrison and Jim Brewster. Seated — Fred Tabuteau and Halsey Williams

Launching "The Glacier Belle" on Glacier Lake, 1902

Soapy Smith at rest

Bill Peyto's calendar

Elliott Barnes in his cabin at the Kadoona Tinda Ranch

Tom Wilson on snowshoes   *Jim Simpson after "big game"*

Alpine Club founding meeting. Rear — Tom Martin (2nd left), A. O. Wheeler (3rd left), Tom Wilson (3rd right), Bob Cambell (right). Front — Dan Campbell (left), Syd Baker (2nd left)

Mary Schäffer at the Kootenay Plains

Chapter VII
Away to the Athabasca

*I*f not for a trick of fate, the country around Jasper and not that in the vicinity of Banff would have become the mecca for tourists, sportsmen and climbers in the years after 1885. Historically and geographically, the Jasper area held all the advantages. After David Thompson's discovery of Athabasca Pass in 1811, it had replaced Howse Pass as the primary fur trade route to the Columbia River country and the Pacific coast. Situated astride the transcontinental route of commerce, the Athabasca Valley saw early development not present along the Bow. To aid in provisioning the fur brigades, a North West Company post was established at the north end of Brûlé Lake about 1813. Later relocated to a site on Jasper Lake, the post became known as Jasper House after Jasper Hawse, the trader placed in charge. Complementing it was a somewhat smaller post known as Henry House, which seems to have occupied several different locales near the junction of the Miette and Athabasca Rivers. Iroquois natives, first brought west by the North West Company as canoemen, gradually settled in the surrounding area, earning a livelihood working on the fur brigades, trapping and trading with the company.

In addition to those connected with the fur trade, the region was also visited by a variety of other travellers during the years between 1835 and 1870. Among others, these included the artist Paul Kane and the Belgian Jesuit Father Pierre J. de Smet in 1846, Dr. James Hector of the Palliser Expedition in 1859, the Overlanders of 1862 and the Milton and Cheadle expedition of 1863. Following close on their heels were the early surveyors for the CPR. Beginning about 1830 some of the fur trade's attention which had been exclusively focused on Athabasca Pass had shifted to the lower, more easily traversed Leather or Yellowhead Pass at the head of the Miette River, and the CPR, anxious to find a suitable route through the barrier of the Rockies, became intent on examining its feasibility for the proposed line. After its exploration by Marcus Smith, Walter Moberly, Henry McLeod and several other CPR surveyors in the years between 1871 and 1880, the Yellowhead was indeed found to be the most practicable pass, and it seemed as though the area would once again enter a new era of development. But two factors combined to plunge it into relative obscurity for the next thirty years. These were the unexpected and controversial 1881 decision by the CPR to abandon the proposed route through the Yellowhead in favour of a more southerly line up the Bow and down the Kicking Horse, and the final closure of Jasper House by the Hudson's Bay Company in 1884. After these debilitating events, the area was left solely to its few inhabitants — the ancestors of the original Iroquois, their half-breed relatives and Lewis Swift and his family.

Among the outfitters along the CPR line there was only very limited knowledge of the country north of the confluence of the Sunwapta with the Athabasca. The only group visiting the region from Banff was the Moore-Hussey party outfitted by Brewster Brothers in 1904. There was also some information available from the Stoney and from the reports of A. P. Coleman, who had made several trips in search of Mounts Hooker and Brown in the nineties. Despite their lack of detailed knowledge, though, it was not long before the pressure of competition began to turn some trailmen's eyes toward this undeveloped region as a scene for their activities. As mentioned, the Otto brothers were among them, but the distinction of being the first to make the move went to Fred Stephens.

The impetus for Stephens's first attempt to reach the Athabasca country was provided by his friend and frequent client Stanley Washburn. While at college he had done considerable reading and research on the mountains of western Canada and was puzzled by the blank spaces north of the CPR on most maps. Unable to find any information on the area, he soon decided to examine it for himself. Contacting Fred in early 1901 to arrange for an outfit, Washburn received a rather skeptical reception as he maintained that the country was "out of his beat." Nevertheless, he agreed to go, and along with two helpers and a fifteen horse pack train met Washburn at Laggan. If Stephens had a fault as an outfitter and guide it was that he failed to take along enough supplies, relying too heavily on the killing of game en route. On this occasion, the grub pile was already low soon after crossing the Saskatchewan, and the party had to lay over in order to hunt sheep. They were able to take five, but in the process Washburn badly twisted his ankle and had to rest in camp for almost two weeks before being once again fit for the trail. The shortage of food and this forced delay made any further attempt to proceed northward out of the question and the party returned, ingloriously, to Laggan. But the failure of 1901 only whetted Washburn's desire to achieve his objective, and when he approached Stephens again in 1903, Fred also expressed a keen desire in seeing his client's goal successfully achieved. Again the party set out from Laggan and again shortages and delays conspired to throw the trip off schedule. This time Wilcox Pass was gained before Washburn's companions decided they wished no more of horses and trails, and the pack string was once more turned around.

In spite of the failure of these two trips, they did awaken in Fred a determination to visit and explore the Yellowhead country for himself. About 1905 he finally succeeded in doing so after setting out from his home at Lacombe, and was so impressed that it became his habit to make a yearly visit. Since there weren't any parties immediately available to outfit in the vicinity, he filled his time timber cruising and prospecting around the headwaters of the Fraser River. While doing so in the summer of 1907 he paid a short visit to Tête Jaune Cache and there made the acquaintances of Bill and Mort Teare, two veteran prospectors, and their young understudy Ted Abrams. Some sixty-five years later Abrams could still clearly recall the event, as while camped with them Fred made the biggest saskatoon berry pie he had ever laid eyes on — two inches deep and a full fouteen by seven inches across! More importantly, the chance meeting with the Teares resulted in the forming of a close relationship, and thereafter Fred spent much of his time in their company.

While these events were transpiring, the long dormant Jasper area was once more on the verge of coming to life with the decision of two new transcontinental railways, the Grand Trunk Pacific (GTP) and the Canadian Northern (CNR), to utilize the Yellowhead Pass for their lines and with the creation of Jasper Forest Park (later Jasper National Park) in September, 1907. This meant that guiding and outfitting was likely to become a viable occupation in the district, and Fred prepared himself by learning as much as possible about the areas which would prove interesting from a tourist point-of-view. As he was now permanently located at Lacombe, he would have to bring in parties from that point, but he had now travelled the mountain trails linking the two locales on several occasions and was convinced that it was feasible. Not surprisingly, his first customer was Washburn in 1909.

Fred had made plans the previous fall to meet the Teare brothers at their mining claim some sixty miles down the Fraser from Tête Jaune Cache and his client eagerly fell in with the idea. The party included a young mining engineer named Sawyer, a cook and Fred's brother Nick. Nick Stephens had worked throughout the western United States as a lumberjack before returning to the family homestead in Michigan, from where he came once every few years to join his brother on a pack trip. Washburn took an immediate liking to him, describing his as "a-day-in-and-day-out, smile-in-the-rain, stick-with-you-in-trouble kind of a companion." The journey turned out to be an epic one lasting from June to October and covering a vast extent of territory. Beginning at Lacombe, they proceeded to the North Saskatchewan and then via the Front Ranges to a tributary of the Brazeau River, which they followed for several days through extensive muskegs. Leaving it and gaining the main branch, they met a mining engineer prospecting the Brazeau basin for coal. This was likely D. B. Dowling of the Geological Survey of Canada, who inspected the area north of the Brazeau in 1909 under the guidance of Tom Lusk, now also outfitting on his own out of Morley.

Fred had hoped to reach the Athabasca by crossing the little used Jonas Pass, but a landslide blocked the trail and necessitated heading south over Nigel Pass at the head of the Brazeau to the North Fork of the Saskatchewan and then north by the more conventional route through Wilcox Pass. On reaching the Athabasca it was found to be in full flood, and ten days were spent in laboriously cutting downed timber and fording torrential streams before reaching the GTP survey line near the Miette. During this, the most trying period of the summer's odyssey, the evening campfires seemed to bring out the best in Fred as he entertained the assembly not only with tall tales but with dissertations on Darwin, international politics, religion and countless other topics that Washburn never expected to hear coming from the lips of an unschooled guide. Fred also expounded on his philosophy of life, which was fairly typical for one guiding, trapping and prospecting in the wildest reaches of the mountains:

Life is too short to worry about money. If I lose all I have tomorrow, I can get a couple of bear traps and by next spring I'll be on my feet again. The mountains are always here, and I know where there's a bunch of bear and a colony of beaver, and I can get along out here and live like a prince, while Morgan, Rockefeller, and these other poor millionaires are lying awake nights lest someone come and steal their money.[1]

After crossing the Athabasca, six days of recuperation were taken at Swift's homestead before pressing on to Tête Jaune Cache eighty miles westward through Yellowhead Pass. Following a well-worn path, which in parts vied with the old "Golden Stairs" pack trail through the Kicking Horse in treacherousness, the summit of the Yellowhead was crossed. Once over it Fred proposed to examine a reportedly excellent stand of timber in the upper Fraser Valley, but it was quickly found to be completely burned over and the party was soon once again on its way to a rendezvous with the Teares. The brothers were found at Tête Jaune Cache, and the combined group then boated down the Fraser to the Beaver River, where the mineral claim lay. However, as it was now late August and Washburn was soon due back at his office desk, little time could be spent in prospecting. Consequently, the party had soon returned to Tête Jaune and then set out at a hectic pace back toward the Athabasca. Then, with time of the essence, it was determined to follow the old fur trade trail from Henry House and deliver Washburn to the railhead of the GTP, now some sixty-six miles west of Edmonton. The dash eastward proved easy going in comparison to the experiences of some of the summer's other trails, particularly after striking first the tote road and then the newly prepared grade for the line. On the first of October, Washburn was safely deposited on the caboose of a construction train headed east, content at last that he had achieved his eight year dream of experiencing the wilds of the Yellowhead country before the encroachment of civilization.

Retracing the now well-worn route homeward after leaving Washburn, Fred could not foresee that it would be his second to last journey over that piece of ground for some time. While he had every intention of outfitting from Lacombe again the next season, circumstances intervened to make it impossible. Over the winter of 1909-10 Fred and his wife were separated, and she was award-ed custody of their young son, Jesse. This decision did not sit well with Fred and one moonlit night early in the spring he kidnapped the boy from his brother-in-law's ranch on the Medicine River west of Lacombe, tied him on a pack saddle and headed for the Brazeau River. The police followed in hot pursuit, but once into the mountains he had no trouble in eluding them and striking north to his old haunts. The following summer he left the lad in the care of friends while out on the trail, but in future years some-times took the boy out on some of his trips. Eventually he was left to stay with an acquaintance in Centralia, Washington where he could pursue his passion of music, becoming an accomplished pianist and violinist. Fred, unable for obvious reasons to return to Lacombe, spent the next few years timber cruising and prospect-ing with his friends the Teares around Tête Jaune Cache and out-fitting from a location near Entrance.

At the same time, some important developments had been underway in connection with the two competing transcontinental railways that were planning to use the Yellowhead as their route to the coast. The Canadian Northern had been able to get the jump on its rival as its rails reached Edmonton in November, 1905, while the Grand Trunk Pacific's were still several hundred miles to the east. From Edmonton the CNR had pushed on twenty-five miles westward as far as Stony Plain by the spring of 1907, but then main line construction had come to a halt while its surveyors and engineers concentrated on laying out various branch lines. This long delay allowed the GTP, whose tracks had not even reached Edmonton until the summer of 1909, to forge ahead and begin the laying out of preliminary survey lines up the Athabasca and Miette valleys. As in the earlier construction of the CPR, the initiation of this work brought with it a large influx of manpower. Of course, the surveying and later the construction lifeline past the railhead was the horse, and horses naturally meant that a good many of the men who came were packers. Again, as with the CPR, the majority made only a brief appearance and then moved on, but a few found the Jasper country to their liking and decided to remain and engage in guiding and outfitting. Among their number were John Yates, James Shand-Harvey and Alex Wylie, all of whom would eventually gain strong reputations working with the first tourist-explorers venturing into the region.

John Yates was a tall, angular young man who had been born in Blackburn, England in 1880 but had emigrated to California with his parents and five siblings when only a lad of four. He had been raised on a ranch near San Diego, and after completing high school had received $500 from his father to help make a beginning in life. Eventually he followed his older brother to Alberta and, about 1906, joined him on a homestead he had taken out with a partner, Allan McConnachie, on the west side of Lac Ste. Anne some forty-five miles west of Edmonton. This homestead became known as the Hobo Ranch because of the partners' generosity in providing a temporary home for footloose young men who were coming into the district to find land of their own. In addition to their work on the ranch, the partners were involved in packing supplies for the railroad surveys, Yates's original trip in this capacity being to Prairie Creek in the fall of 1906. However, he first came into real prominence in 1907 when he was able to outmaneuver, outride and outdrink his opponents in a contest to carry the mail to the railroad construction camps west of Edmonton. The contract required John to regularly traverse the trail to Tête Jaune Cache, and while doing so in the fall of 1907 he chanced to meet the A. P. Coleman party in retreat from Mount Robson.

Coleman, his brother Lucius and the Reverend George B. Kinney of Victoria had been convinced by A. O. Wheeler at the founding meeting of the Alpine Club of Canada to attempt to capture Robson, the highest peak in the Canadian Rockies at 12,972 feet, as a fitting inauguration of the club 's mountaineering activities. Unable to proceed with their plans until 1907, the party had succeeded in making the difficult journey from Laggan to the Yellowhead only to arrive too late in the season to make a determined bid on their objective. Due to the fast approaching snows of winter, a return trip via Edmonton as quickly as possible was imperative, but as they went along some of their pack horses, worn out by the hardships of the summer's trails, were of necessity left behind. The trio was therefore in fairly dire straits by the time they happened upon Yates at the Big Eddy construction camp on the McLeod River. As Coleman's immediate return to his teaching post in Toronto was imperative and John was bound for Edmonton on the mail run, he lent the professor a horse and took him along. Coleman much appreciated the favour and was so impressed with John that he requested his services as a guide for a renewed attempt on Mount Robson the following year. Yates readily agreed.

On August 4, 1908, the previous year's party regrouped at the Hobo Ranch and set out for the Yellowhead, complete with "an obstreperous set of ponies" and Hoodoo, the ranch's pet bulldog. Before travelling far it became apparent to Coleman that his decision to employ Yates had been a wise one as "he was the most resourceful man with horses and in the general conduct of camp

181

life in the wilderness imaginable: strong, courageous, and alert in all emergencies of a life made up of major and minor emergencies. His skill in packing a horse so as to avoid a sore back on the trail was only equalled by his versatility in turning dried goat meat, smoked fish, desicated potatoes, and odds and ends of rice, oatmeal and bannocks into flavoursome 'bouillon' or 'Mulligan'."[2] The approach to the massive bulk of Mount Robson was made by way of the Moose River, a tributary of the Fraser, over Moose Pass at the head of its east fork, onto the headwaters of Smoky River via Calumet Creek, and finally over Robson Pass to the foot of the Robson Glacier. This route was followed on the advice and with the assistance of Adolphus Moberly, one of the half-breed descendants of one time Jasper House trader Henry Moberly. As a tribute to his invaluable help, the picturesque lake on the north side of the pass was named Adolphus. And on reaching the summit of Robson Pass, the view of a crystal clear lake to the south with an iceberg afloat in it provided the inspiration for another piece of nomenclature — Berg Lake.

Unfortunately, the party was already more than a week behind schedule when it gained the foot of Robson Glacier on August 29th, and then continuous rain and snow made an immediate assault out of the question. Five days of impatient waiting ensued, during which it became apparent that the food would only hold out another week. Yates was dispatched back to the Athabasca in order to replenish the larder, a mission which undoubtedly would have taken an entire week except for another chance meeting with Moberly's band of half-breeds a day's journey down the Moose Valley. Moberly's people had just completed a successful goat hunt and were able to supply a sufficient quantity of meat and other necessities to temporarily alleviate the food problem. By September 4th John was back in camp eager to discover what his clients found so exhilarating about climbing a mountain. His opportunity would come the next day.

Yates's eager, almost light-hearted approach to mountaineering was quickly replaced by a stark realization of its rigours. He lacked all the essential equipment, being shod in thinly soled boots

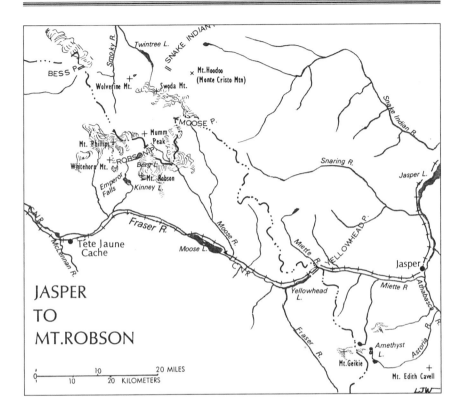

into which he had inserted hobnails and using an alpenstock roughly fashioned from a pole and a heavy wire nail. Proceeding across the glacier was a long, tiring grind but caused the few difficulties until a steep snow slope was encountered at its upper end. This required some step cutting, and as Coleman had injured his knee, John had to take his turn at hacking out the rather fragile-looking footholds while clinging precariously to the fifty degree slope. Soon his makeshift climbing boots proved more of a hindrance than a help, the hobnails acting as a conductor taking all the warmth away from his feet. By the time the climbers had reached the next obstacle, an almost vertical cliff at the top of the snow slope, his feet were completely numbed. Because of this situation and the unexpected length of time required to reach the 10,000 foot level, Coleman decided that discretion was the better

183

part of valour and, after a short break for food and photographs, the weary and dispirited group began an equally painful and hazardous descent. Several hours later the main camp was regained and as Yates thawed out his toes beside a roaring fire the party's spirits revived to the point where they were able to joke about his having got "cold feet" on his maiden mountaineering venture.

The experience led him to conclude that, for the time being at least, his place was with the horses and not the climbers, and when invited to participate in a second attempt he showed little enthusiasm. As for the remainder of the party, they mounted two more assaults, and then Kinney, the most accomplished alpinist among them, tried a solo attempt. All failed, mainly because of the inclement weather that was typical of the Robson area. Of the twenty-one days spent in the mountain's vicinity, only twice were there two in succession that proved suitable for climbing. By September 18th the weather at last seemed to be clearing, but the advanced season and the continually dwindling food stocks required an immediate return to civilization. A record time for the 250 mile trip over the trail to Lac Ste. Anne was accomplished before switching to a wagon for the remainder of the journey to Edmonton. There John saw his clients safely boarded on trains headed for their homes before setting out once more for the Yellowhead on the mail run.

Experience gained outfitting and guiding the Coleman party in 1908 stood Yates in good stead the following year. Kinney, determined to be the first to reach Robson's lofty summit, contacted him during the winter with plans to launch a new expedition the next summer. However, early that spring Kinney heard rumours that "foreign parties" also had designs on the peak and he decided to move his timetable forward to ensure an attempt ahead of them. Telegraphing his guide to prepare for an early June departure, he left Victoria bound for Edmonton. Upon arrival he found a letter from Yates in which he outlined his refusal to go because he felt it was too early in the season after the particularly heavy snowfall of the past winter. Dismayed but undaunted, Kinney set out on his own.

Yates was by that time packing for a survey party working on the 15th Base Line. At the end of July he unexpectedly received word that there was a party requesting his services en route by buggy for Wolf Creek, where they hoped to rendezvous with him. Leaving the survey immediately, he was unable to meet the party before they left for the west with another packer, but did manage to catch them on the Athabasca. On making their acquaintance, he realized that this was the "foreign party" whom Kinney had so feared, consisting of Arnold Mumm, Leopold Amery and Geoffrey Hastings, all members of the Alpine Club (London), as well as Hasting's friend A. G. Priestley and Mumm's personal Swiss guide Moritz Inderbinen. They had been specially invited guests at the Alpine Club of Canada's camp held at Lake O'Hara that year but had decided on their way overseas that it would be only a prelude to a more extensive expedition to Mount Robson. In order to make arrangement, Amery had paid a brief visit to Edmonton before joining his friends at O'Hara. Contacting an acquaintance, Harry Evans of the Hudson's Bay Company, he was told that something could probably be worked out with Yates. When told that he had been Coleman's guide the previous year, Amery had agreed, but when the entire party reached Edmonton on August 7th, Evans infomed them that he had been unable to contact Yates and would supply another man. Amery insisted that he must have the guide who had accompanied Coleman, and Evans agreed to send a messenger to see if John could be convinced to join the party.

Soon after their meeting on the Athabasca, Mumm's insistence was shown to be well placed, as he later wrote "we could not have been in better hands." Under Yates's able guidance he felt the party would have no difficulty reaching a location at the foot of Robson from which the first ascent could be launched. But at that time he was unaware that an unwelcome surprise awaited them further up the river. At the ferry above Jasper Lake on August 23rd they encountered an excited George Kinney, who claimed to have just completed the conquest in the company of a young guide he had encountered on the trail. The guide, Donald Phillips, was not known to Yates but was not to remain so for long. In fact, within a short few years he would be acknowledged as one of the foremost guides and outfitters of the entire Jasper-Yellowhead region.

Known as "Curly" because of his mop of brown hair, Phillips was a stocky, somewhat baby-faced youth of twenty-four. A native of the heavy bush country around Dorset, Ontario, he had learned as a boy the secrets of hunting , trapping and canoe work from his father Daniel, an experienced backwoodsman. As early as 1902 he had begun trapping both on his own and in partnership with his brother-in-law Bert Wilkins in the vicinity of Temagami, and later began to work with his close friend Ed Britton on a trapline out of Biscotasing. Over the winter of 1907-08 he and Britton had set out in search of adventure, boarding a train for the west on April 15th, Curly's birthday, but parted company on reaching Calgary. Phillips headed for the mountains, and although on reaching Field was able to secure a job with the CPR working on the construction of the Spiral Tunnels after one look at the damp and dangerous working conditions decided it was not for him. Returning to Banff for a brief stopover, he had a conversation with Bill Brewster, possibly with regard to employment with Brewster Brothers, but quickly came to the conclusion the country was too crowded for his liking. He soon departed for Edmonton and spent the winter of 1908-09 working on the construction of the GTP line for George Kaywood, a tie contractor. The following spring he bought a few horses and set out for the Yellowhead in the hope of discovering some trapping territory and perhaps even the odd hunting party to guide. Although his experience with horses was limited, he had training guiding by canoe in Ontario and felt that he could adjust to the new circumstances. He soon had the chance to prove himself as fate brought him into the company of Reverend Kinney.

As mentioned, Kinney's almost paranoic fear of being beaten to the summit of Robson had led him to set out for the great peak on his own. On June 17th he left Edmonton with three pack horses, three months provisions and few dollars in his pocket, hoping to meet someone on the trail willing to share fortune. Struggling through to the McLeod River he encountered an old prospector named McBride who agreed to join forces, whereupon Kinney sold him a horse and half of his provisions. The partnership proved shortlived for, as Yates had predicted, the Athabasca's tributaries were found to be in full flood and, after almost drowning in the Rocky River, McBride made for safer ground. Kinney pressed on, losing more of his supplies and equipment in other flooding streams and finally being forced to seek refuge on a small island in the Athabasca itself when it rose to unprecedented heights. As the water began to recede he discovered a high water trail which led him to the home of John Moberly, about seven miles above Jasper Lake. There, on July 11th, he found Phillips, who like himself had been marooned on an island in the Athabasca for six days before heading for the same high ground at Moberly's. Soon after their meeting the persistent Kinney had the young greenhorn convinced to accompany him to Robson.

As it turned out, Kinney had taken advantage of Phillips's inexperience to dupe him into participating in the venture. Curly was himself short of supplies and had been planning to return to Edmonton for a restocking, but Kinney glibly assured him he had sufficient for both of them. By the time the pair reached Yellowhead Pass, Curly had sized up Kinney's grub pile and it was apparent that he had been, at best, stretching the truth. According to his calculations, they only had enough for one month and was only willing to continue on because he felt that Kinney's rifle would enable him to supplement the larder with some game. Once more his faith proved misplaced as he found, after firing nine successive misses at a caribou only fifty yards distant, that the barrel was bent a quarter-inch out of line. These drawbacks made chances for success rather remote, but their proximity to Robson and the reverend's determination to have his day persuaded Curly to continue to accompany him Arriving at the foot of Robson's north shoulder, Kinney's silk tent was erected on a bench of land overlooking the river and preparations were made for the assault.

The following afternoon when the pair began the ascent Phillips's situation was much the same as Yates's had been a year earlier. Except for his visit to Field and Banff, he had never even been in the mountains, much less climbed one, and his equipment was of the crudest variety. He wore light, unnailed boots, a pair of thin gloves over which were pulled woollen socks for extra warmth, and carried a five foot branch as an alpenstock. Only ignorance of what was entailed in ascending a peak of Robson's immensity would lead a man to undertake it in such conditions and, of course, Kinney was not wont to enlighten him. Even he might have had some second thoughts if he could have foreseen what lay ahead. Probably no ascent in the history of the Canadian Rockies required more sheer guts and determination in the face of hair-raising brushes with death by avalanche, exposure and starvation.

Beginning by establishing what was named "Camp High Up" at the 9,500 foot level, two tortuous but unsuccessful bids were launched on July 27th and 29th. While attempting these the alpinists alternately returned to the main camp to restock their rucksacks or slept covered with the thinnest of blankets at their fly camp on a ledge so narrow that a little wall of stones had to be piled up to prevent them from rolling off into the abyss. After the second attempt, the weather turned foul, and Curly took the opportunity to do some hunting and fishing to try fill out the perilously scant larder. Seven days of effort earned him no more than two spindly grouse and a few marmots for the stew pot, and it was apparent that if success was going to crown their efforts it would have to be soon. This seemed doubly so after a third foray on August 9th was turned back at 10,000 feet by heavy snows and avalanches tearing past at frequent intervals. Finally, on August 12th, the weather appeared to be lifting, and for the fourth time they toiled up to the fly camp. It was obvious that this was to be a last ditch effort and, in order to get a jump on their objective, they decided to forsake the fly camp in favour of a bivouac at the highest possible altitude, 10,500 feet. Here an impromptu ledge was hacked out of the snow and lined with flat pieces of cold grey slate.

Dawning cold and clear, the morning of Friday the 13th seemed to offer tolerable possibilities for success, although these soon dimmed as telltale storm clouds began to gather in the south. As they made their way up the steep cliffs of the west slope from the bivouac, the storm overtook them and for a time it appeared as though further progress would be impossible. But, almost miraculously, the storm abated somewhat and one by one the treacherous series of cliffs leading to the summit, many sloping over sixty degrees, were scaled by ice-coated hands and feet. On the summit ridge the wind had corniced the snow, but, according to Kinney's later report, this too was overcome and victory finally gained. His long sought ambition seemingly achieved, Kinney treated the moment with suitable reverence for a man of the cloth: "I was on a needle peak that rose so abruptly that even cornices cannot build very far out on it. Barring my head I said, 'In the name of Almighty God, by whose strength I have climbed here, I capture this peak, Mount Robson, for my own country and for the Alpine Club of Canada'."[3] His moment of joy was shortlived, however, as the perils of descent now had to be faced and it was already five o'clock in the afternoon. Due to a late arriving chinook the temperature had risen and had all but erased their laboriously cut steps, requiring an additional seven hours of climbing to bring them safely to their upper camp. Here the remaining bits of marmot were ravenously consumed and a short rest taken before returning to the main camp, completing a twenty-hour day of continuous activity.

Because there were only three or four days of half rations left and it was seven days journey to Swift's where more could be obtained, there was no time for rest the next day. Proceeding towards Moose Pass, Curly's luck at hunting improved marginally as he secured a few grouse, ptarmigan and ground squirrels for the interminable stews. Unfortunately, any advantage gained by his success was wiped out the next day when Kinney, who insisted on leading on the trail as well as the mountain, guided them into muskeg and heavy timber and in the wrong direction as well. Curly thereafter demanded to do the guiding and luckily was able to get them back on the right track. Good fortune again smiled a few days later when they happened on a trail party heading in the same direction who offered to share their food and company. After crossing the Athabasca near Jasper Lake and informing the British party of their triumph, a few necessities were purchased at John Moberly's and the trail eastward resumed. Arriving at Medicine Lodge on the McLeod River on September 1st, Kinney sold Curly the few remaining bits of his outfit and bade him farewell.

Within a few years, the issue of whether Kinney and Phillips had actually gained the true summit of Robson was being actively discussed by various members of the alpine fraternity. Kinney steadfastly maintained they had, and probably experienced little difficulty in convincing Curly, who at the early date of 1909 was completely unfamiliar with mountaineering etiquette, that a matter of a few feet made no difference. A joint account of the expedition and ascent appeared in the *Canadian Alpine Journal*, but in it Curly's remarks were confined mainly to a description of the trails and camp life while Kinney elaborated on the details of the actual climb. Strangely, during the next few years, Curly was not called upon to confirm or deny success as no one took the trouble to ask him. But at the 1913 Mount Robson Alpine Club camp, which he helped to outfit, his friend Conrad Kain took part in what was supposed to be the second ascent of the peak. On returning victoriously to camp, Kain was informed by a now older and wiser Phillips that it was, in reality, the first ascent since he and Kinney had fallen short of their goal: "We reached, on our ascent (in mist and storm), an ice dome fifty or sixty feet high, which we took for the peak. The danger was too great to ascend the dome."[4]

Despite this revelation, Curly deserved a great deal of credit for the pluck and determination he showed as a rank amateur in the face of such a formidable conditions as those encountered on Robson. Kinney reported that throughout the whole ordeal he never heard a word of discouragement, and this was soon to become the mark of the man in other trying circumstances. All in all, the climb was a feather in the cap for a young guide attempting to establish a reputation for himself, particularly when news of it reached the ears of other mountaineers and explorers anxious to come to grips with the little known country north of the great peak. Certainly it must have gone a long way toward convincing him to remain in the area and to attempt to earn his livelihood from outfitting and guiding. At any rate, remain he did, spending the next two winters working for railroad timber contractors between Obed and Brûlé and picking up guiding jobs during the summer and fall. In 1911 Curly ran his pack trains from Edson, but by 1912 was well established at Fitzhugh (renamed Jasper in 1913) with corrals, a cabin and a rather unique two-storey pack and saddle shed along the trail that would one day become Pyramid Drive.

The site of his headquarters in Jasper was no accident as it conformed to a newly enacted government regulation which had resulted from experience with stables at Banff. There they tended to be spread all over the main business area causing tourists to complain of the noxious odours. Starting with a clean slate at Jasper, the government decided to "debar from the townsite all stables and their attendant smells and flies."[5] To compensate for this ruling, steps were taken to have six sites surveyed near the foot of the hill at the rear of the town, one lot of two acres for a government corral and stables and five of one acre each to be apportioned to outfitters as the need arose. Phillips, being first on the scene, was given his choice and took the second plot northeast of the government site.

When the outfitters along the CPR learned of the ascent of Robson, it was only the most current in a series of exciting reports emanating from the more northerly region. By 1909 Fred Stephens's activities were well-known to his old friends at Banff, Lake Louise and Field, and every month brought fresh news of the supposed great opportunities provided by the building of the GTP and its rival the CNR. It was undoubtedly the lure of these opportunities, in combination with the interest of some of their steady clients and the continuing pressure of competition, which were the major considerations in the decision of the Ottos to abandon their apparently secure footing at Field in favour of the Jasper area. Within a short time some of these considerations would also play an important part in the appearance in the same locale of another well-known outfitting name — Brewster. However, in this case it was not Bill and Jim Brewster but their younger brothers Fred and

Jack, who were spreading their own wings.

Oddly enough, the Ottos' announced intentions of departing from Field and the sale of their interests just before the 1910 Alpine Club camp did not result in an immediate move to the north. They handled the outfitting from the Consolation Valley camp and in addition continued to outfit some parties from Field during the 1910 season. This was undoubtedly by arrangement with Jim Brewster as the Ottos were already committed to taking out parties with whom it was too late to make other plans. One of these was a rather cosmopolitan group headed by J. E. C. Eaton, a colleague of Collie's in the Alpine Club, and including his Italian cousin Captain Marocco and the Swiss guide Heinrich Burgener. Eaton had previously corresponded with Jack Otto about setting up the trip which he had decided, after consulting Collie, should be destined for the Freshfield Group. Bruce Otto was assigned to them as guide and within a short time Eaton was able to pronounce "I do not think that the British Empire contains a better fellow."[6] After leaving Field on July 15th with Otto, a cook and ten horses, the climbers succeeding in conquering Mounts Pilkington, Walker, Dent and Freshfield before returning to Laggan on August 5th.

Meanwhile, Jack and Closson Otto had delivered forty-seven head of horses with saddles and a few carriages to Jim Brewster as per their agreement and had then gone to Moberly where a few pack animals were purchased for their trip through the mountains. Joining Bruce, fresh from his exploits with the Eaton party, the brothers headed north by way of Wilcox Pass and the Athabasca, arriving at its junction with the Miette some twenty-one days later. Being unfamiliar with the terrain they were unsure of their bearings, so Jack climbed part way up Signal Mountain and, with the aid of his spy glass, was able to pick out the Swift children playing in their yard several miles downstream. After visiting at Swift's for two days and learning something of the lay of the land, they continued eastward down the Athabasca. At the mouth of Solomon Creek they stopped and set up a temporary headquarters before pushing on to Edmonton, where they spent the following winter.

Away to the Athabasca

While in Edmonton, the brothers accepted an interesting proposition put to them by Howard Douglas, the former superintendent at Banff who had just taken on the new position of commissioner of Dominion Parks. At the request of D. B. Dowling, Douglas had agreed to have thirty miles of trail cleared from the proposed new railway line into Maligne Lake. The discovery of the lake by Mrs. Schäffer's party had brought it a great deal of attention as a location that the tourists soon expected in the area would be interested in seeing, and Dowling wished it to be properly surveyed. Leading the party to carry it out was none other than the selfsame Mary Schäffer, accompanied by her sister-in-law Mrs. H. H. Sharples and her nephew Paul Sharples. Mrs. Schäffer had become well-acquainted with Jack Otto during his days at Field and since the trail clearing contract also involved guiding her party, the Ottos were a logical choice.

Early in the spring of 1911 the brothers acquired more horses in Edmonton and shipped their outfit to the railhead at Hinton. On reaching Solomon Creek they re-established their former camp, hired a few men and then headed out to begin the task of trail blazing. It proved to be slow work as the route to be followed went through heavy timber from the future site of Jasper to Buffalo Prairie on the Athabasca near the mouth of the Whirlpool and then over a high, unnamed pass into Maligne Lake. An additional delay caused by late spring storms meant that the work was far from completed when Jack Otto met the party, who were accompanied by Sid Unwin, at Hinton on June 7th. Nevertheless, after a night spent at Prairie Creek, Jack began guiding them over the GTP tote road, which was in such poor condition that a horse and an ox had recently been reported to have drowned in its mud. After reaching the part of the trail that his men had cleared, the going proved to be easier for a time, but a constant irritation was provided by several sixteen foot pieces of cedar for a boat that one of the pack horses, Jonas, was forced to carry: "His burden had been lashed to his unprotesting sides, a rope had been looped across the front end of the boards, Jack had assumed the position of steering gear, and with Jonas acting as propeller the pair had taken the lead of the small procession. . . . The sight of him under the best of conditions was trying, for when the boards were not striking the inoffensive horse in the cheek, or nearly knocking the steersman down, they were slipping from their guiding ropes, going fore and aft according to the lay of the land, and having to be shifted back into place."[7]

Additional hardships were encountered when ten feet of fresh snow was found on the pass. A day's halt was called while Jack's crew broke a path, but on travelling it the next day it proved so narrow that one of the packers had to walk ahead of poor Jonas and hold the lumber vertically to enable him to gain passage. Coming to the top of the pass two objects thought to be goats were spotted by the ladies, but on closer inspection they were found to be snow shovels fashioned from trees and left behind by the trail clearers. Accordingly, the defile was immediately given the name of Shovel Pass. Difficulties continued to plague the pack train until Maligne's shore was finally gained on June 20th. Immediately the Ottos set to work to build the boat necessary for the survey, which was completed just in time to coincide with the start of a further two week period of rain and snow. Combined with the discovery that a spool of wire needed for the survey work was missing, events conspired to create an almost three week delay in actually commencing the party's work. However, Mrs. Schäffer and her companions put the time to good use in a thorough exploration of the lake and its surrounding peaks and valleys.

During this period, Jack was not found to be wanting in any of the skills demanded of a good and faithful guide. Rowing the boat or exploring on foot for up to twelve hours a day did not daunt him, and still he found time to do the thousand and one jobs that maintenance of a camp in the wilderness required, from baking bread in the campfire to mending Mrs. Schäffer's broken glasses with tools fashioned on the spot. Food stocks had to be replenished by hunting after the other chores of the day were completed, yet by six o'clock the next morning he was awake with a cheery fire burning to greet the ladies when they arose. However, work was finally completed on July 25th, and he quickly packed up, escorted his charges to the railhead and then accompanied them back to Edmonton. Although the survey had taken much longer than anticipated, permitting he and his brothers to outfit few other parties that summer, it was to ultimately prove highly beneficial. As in the case of Phillips's work for Kinney, word of the excellent service provided the well-known Mary Schäffer would stand them in good stead with future parties wishing to outfit in the region. Soon the Ottos had an excellent foothold in Jasper with corrals located on the site between those of Phillips and the government.

Before long the Ottos and Phillips were to be joined by another outfitting interest who would gain a reputation as large as their own, but Fred Brewster's arrival at Jasper followed a somewhat more circuitous path. Frederick A. Brewster, the third son of John Brewster, was born on December 21, 1884 at Kildonan, Manitoba, and like his two elder brothers received his early education at St. John's College, Winnipeg. On completing his course in 1905, he was not sure what to do with his life, but while thinking about it accepted an invitation from his uncle George Brewster to accompany him on an exploration trip. Starting from Ashcroft, 160 miles east of Vancouver on the CPR line, the pair travelled with pack horses by way of Quesnel, Fort St. James, Omineca River and Babine Lake to Hazelton. Here the horses were abandoned in favour of a canoe, which took them the remainder of the way down the Omineca to the Finlay River and then to its headwaters where the winter was spent. Early the next spring the Finlay was followed its full length and Edmonton finally reached via Peace River Crossing and Athabasca Landing, requiring the building of three different boats in the process. When he reached Edmonton in June, Fred had been on the trail for almost a year, yet within a few days, this time in the company of Fred Hussey, departed for the coast to do it all over again. After he arrived back in Edmonton three-and-a-half months later, he felt he had experienced enough of trail life for quite some time. In the fall of 1906 he began attending Queen's University, Kingston and graduated with a B.Sc. in Mining Engineering in 1909.

During the summer of 1908, while on holiday from university, Fred had gained his first practical mining experience working for the Consolidated Mining and Smelting Company examining some copper and silver claims on Vancouver and Queen Charlotte Islands. After graduation he returned to do more prospecting in these regions on his own, but the good claims were already tied up and by the late fall of 1909 he was once more back at Banff. Undecided what to do next, he spent some time on his uncle James Brewster's ranch near Bowden, south of Red Deer, before returning home to work on the trail. This he continued to do until 1910 when he was approached by this brother-in-law Phil Moore about forming a partnership. Fred agreed, and along with his brother Jack Walker Brewster, only a lad of seventeen at the time, a company known as Brewster and Moore was created. Its initial endeavour was working on the construction of a branch line from the Calgary and Edmonton Railway into the Nordegg coal fields in the winter of 1910-11. Working out of Red Deer, they were mainly involved in the freighting of ties and other supplies to the railhead, although they briefly ran a stagecoach to Rocky Mountain House and Moore also operated a store at Nordegg for a period. Meanwhile, Fred began to hear of the possibilities along the GTP line, probably from his uncle's acquaintances Pres and Charlie Berry, who had begun to make yearly pack trips to the Yellowhead region from their ranch at Raven, west of Innisfail.

In February, 1911, Fred took a trip as far as Edson and determined that prospects appeared so bright on the GTP line that in the spring Brewster and Moore moved their horses and freighting equipment to Bickerdike. Little difficulty was experienced finding work freighting and packing on the construction of a branch line into the Coal Branch district and hauling coal for British American Colleries. Headquarters were quickly moved on to the end of steel at the rough-and-ready town of Prairie Creek, where temporary corrals were erected and tents put up to serve as living quarters. Soon the Brewster brothers were joined by their younger siblings, George and Pat, who supplied some much needed manpower. Although freighting provided most of the work, Fred believed that much of their business would eventually be supplied outfitting tourists, as it had been for his brothers when they started out at Banff. Early in the summer of 1911, he set out to explore the country north of the proposed rail line, travelling over Moose Pass, down the Moose River and then up the Fraser and through Yellowhead Pass. From there he headed east down the Miette River and met his brother Jack at the future site of Jasper, which he described as "a boulder strewn flat with a second growth of Lodgepole Pine about four feet high."[8] Although he didn't realize it at the time, this seemingly unlikely spot was soon to become his lifelong home.

Prairie Creek was maintained as the headquarters for Brewster and Moore operations until late in 1912 when, falling in line with most of the other outfitters, they moved on to Fitzhugh. After the growing clan of Brewsters was joined by Moore and his wife Pearl, construction was begun on a stable and corrals on one of the plots northeast of Phillips and the Ottos. Conforming to a government request for a rustic style of architecture, using either logs or boulders, their structure was designed "on the lines of the old Fort David Thompson of the Hudson's Bay Company" and was thought to be "a decided acquisition to the beauty of the townsite."[9]

Chapter VIII
Joining Up in Jasper

The trailmen working in the Jasper-Yellowhead region after 1909 were in some respects quite different from those plying their trade along the CPR line. They tended to operate smaller scale guiding and outfitting businesses than their southern confreres and were also more diversified. The main reason for this had to do with the fact that most of those working along the CPR line had come into the business after the tourist trade was well-established, while those setting up on the Athabasca were doing so while the GTP and CNR lines were being built and in advance of the development of tourism in the area. This meant that for a number of years more attention would be devoted to securing contracts that were readily obtainable from railroad contractors competing for manpower and equipment than to outfitting tourist-explorers. Because these contracts mainly involved the cutting and hauling of ties and bridge timbers, this work demanded the use of heavy teams and wagons rather than cayuses and pack saddles. Phillips and Brewster and Moore relied heavily on such activities for their livelihood and soon the Ottos did as well, working with a tie cutting outfit up the Moose River. As for Stephens and Yates, while they were not directly associated with railroad construction, they also were small operators as a matter of choice. Stephens preferred to spend much of his time timber cruising and prospecting, and Yates soon had a new homestead and a coal mining lease near Brûlé Lake to occupy him.

In these circumstances, these outfitters, with the possible exception of Brewster and Moore, were faced with choosing one of two alternatives when a tourist party was secured. They could either find additional men and stock to assist them on an interim basis or form an ad hoc arrangement with one of their peers. The first choice was perhaps the most logical, but in all except a few cases their clients required more horses and equipment than one outfitter was able to access on short notice. For this reason, temporary partnerships became the most favoured means of compensating for small size.

Generally speaking, there tended to be little of the competitiveness in outfitting that was so evident along the CPR on the Jasper scene in its early years. This was at least partially due to the absence of concessions such as those associated with the CPR hotels, concessions that had played a role in the decision of some outfitters to abandon the CPR line in the first place. According to its promotional material, the Grand Trunk gave equal opportunity to all. In a brochure published about 1913, entitled *The Canadian Rockies, Yellowhead Pass Route*, an entire page was devoted to recommending different guiding and outfitting services, with Brewster Brothers (Brewster and Moore), Donald Phillips and Otto Brothers heading the list. Other factors accounting for the situation were, perhaps, a realistic assessment by those in the business that there was a need to help one another in order to survive and a feeling that there would eventually be enough business for everyone. Whatever the reasons, the resulting partnerships were often quite diverse involving combinations of up to three interests to handle particularly large groups.

Of all the impromptu cooperative efforts at this time the ones that came closest to resulting in a more permanent business relationship were those of Fred Stephens and John Yates. This was not surprising as these two had the most limited pack strings and could only rarely provide the necessary horseflesh to outfit a party completely on their own. There is no doubt that by 1910 the two had crossed each other's paths and quite possibly could have come to some agreement to handle a rather interesting party that was due to arrive that summer. However, it is even more likely that their combination of forces resulted from the make-up of this group itself, composed as it was of A. L. Mumm, his Swiss guide Inderbinen and J. Norman Collie, back to his beloved Rockies after an eight year absence. Mumm's expectations of a first ascent of Robson in 1909 had, of course, been dealt a crushing blow when he and his companions met Kinney and Phillips returning from their purported conquest. Nevertheless, the party had continued on and succeeded in carrying out an exhaustive reconnaissance of the peak without gaining the summit. But Mumm, a man not easily daunted, was determined to launch a further attempt and examine the area seen from Robson's slopes. As he had found Yates such a valuable asset in 1909, he could see no reason to look further for an outfitter and guide on his return trip. Collie too had wanted to explore the area north of the Yellowhead but could not afford the time to do it until the construction of the GTP made the country more accessible. During the period since his last visit to Canada his friendship and exchange of correspondence with Stephens had continued, and his 1902 pledge to go out with no-one else meant that Fred would provide for his guiding and outfitting.

The long anticipated reunion between Collie and Stephens took place at the end of steel on July 17, 1910. Upon embarking from the train the mountaineers found their guides ready to proceed accompanied by Allan McConnochie, Yates's former partner in the Hobo Ranch, and George Swain. As Robson was the main objective, the standard route up the Athabasca and Miette rivers was followed to Yellowhead Pass, at which point it was decided to retrace the trail blazed by Yates while with the Coleman party in 1908. Following this trail was the simplest way to reach the Robson Glacier, as once over Moose Pass it was only a matter of following the Smoky River to its source, a route that took them across a small creek subsequently known as Yates Torrent issuing from the snout of the Coleman Glacier. After twenty-three days of travelling, they pitched camp on the shore of Berg Lake, but as usual Robson was shrouded in cloud and snow. While waiting for it to clear several lesser peaks in the vicinity were ascended, including two that would ultimately bear the names of Mumm and Phillips. But as was so often the case, the weather continued to deteriorate rather than improve and, growing impatient, Mumm and Collie decided to focus attention on an exploration of the Smoky River Valley and some of its tributaries which might hold passes over the Divide. The second valley examined proved to be the most intriguing as it contained a rather easy pass into British Columbia and "a splendid snow mountain" christened Mount Bess by Yates, after a daughter of Peter Gunn, the Hudson's Bay Company factor at Lac Ste. Anne.

At this point it was necessary to begin the return journey to the railhead at Wolf Creek and the question immediately arose as to which route to follow. Returning the same way they had come would undoubtedly be the easiest course to follow but it would also be the least interesting. Since Yates knew the area well, it was left to him to suggest an alternative. He favoured following the Smoky to where some natives had told him of a pass to the Stoney (Snake Indian) River, which in turn would lead them back to the Athabasca near the former location of Jasper House. Although he had never made the passage himself he had an uncanny sense of direction which greatly impressed Collie:

. . . *on September 2 we started down the Smoky River, intending to turn E. up the first promising looking valley, in the hopes that we should find a pass at its head over which we could take the horses. We found a very beautiful lake [Twintree Lake] in our side valley with two infinitesimal islands, on each of which was one fir tree. Yates, who is the best guide in unknown country I have ever met, by some unaccountable instinct refused to follow the valley to its head and turned up a side valley ; two days later he proved to be right, for we crossed an easy pass [Snake Indian Pass] above tree-line on the old and well-worn Indian trail, descending on the other side into a beautiful valley down which a fine stream ran through the pine woods.*[1]

Arriving back on the Athabasca on September 16th after a comparatively short return trip of two weeks, Mumm and Collie immediately decided to come back the following year and explore more thoroughly the new country which Yates's trail had brought to light.

John's keen guiding ability used in conjunction with Fred's

renowned axe work had made the pair a perfect team. In fact, their combination of forces had proven so effective that there was no question but that they would repeat it in 1911. When Mumm and Collie reappeared in July, they were once more at the ready, with Allan McConnochie again assisting. Striking up the Stoney River, it took seven days of chopping downed timber to cover a mere twenty-five miles, but thereafter the going was easier and the weather unusually good. On August 4th the pass discovered by Yates was regained and time allowed for Collie to commence a plane table survey. A peak on the east side of the pass was ascended for this purpose, and upon reaching its summit Mumm immediately proclaimed that it would be named Mount Hoodoo in honour of Yates's loyal bulldog. This amazing animal accompanied his master on all his travels and on this particular occasion had set off with him on the climb. Even at a point near the summit where there was a steep cliff he could not bear to be left behind and had to be tied to a rope and pulled bodily up the final precipice.

From its summit the climbers spied an interesting group of mountains around Mount Bess and decided to give them some attention. Down on the Smoky again they examined the Resthaven Icefield and then attempted to look into some of the valleys entering onto the river further north. However, the muskeg and burnt timber proved so overwhelming that the brief time at their disposal rapidly dwindled away. With but one week remaining they decided to spend it near Mount Bess, and on August 26th Mumm, Collie, Inderbinen and Yates succeeded in making its first ascent. The accomplishment was particularly notable for Yates as with it he established a reputation as a fine mountaineer, a rare exception among trail guides. Following this success the party crossed Bess Pass on another old Indian trail and made a brief reconnaissance of its western side before commencing their return trip to the railhead. For the next two weeks the party maintained a leisurely pace in the best weather that Collie had experienced in the six summers spent in his Rocky Mountain travels. It was fittingly so, for when they reached the railroad at Prairie Creek it would mark the end of his explorations. Henceforth, he would have only his memories: "As one sits in one's armchair on the winter evenings and dreams of the camp life return once more, the teepee with a roaring fire and the door snugly closed; of Fred's stories, of John's leisurely method of playing poker, of Moritz's fears that we were lost in a strange land and that the 'grub pile' was low; all these small happenings, as they come back to one, stir the remembrances of the life in the wilds."[2]

The completion of the 1911 Collie-Mumm expedition also marked the termination of Yates's and Stephens's cooperative efforts, although it was not the last time they were on the trail together. In 1913 Yates was once again engaged by Mumm while Stephens was hired by Geoffrey Howard, another Englishman, with both guides being assisted by two packers. Howard, with no definite plan and a limited amount of time at his disposal, was invited by Mumm to accompany him on a brief exploration of the Mount Geikie (Edith Cavell) region, a proposition which found much favour with the outfitters. However, there was no formal combination of their outfits as each man ran his pack string and camp independent of the other. While for a time it seemed as though the relationship developed between the two would result in a more lasting partnership, their fierce independence and outside interests gravitated against it. Failing to grasp the opportunity ultimately cost them their chance for viability as within a few years both had disappeared from the Jasper guiding and outfitting scene. Small size was the norm and could even be regarded as an advantage in the early years when tourism was still on a minor scale, and it would again have some advantages during the mid-twenties. In the interim, though, larger interests were the order of the day, and neither Stephens or Yates changed with the times. On the other hand, outfitters such as Phillips and the Ottos teamed up only as a temporary way of carrying on business while they were expanding to prepare for an expected busy future.

Curly Phillips's first big break as a guide and outfitter came about as a direct result of his participation with Kinney in the assault on Mount Robson. Kinney was a leading member of the

Alpine Club of Canada and, as mentioned, the club was beginning to look northward for new challenges by 1910. A. O. Wheeler, never one to be far from the action, was enthralled by the reports emanating from the Yellowhead and was determined that the club should make its own investigations "in accordance with the propaganda laid down in its constitution, viz. the encouragement of mountain craft and the opening of new regions as a national playground."[3] By 1911 he was once more at work as a private surveyor, but managed to convince the government that some phototopographical work in the region would be beneficial. In addition, the GTP, about to embark on a publicity campaign similar to the CPR's, agreed to lend some financial support to an investigative expedition through the area. Wheeler's personal objective was to look into the possibility of holding one of the club's future annual camps in the vicinity of Robson. As he was unfamiliar with the country, he was glad to follow Kinney's advice for a guide and outfitter to handle this important undertaking.

Phillips was equally happy to receive the opportunity to conduct the prestigious party, consisting of Wheeler, Byron Harmon, the club's official photographer, and Conrad Kain, its official climbing guide. He initially believed he would have no difficulty handling this group with the help of one man to cook, but had to drastically alter his plans when some major changes took place in the party's composition as the time for departure drew near. First of all, Kinney was added as an assistant, and then with the cooperation of the provincial governments of British Columbia and Alberta funds were made available to add a team capable of reporting on the area's geology, flora and fauna. Through contact with Dr. Charles D. Walcott, secretary of the Smithsonian Institution in Washington and a long time investigator of the Canadian Rockies, Wheeler was able to secure the desired scientists. Headed by Ned Hollister, assistant curator of mammals at the United States National Museum, the group also included J. H. Riley, likewise from the National Museum, Charles Walcott jr. and Harry Blagden, the latter two whom were charged with the responsibility for collecting the larger specimens of mammals.

Faced with more than a doubling of the size of the party, Curly had to do some quick scrambling to find assistance.

Luckily, help was immediately available in the person of James Shand-Harvey, one of the packers who had come into the country during the construction of the railroad. Shand-Harvey had arrived at Edmonton from his native Scotland in 1905 and after a brief stint at homesteading had gone to work packing on a survey party. Most of his experience was gained during the survey of the 14th Base Line west from Lac Ste. Anne to Jasper, but he had made one brief appearance with a mountaineering party when he guided Mumm's 1909 group from Wolf Creek to their rendezvous with Yates and then accompanied them on to Robson. By 1911 he had managed to acquire a few horses of his own and with Fred Kvass, a well-known trapper, spent the spring hauling supplies from Lac Ste. Anne to Tête Jaune Cache. It was on the completion of this venture that he encountered Phillips and accepted his proposition to cooperate with him in the outfitting of the Alpine Club-Smithsonian expedition. Since the enlarged party would demand a substantial number of extra horses, Curly sought additional assistance. Fred Stephens agreed to help and added his horses to those of the other two outfitters when they set out from Brûlé Lake in early July. He was given the task of handling the combined pack strings while Phillips and Shand-Harvey scouted ahead, and soon his penchant for giving primary consideration to the horses' welfare got him in trouble with Wheeler.

Near the mouth of the Miette River, the director found himself in a particular hurry and informed Fred that he would push on with a few of the men, choose a campsite and expect him to bring up the horses and equipment later in the day. Fred had other ideas and on seeing some good pasture early in the afternoon he stopped, forcing Wheeler to spend the night in a makeshift shelter. Beginning the next morning "without soap or breakfast," Wheeler quickly worked himself into a temper and furiously backtracked to Fred's camp, arriving just in time to see the pack train pulling out. Accosting the outfitter he snapped, "Stephens, I always heard that you were a damn good man, but you're not." Unabashed,

Fred retorted, "Wheeler, I always heard that you were an s. o. b., and you are."[4] The party continued on in icy silence to near the mouth of the Moose River where, after turning the horses over to Phillips, Fred, understandably, took his leave.

Phillips and Shand-Harvey carried on, stopping the next evening at the raucous railroad construction camp known as Moose City. Here Conrad Kain, still rather new to the ways of the trail but eventually to be the only individual in the Rockies to combine mountain guiding and trail guiding, had a rather rude introduction to the habits of some of the camps inhabitants. Slipping out of his tent for a brief moment, he returned to find his clothes, some of his food and his cook stove slickly extracted in his absence. Fortunately, the loses were easily replaced and the party was soon once again underway, with each of its members involved in their own particular pursuits. As Wheeler was experienced in topographic work, he and his assistants had little difficulty in carrying out their surveys, but the young American scientists, at least initially, proved not quite so adept at their collecting. Attempts to shoot game specimens proved a constant source of hilarity for Phillips and Shand-Harvey, who went to the extent of driving flocks of sheep and goat into range so that the "experts" might obtain something suitable to stuff. Kinney, at a later date, remembered one particularly vivid example of their ineptitude:

Our climbers were having a day off from strenuous work, and had been busy here and there, when Harmon, who had been up Robson glacier after pictures, came rushing into camp wildly shouting "bear, bear." Out tumbled the "Big Game" hunters wildly scrambling after Harmon, the guide. Conrad and Curlie seized what weapons were handy and I trailed behind efficiently armed with two ten-inch twenty-tews. We were making a comedy for what was a serious matter for the hunters.

At last we discovered the black bear on the mountain side above us. The big game hunters knelt and began filling the mountain side with lead. Their magazines were soon emptied and Conrad and I each got behind one of the hunters and pulled the shells out of their belts and handed them the ammunition as needed during the terrific bombardment.

The bear, in the meantime, dodged here and there or watched curiously what was going on. He was finally hit by a stray shot and scurried out of sight.[5]

Despite such setbacks, the required fauna, varying from miniscule voles to rangy bull caribou, were eventually obtained, often by the intercession of the accurate marksmanship of Phillips or Shand-Harvey.

The guides accompanied the party as far as Berg Lake where the steep cliffs of the Valley of a Thousand Falls on the upper Grand Fork of the Fraser (Robson) River prevented them from taking the horses further. As a consequence, they were forced to retrace their route and then push on up the main Fraser Valley and the Grand Fork Valley to Kinney Lake, where they were to meet the rest of the party below the offending cliffs. Effectively, this meant that they completed the equivalent of another full circuit of Robson while the others leisurely awaited their arrival. Kain, for one, could not stand to be idle in the midst of so many unclimbed peaks. Wheeler had intimated that his assistants would get a crack at Robson, but as time went by his constant stalling made it apparent that he was saving the supposed second ascent for a future Alpine Club camp. Realizing that a Robson climb was not to be, Conrad vanished one afternoon and did not return that evening. The next morning he reappeared and informed a chagrined Wheeler that he had climbed, partially in darkness, the magnificent neighbouring Whitehorn Mountain, a peak he had also been hoping to save for a club ascent.

It took Phillips and Shand-Harvey five days of hard travelling, much of it through country where no pack trails existed, to attain their destination of Kinney Lake. There, on August 9th, Curly constructed a sizeable raft, ferried his waiting passengers and their gear across its expanse, and then brought them down some three miles to a camp he had established on the Grand Fork. After a short stay, while the survey party occupied a few more camera stations, the return trip was commenced and Fitzhugh was regained in early September. From there it was Wheeler's intention to press the survey work on to Maligne Lake and then to cap of the season's successes by pushing the pack train right through to Laggan, thereby completing the first trip from the new Grand Trunk Pacific to the Canadian Pacific. At the time, he prophesied that this route would one day be one of the most popular scenic trips in the Canadian Rockies, and, indeed, he was correct for it was the route eventually followed by the Banff-Jasper Highway.

While Phillips resupplied at Fitzhugh in readiness for the proposed journey, Shand-Harvey forged on ahead to Maligne Lake with Walcott, Blagden and Harmon. En route, Blagden redeemed his earlier inaccuracies by bagging a bighorn ram measuring 18 1/2 inches around the base of the horns, the biggest ram ever taken in the lands that formed Jasper National Park and eventually to go on display in the Smithsonian Institution. Phillips followed close behind Shand-Harvey's group with his cook, Casey Jones, and the remainder of the party, except for Riley and Hollister who stayed at Swift's to collect birds. It was Curly's first trip into the Maligne Lake country and to his surprise he found it easy going, due in large measure to the trail cut by the Otto brothers earlier in the season. Arriving at the lake, he had further reason to be thankful to the Ottos, as his party was able to make use of the boat which they had conveniently left behind. Such good fortune allowed he and Shand-Harvey to spend their time clearing a new piece of trail from the foot of the lake to its outlet into the Maligne River.

September 17th was the proposed date of departure for the remainder of the journey to Laggan, but it proved an inauspicious choice as it marked the beginning of what was to be a five day period of rain and snow. Faced with these conditions and on a tight schedule, Wheeler was forced to abandon his plans and return to Fitzhugh with the collecting party under Shand-Harvey's care. However, he believed that "Phillips could get through if anyone could" and delegated to him the responsibility of seeing Harmon, Kinney and Kain safely to the CPR line. This he was able to accomplish in twelve days, but not without inflicting severe hardship on himself and his livestock in the snow-choked passes. Immediately on reaching Laggan on September 30th, it was necessary for him to turn around and retrace the 120 mile route just completed in order to reach home before the passes were completely blocked for the rest of the winter. Not wanting to make the trip alone, he was able to convince Kain to accompany him with the promise of sharing his winter trapline at the head of the Smoky River. Showing characteristic fortitude, the pair travelled long hours in deteriorating conditions and arrived back at Fitzhugh in the amazingly short time of thirteen days. Before departing for the trapline, Phillips prepared a report for Wheeler in which he concurred in his employer's optimism about the route's future and estimated the cost of constructing a decent trail over it:

When a good trail is put in from steel to steel it will be a very popular trip. The cost of the trail will not be very great. There is about five or six miles of it that will have to be graded and "switchbacked" but very little bridging to do. Going back we had a lot of trouble on the Sun Wapta and Athabasca, but a very fair trail can be put up all these streams to the foot of Wilcox Pass for about fifty dollars per mile.[6]

Wheeler's plan to hold an Alpine Club camp at the foot of Mount Robson had to wait until 1913 to come to fruition, but when it did he had no doubt about who should be placed in charge of the outfitting. Curly had performed all that was asked of him with speed and efficiency in 1911 and had earned the right to handle the potentially lucrative 1913 venture. However, both he and Wheeler realized that, as in 1911, additional assistance would be required. The choice fell on the director's old friends the Otto brothers. Phillips and the Ottos were already well-acquainted and it was even their practice to share each other's facilities and equipment on occasion. For example, when outfitting the famous American sculptor Phimister Proctor and his friend G. D. Pratt on a hunting trip in the fall of 1911, Curly noted in his diary that he stopped at Ottos's shack at Mile 111 (Cabin Creek) in order to pick up his toboggan, bear traps and folding stove.

When the time came to make arrangements for the Alpine Club camp, Curly had to leave his trapline in early April to go to

Edmonton, where Jack Otto spent his winters. Together they decided on what remuneration they hoped to obtain from the camp and on April 4th began negotiations with Wheeler. Apparently, an agreement was reached quite easily, for on that day Curly made a cryptic note in his diary: "John Otto and I closed a deal with A. O. Wheeler, director of the Alpine Club, to handle the Club Camp at Robson Pass in July and August. Taking the 10 p.m. train for the west tonight."[7] But the closing of this deal was not the only groundwork that had to be laid to ensure a successful camp at the chosen site. A major difficulty presented itself in the form of the forbidding cliffs of the upper Grand Fork Valley which had so vexed Phillips and Shand-Harvey in 1911. Descending 1,600 feet in less than a mile, the waters flowing out of Berg Lake formed a series of beautiful waterfalls, the most spectacular of which was Emperor Falls, which made the building of a pack trail a seeming impossibility. Yet if such a trail were not constructed, the usual route up the Moose Valley and over Moose Pass would make the task of transporting a large camp to be set up between Berg and Adolphus Lakes, the ideal location from a mountaineering stand-point, too expensive and time-consuming. Negotiations with the GTP and the British Columbia government were carried out by Wheeler and in the spring of 1913 the latter agreed to pay the costs of having a trail built, if such were possible. Curly was awarded the contract at a reported $50 per mile, and with customary zeal and inventiveness went to work on the problem. With the assistance of Frank Doucette, his trapping partner and sometimes pack-er, he fashioned a switchback trail, involving extensive cribbing and tilling, up the steep precipices. The crowning glory of this engineering feat was a flying trestle bridge built around the rock face leading to Emperor Falls, an edifice that never failed to elicit comment from those who used it.

After finishing this work in early July, it was time for Curly to join with the Ottos to begin the job of packing in the camping equipment and gear. Although attendance was to be restricted to the most proficient of the club's members, it was nonetheless fair-ly large with seventy-three participants. Since it was to begin on

July 28th, little time was available to get everything to its appointed place, and the new trail immediately proved its usefulness. It was equally appreciated by those attending the camp, who not only escaped the long pack trip over the Moose Pass route but were also treated with a view of the splendours of the Valley of a Thousand Falls. At the camp itself, which lasted until August 9th, thing ran extremely smoothly. Phillips and the Ottos were kept busy ferrying members back and forth to two subsidiary camps placed six miles down the Smoky and near Moose Pass, aided in their work by perfect weather throughout. On July 31st the ascent of Robson, the main objective of the proceedings, was made by Kain, Albert H. MacCarthy and William W. Foster, and on returning from the conquest they were greeted by Phillips with the information that its was in actuality the first ascent and not the second as they had supposed. All in all, the decision to combine outfitting forces was once again shown to be the most practical means of making a success of such a large undertaking.

Be that as it may, there were, of course, occasions when the early Jasper trailmen handled parties completely on their own. If a group was composed of only one or two patrons, it was often possible to hire some stop-gap help and take care of them single-handedly. This became progressively more feasible as pack strings, equipment and supplies were built up over a period of time. Fortunately, there were also some dependable sources of personnel available who were willing to work on a trip by trip basis. One of the best places for an outfitter to find this type of help was from among the ranks of the half-breed population of the region. Born and raised in the wilderness, they knew the country to the north of Jasper as no one else, and from their earliest youth worked with the Indian cayuses used as pack animals, attributes not easy to find in white men.

The first half-breeds to come into prominence on the trail were Tommy Groat, son of respected Edmonton resident Malcolm Groat and an early packer on the GTP, and Adolphus Moberly, who in 1908 had aided Yates in finding a route into Robson Pass for the Mumm party. Moberly was only one among a number of half-breeds of that surname who along with several other settlers of mixed blood and the Swifts inhabited the area enclosed within he boundaries of Jasper Forest Park, a 5,450 square mile reservation created by the federal government in 1907. Such settlement was incompatible with government plans for the park and in December, 1909, J. W. McLaggan, chief forest ranger and acting superintendent, took on the task of trying to remove them. Swift would not budge, but the half-breeds came to terms fairly easily and most of them moved northward to the Grande Cache district, one of their favourite hunting and fishing grounds. But the move did not preclude their continuing to frequent the park area in their wanderings and soon several others, in addition to Groat and Moberly, began to come to the attention of local outfitters as trail hands.

Relatives of Adolphus Moberly predominated with Frank, Dave and Ed Moberly and Felix Plante being some of the most noteworthy. But it was to be Adam Joachim, a Moberly-in-law, who would gain the most lasting reputation. Joachim, a descendant of both the original Iroquois canoemen brought out by the North West Company and the famous Hudson's Bay Company trader Colin Fraser, was born at Berland lake in 1875 and had rather an interesting upbringing for one who eventually would make much of his livelihood working on the trail. At an early age he came to the attention of the Catholic missionary Father Albert Lacombe who provided an education for him at the St. Albert Mission School. While living at the mission he also served as an altar boy and upon completion of his schooling was sent to the seminary in Montreal to study for the priesthood. However, a family crisis intervened and, abandoning three years of hard work, he returned home and was soon married to a daughter of Ewan Moberly. A man of his education, proficient in several Indian languages as well as English, French and Latin, was eventually bound to attract attention, landing him jobs with a number of outfitters when he was not hunting or trapping on his own.

Supplementing the half-breeds as temporary help were discontented railroad construction workers and the odd down-and-out prospector wanting to make a grubstake. Life in the construction camps was somewhat less than glamorous and combined with low wages made for what one observer claimed were three equal bodies of men — those actually working on the line, those fed up and heading back to Edmonton, and those replacing them heading out. Although few of these remained in the vicinity for any length of time, some did stay long enough to take one or two pack trips. By employing them as well as their more permanent men, the Jasper outfitters were able to make a few important hunting and exploring trips in the years prior to the First World War.

Perhaps the most celebrated of these expeditions were the three trips of Samuel Prescott Fay outfitted by Brewster and Moore and guided by Fred Brewster between 1912 and 1914. Fay was the type of client an outfitter dreamed about, hiring the outfit for three to four months and returning for several years. A native of Boston and a Harvard graduate, he had first visited the Rockies at Lake O'Hara in 1906. At least two other visits to the Banff vicinity took place prior to 1912, but unlike his relative, Professor Charles Fay, he was more interested in hunting than climbing. It was therefore not surprising that when he heard of the excellent sport to be had along the new GTP line he would be attracted to the scene. Certainly the reports were not unfounded, as the wilderness north of the line abounded in bear, deer, moose and goat and had the added attraction of caribou, not plentiful in the south. But what interested Fay the most was solving the question as to the variety of sheep inhabiting the region north of the Athabasca River and south of the Peace River. Bighorn sheep (*Ovis Canadensis*) were known to range south of the Athabasca and Stone Sheep (*Ovis Stonei*) north of the Peace, but the species or sub-species roaming the country between was still a mystery to naturalists.

Fay appeared at Hinton in early August, 1912, and contracted Fred Brewster to outfit his proposed trip. Since this was to be the first hunting trip handled by Brewster and Moore in their new location, Fred decided to guide it himself with one of his most trusted men, J. Beaumont Gates, assisting. On August 8th, with a seven-horse pack train, the three set out, intending to get as far as

213

possible beyond the Smoky River in the time available. Fred believed that this was the first attempt by white men to penetrate the country west of the Smoky for purposes of big game hunting, and the trail seemed to support this assumption. Struggling through downed timber and treacherous muskegs south of the Muddywater River, they easily bested Yates's and Stephens's 1911 mark of taking seven days to cover twenty–five miles by consuming twice as much time for the same distance. The Muddywater and Jackpine rivers, as well as Sheep Creek, were hunted unsuccessfully but not without profit, as in the process the environs of Mount Bess were examined in detail and a good view obtained of a peak some thirty miles away to the northwest which rivalled Mount Robson in its magnificence. Further examination of this mountain proved fruitless, however, for although they were able to get within ten miles of its supposed location the weather proved too foul to even get a glimpse of it for the next two weeks. Bad weather, a shortage of supplies and a complete lack of success at hunting also greeted the end of September, the date Fay had been expecting to arrive back in Hinton, necessitating the abandonment of both sheep and mountain hunting for 1912. Starting down the Porcupine (Kakwa) River in an endeavour to find a way home that would avoid the high, snow-covered passes, the party continued to be dogged by the weather's persistent inclemency. After striking the Smoky River, snow fell incessantly, and it was not until the end of October that Hinton was finally reached, with both men and horses completely exhausted.

Undaunted by his failure, Fay laid plans to return the next summer to continue his quest, and Fred again expressed a desire to act as guide. In the interim, though, Fay underwent a serious operation and when the time came to resume the investigation he was in no shape to undergo its difficulties. As a consequence, Fred suggested a shortened trip that would proceed at a more leisurely pace. Beginning from Brewster and Moore's new headquarters in Jasper, a few weeks were spent in the vicinities of Mounts Robson and Bess. Later, two months were taken to hunt sheep as far south as Laggan and caribou along the Divide above Fortress Lake.

Joining Up in Jasper

This trip in no way compensated for Fay's real objective, and elaborate plans were once again laid with Brewster for the 1914 season. That year's expedition took on an added dimension when Fay received a commission from the Biological Survey of the U. S. Bureau of Agriculture to make collections of animal skins and detailed reports on the birds and mammals of the region. Support from the Biological Survey allowed for extensions in both the range and time limits of the trip, and when Fay arrived in Jasper in June, 1914 it was with the intention of pushing right through to the Peace River. The proposed lengthening of the expedition and the fact that Fay brought along a friend, C. R. Cross of Boston, made the need for an enlarged outfit and more men apparent. Sixteen pack horses and five saddle horses were supplied, taxing Brewster and Moore's comparatively small pack string to the limit, and to handle them two green but willing men were hired. They were Bob Jones, a former railroad worker who in later years would achieve a fine reputation as a park warden, and Jack Symes, an ex-North West Mounted Police constable.

Leaving Jasper on June 26th, the party was guided for the first two weeks by Jack Brewster, as Fred was tied up helping Phil Moore get started on a contract the company had to clear a trail into Medicine and Jacques Lakes. However, he was replaced as guide by his more experienced brother at the head of the Sulphur River. Two days hence Fred and Fay again glimpsed the intriguing mountain they had seen in 1912 and decided to detour in order to study it in more detail. The peak, when sighted, was still a long way off to the northwest, and getting close enough to obtain good views was not an easy matter. After passing through the settlement of Grande Cache at the confluence of the Sulphur and Smoky Rivers, the Smoky was crossed and the trails were found to be either old or non-existent. As Fay noted in his diary, this situation demanded great skill on the part of their guide and patience on the part of all:

We found the old trail but no one had been over it for years, — probably not since the big fire burnt it over. It has fallen in so anyone coming this way avoids it. The only people who go this way are breeds and one or two trappers. Fred and Bob Jones went ahead to chop the trees away and it was slow work. Signs of the old trail appeared now and then and how Fred followed it the way he did was a mystery to all of us. It was a fine exhibition of a guide's seventh sense. Finally, we decided to hit across the top of a hill to find the old trail and here was our mistake, as the trail turned out to be ahead of us some ways. From here on we had lots of chopping and it was slow, tiresome work. Pack came off and sometimes three or four horses had to be repacked at once. Roachy fell under some logs and could not move until the logs were cut away. Snowball's pack went over his head but the ropes held him so he couldn't move. One trouble after another turned up and it was 8 p.m. before we made camp in a mess of down timber, with no feed for the horses. After a while we picked out spaces between the fallen logs, unrolled our blankets, and were soon asleep.[8]

Fighting their way up Sheep Creek, they finally caught sight of the mountain again and estimated its height at 12,000 feet. On August 3rd another excellent, but unexpected view was obtained from what was appropriately named Surprise Pass, and for the next ten days the peak was constantly in sight while the party continued northward. Fay was completely distracted by its great size and beauty and, in consultation with Brewster, decided to name it Mount Alexander in honour of the intrepid fur trader-explorer Alexander Mackenzie. Later the name would be modified to Mount Sir Alexander, at 10,700 feet the highest peak in the Rockies north of Mount Robson.

Fay's two year old interest in the great mountain finally satisfied, his attention turned to the biological survey and the question of the sheep. Specimens similar to those taken by the 1911 Smithsonian party were shot or trapped and then carefully skinned and preserved in the interests of science. The fact that the collecting occurred in all kinds of weather and while travelling through difficult and unfamiliar country often led to uncertainty and frustration. On particularly bad days these feelings showed up in Fay's diary: "Why any sane man comes to these mountains

is a mystery to me when he knows the misery he has to endure —
yet we all do it again and again."⁹ The plan of the expedition had
been to get to Pine Pass and then across country to the Peace River,
but by the beginning of September it had become obvious that the
pass was going to be impossible to reach. As an alternative, it was
decided to head immediately for Hudson's Hope on the Peace and
from there return to Jasper by way of Pouce Coupe, Grande Prairie
and Edson. Although this would not allow for a complete study
of all possible sheep ranges, Fay felt that he had already satisfac-
torily answered that question. From his observations he concluded that there were no sheep between the Peace River and the heads
of the northern tributaries of the Smoky River, and the sheep south
of this line were of the same species found between Banff and
Jasper, conclusions supported by the reports of natives and half-
breeds met in the course of the journey.

A change in the excellent weather pattern and a growing difficulty in filling out the larder immediately illustrated the wisdom
of their decision to head for Hudson's Hope. Sixteen days of continuous rain and snow cut progress to a minimum, and the accom-
modation situation suffered a serious setback when Symes acci-
dentally burned down the portable lean-to shelter, "the most useful article in the whole outfit." Fourteen weeks on the trail had
also taken a rather devastating toll on the men's personal apparel,
and by early October a day had to be taken to sew themselves back
together:

*Fred, whose outfit is usually in pieces, at present is sewing his hat, the
crown having been slowly torn off until it is held by one corner only.
Yesterday when he faced the wind his lid stood on end, making him look
like some crested creature. His trousers are continually in need of repair
as his supply is limited to two pair. If he had more these wouldn't be
worth repairing. The ordinary person if assigned to such a job would be
at a loss to know which piece to sew onto which, so many are there of
them. He spent the morning sewing his socks, the repairing of which was
similar to a picture puzzle. However, the results were excellent.*¹⁰

These repairs were necessary at this juncture because the party soon expected to meeting white men, a pleasure they had not experienced for almost four months. When they finally did, a startling piece of news greeted them. On October 7th they encountered a trapper named Nelson, and when questioned as to the latest news he commented that the war was still the main topic of interest. At first thinking that the United States had gone to war with Mexico, they queried him further and finally realized that the First World War had already been raging for two months. After learning this disquieting information, they party hurried on to Hudson's Hope, reaching it on October 16th after sixteen weeks on the trail. From there they began the return to Jasper following the road through the farming districts of Pouce Coupe and Grande Prairie, utilizing a wagon to carry much of their equipment. At Beaverlodge they split up, Fay and Cross continuing by road to Edson while Brewster, Jones and Symes cut across country with four pack horses and three saddle horses. Battling the first winter snows, they finally reached Jasper on November 21st, completing in five months the longest recorded tourist pack trip in the Rockies to date

Although perhaps the most important of these years, Fred Brewster's three expeditions with Fay were not the only ones handled by an outfitter on his own. In 1914, Curly Phillips too guided and outfitted an interesting party that wished to examine the same mountain which has so captivated Fay. As mentioned, Curly was an inveterate trapper, and over a period of years he explored most of the territory between Mount Robson and Jackpine Pass. During the winter of 1913 he ran a trapline to within a few miles of what he called "Big Mountain" and thereby became completely familiar with the entire Sir Alexander region. Elsewhere, Mary Jobe, a wealthy young New York woman who taught American history at Hunter College, had heard reports of the magnificence of the peak from those who had seen it while climbing at the Mount Robson Alpine Club camp. Since Phillips was the only one known to have actually visited the area, her inquiries about reaching the mountain put her in touch with him and a trip was arranged.   Accompanying Miss Jobe was a friend, Margaret Springate from Winnipeg, the two making a party small enough for Curly to handle on his own. During the years between 1911 and 1914 he had constantly been building up his pack string, and the manpower situation had taken a decided turn for the better with the appearance at Jasper of his brother-in-law Bert Wilkins in May, 1913 and both his father, Daniel, and brother, Harry, in early 1914.

It was understood that the trip would be a difficult one for the ladies as it crossed some very rough country where few, if any, trails existed. Consequently, in an attempt to travel as lightly and quickly as possible, only one assistant, Wilkins, was taken along. Beginning early in August, they followed a route to Robson Pass and then went northwestward in what seemed like a dreary procession of passes, until at the Big Salmon (McGregor) River further travel with horses was impossible. Among the obstacles already overcome was timber so thick and ridges so steep that at one point the men had worked twelve hours cutting out three-quarters-of-a-mile of trail, including twenty-four separate switchbacks. From the point where the horses were left they packed all the supplies on their own backs, an equally arduous chore since the mountain was still many miles distant. When they reached its foot, Jobe, unaware of Brewster's and Fay's recent naming, called it "Kitchi," Cree for "great" or "mighty." After two days of bone-wearying walking to a point where an ascent might be made, two plucky but unsuccessful attempts were launched on August 22nd and 25th. On the second try, Curly and Miss Jobe attained an elevation of 7,800 feet before the difficulty of the climbing and short supplies forced a retreat. After this an immediate return to Jasper was imperative, but it was not the last time the mountain would see the two seeking to capture its magnificent, snow-capped summit for they would return for a renewed attempt the following summer. As for her outfitter's performance on the 1914 outing, Miss Jobe gave a flattering assessment: "I wish to say that the main factors in our success were the splendid ability, unflinching courage and determined effort of Donald Phillips."[11]

The Otto brothers too were relatively successful in obtaining some parties to outfit on their own in the immediate pre-war years. Worthy of note were those composed of individuals with wide literary reputations. One of them was James Oliver Curwood, who went out with them on at least five occasions beginning immediately before the war and continuing until the mid-twenties. Curwood had begun his career as a reporter for a Detroit newspaper, but he had later discovered a talent for writing adventure stories and went on to become America's foremost author of this genre. Many of his works, such as *Kazan, The Wolf Dog* and *Nomads of the North*, were transformed into screenplays for motion pictures, and at one time his name on the marquee was all that was needed to ensure a sell-out house anywhere in North America. Because he preferred to set his stories in the so-called "trackless wilderness" of Canada, his books, although in a somewhat inaccurate manner, served to advertise the country. This led the Canadian government to provide him with financial support to allow for further "research." Each summer for about ten years he spent three to four months in the Canadian wilds, at least half of the time in the Rockies, and it was his practice to take extensive sightseeing and hunting trips outfitted by Otto Brothers and usually guided by Bruce Otto. Curwood became so attached to his guide that in a book published in 1917, entitled *The Grizzly King*, Bruce became the main character in the story of a grizzly bear and how he survived a hunt by a crack guide and his dude. In another Curwood epic, *The Hunted Woman*, both Fred Stephens and Mrs. Jack Otto appeared as characters in a melodramatic tale set in the Yellowhead region.

A second and perhaps even more famous author to be served by Otto Brothers was Sir Arthur Conan Doyle, creator of the popular Sherlock Holmes series. Conan Doyle, accompanied by his wife and children, paid a visit to Jasper in the summer of 1914, just in time for the local citizenry to corral him into laying the cornerstone of the town's first church, known as "The Little White Church in the Rockies." During his stay he expressed a desire to take a short pack trip, on which he was guided by Closson Otto.

He was so delighted by the experience that he wrote a poem, entitled "The Athabaska Trail," which read in part:

I shall hear the roar of rivers where the rapids foam and tear
I shall smell the virgin upland with its balsam laden air
I shall soon again be riding down the winding, woody vale
With the packer and the pack horse on the Athabaska Trail.[12]

By 1914 some of the Jasper outfitters had been able to gain a measure of security and prosperity. Their willingness to join in temporary partnerships to assist them through periods when they were still getting established had played a major part in this, as they had allowed for the outfitting of parties that would have otherwise been unmanageable. Already by 1914 the gradual build-up of horses, equipment and manpower was making such combinations less necessary, but the good-will they had engendered would long remain in evidence. At the outbreak of the war the future of guiding and outfitting in the area seemed particularly bright with the newly completed GTP and the soon to be completed CNR making the region much more accessible to tourists.

Chapter IX
Old Trails, New Trails

As was the case in so many fields of human endeavour, the First World War marked a turning point in the history of guiding and outfitting at Banff and Jasper. Essentially, it marked the end of an era when guides and outfitters had provided the sole means for tourist-explorers of all descriptions to see the wilderness of the Canadian Rockies away from the railroad lines. At the same time, it coincided with developments which would see a new type of tourist appearing in the mountains, resulting in significant changes in the mode of operation for those trailmen attempting to attract their patronage.

Of course, the most immediate effect of the war was the departure of many from the field to help defend the freedom they so greatly valued. As soon as word of the hostilities was received at Banff a movement was afoot to form a "Corps of Guide," whose skills, it was believed, would make it admirably suited for reconnaissance work. The response among those following the trail was excellent, but the proposed unit was quickly disbanded because of the need for reinforcements in other battalions. Most of those who responded did not see each other again until war's end, and in the meantime several were wounded or captured in the course of their service. Bill Peyto, Harry Lang and Joe Woodworth were all wounded in action, the latter losing his right arm at the shoulder. Such a debilitating loss would seem to have marked the end of his trail days, but after returning home and being awarded the Military Medal he set to work to rehabilitate himself. Soon he was back working for Simpson, wielding an axe to good effect with his left arm and using his teeth to assist in tying the diamond. Of those captured, Bill Potts underwent the worst experience in a

German POW camp and for a time after his return would occasionally scare the daylights out of his dudes when he woke up screaming from nightmares. But despite their wounds, these men were more fortunate than their fellow guide, Sid Unwin, who made the supreme sacrifice.

On returning from a trip to the Athabasca with Professor Mitchell in the fall of 1914, Unwin immediately enlisted and, with his experience in the Boer War, was immediately assigned to the 20th Artillery Battery at Lethbridge. In June, 1915 the Battery was sent to England, and in January, 1916 he saw his first action in France. Meanwhile, with his brother Art also volunteering, responsibility for his outfitting business had been left in the hands of his sister Ethel, who had sometimes assisted Sid on the trail. With characteristic Unwin determination, she immediately applied to the government for a guide's license, the first granted to a woman in the parks. This was meant to be only a stopgap until her brother returned, but in July, 1917 word reached Banff that such was not to be. At the Battle of Vimy Ridge, Sid was hit by a piece of shrapnel while single-handedly manning an artillery emplacement and later died of his wounds in a hospital at Leeds. His passing came as a great shock to his friends at Banff, particularly the new Mrs. Warren. In August, 1920 she and her sister-in-law Mrs. Sharples dedicated a window at St. George's Church in Banff to him "as an appreciation of his fidelity as a guide and a testimony to his kindly disposition and high character."[1]

At Jasper there was an equally patriotic response to the call to arms among the men of the trail. On arriving back from his trip with Fay in October, 1914, Fred Brewster intended to enlist immediately, but had to delay when he found that his partner Phil Moore had already joined up. Moore had become part of a militia unit, the 15th Light Horse of Calgary, shortly after coming to Canada and had achieved the rank of captain before the war broke out. On call up, he reported for duty at Winnipeg and was promoted to brigade major. He was quickly sent overseas and remained there until transferred home in 1917, promoted to colonel and placed in charge of the garrison for Southern Alberta.

Later in the war he was given the difficult task of running the Alberta conscription branch. Fred did eventually volunteer for service in the Engineers late in the summer of 1915, shortly after he and his brother Jack initiated the subsequently famous Sky Line Trail Rides into Maligne Lake and became involved in a tent camp venture, known as Jasper Park Camp, on the shore of Lac Beauvert. Because of his background and education, he was commissioned as a major in the Second Tunnelling Division and sent overseas in charge of a company made up mostly of miners from the Barkerville district of British Columbia. In 1917 the company was credited with the demolition of Hill 60, a strategic observation post dominating the French countryside, and for this achievement Fred was decorated with the Military Medal and Bar.

Meanwhile, Fred's brothers Pat and George, who had been working for the company at Jasper, also enlisted, Pat in the Royal Flying Corps and George in the Canadian Artillery. This left the still youthful Jack Brewster to shoulder the entire responsibility for the Brewster and Moore operation. He performed exceptionally well, and fortunately was able to rely on the advice of his father, John, who arrived in the vicinity in the fall of 1916 after suffering reverses in his real estate interests at Vancouver. Not only was Jack able to maintain the company's outfitting and freighting interests over the slack period to the war's end, but also managed to buy out their partners in the tent camp, Messrs. Bone and Kenneth of the Edmonton Tent and Mattress Company.

Curly Phillips likewise became a member of the armed forces, but not until later in the war. Early on after its outbreak and before the United States joined in, he was able to continue securing a few parties to outfit, running his pack string in combination with the Ottos' out of the tent camp at Lac Beauvert for a time. Mary Jobe returned in the summer of 1915 for a second attempt on Mount Sir Alexander, during which Curly was able to lead her and a companion to within 100 feet of the summit, and in 1917 she accompanied him on a winter trip to the Wapiti River to supply William Rindfoos, out on yet another collecting expedition for the Smithsonian Institution. On returning from this outing Curly was called up for service in the Canadian Field Artillery, although he was granted a temporary leave early in 1918 which was spent trapping with Rindfoos. Unfortunately, he never got the opportunity to go on active duty as while training at Kingston later that year he had his arm smashed when caught between some kicking horses.

When the trailmen returned home from serving their country signs that the old order was changing were already apparent. One was the continuing departure of veteran outfitters and guides from the business. In Banff, Unwin's death affected many, including his former employer Billy Warren, who within a few years of his marriage had become one of Banff's leading businessmen. In 1919 he began the Cascade Garage and Banff Motor Company in partnership with Bert Sibbald, in 1920 he acquired the old Alberta Hotel and began renovating it, and in 1921 he initiated Rocky Mountain Tours and Transport in conjunction with James I. McLeod, also a former guide. In Jasper, both John Yates and Fred Stephens disappeared from the ranks. Yates's mail contract had ended with the completion of the GTP and having been married in 1910 he moved off the Hobo and took up a new homestead, remaining there with his growing family until his retirement to the Imperial Valley in California in 1920. Fred Stephens had begun to spend much of his time back in Lacombe during the war, having at least temporarily fixed up his "double harness scrapes," and in the twenties abandoned the trail in favour of operating a fox farm in Montana.

But even more significant than the departure of several individuals from outfitting as an indicator of the changing situation at war's end was the growing predominance of the internal combustion engine over the horse as a mode of transportation. Before the war the parks had been largely isolated from the effects of the automobile. In September, 1905, an Order-in-Council had been passed prohibiting the use of automobiles in any part of Rocky Mountains Park, a rather needless piece of legislation as there was no road connecting Banff with the outside world. By the summer of 1909, though, the construction of a Calgary-Banff road had progressed to the point where the occasional adventurer had attempted to make the often perilous journey to the resort. The law came down hard on such violators, and it was not until 1911 that a deputation of Calgary motorists was able to convince the minister of the interior to at least partially lift the restrictions. Motorists were allowed to bring their cars into town, but then the vehicles had to be parked and the keys left with the police until they were ready to return to Calgary. Some members of the Calgary Automobile Club had thumbed their noses at this regulation, and finally, in June, 1914, the superintendent had relented, over the protests of local horse interests, allowing cars to use a limited number of streets and drives at very modest rates of speed.

Although those returning from the war might have expected some further relaxing of the rules, many were undoubtedly amazed at the state of affairs that greeted them. Not only had the government removed all restrictions by 1916, a year which saw 1,016 cars enter the east gate of the park, but it had also begun to push full-steam ahead on a motor road construction program. Concentrating on the road leading west to Castle Mountain and Lake Louise, which was planned to eventually link up with a road to be built over Vermilion Pass from B. C., it utilized all the money that could be scraped together from thin wartime appropriations. At the same time the local population, which had formerly been so opposed to the automobile, began to get on the bandwagon, with dealerships and garages springing up virtually overnight. Evidence of the extent of change was apparent in the spring of 1916 when on one day a train carload of automobiles was being unloaded at the Banff station at the same time as two carloads of horses were being loaded for shipping out.

One of the earliest and most important purchasers of an automobile was Jim Brewster. While living at the coast he had become acquainted with their capabilities and in June, 1915 he acquired a Baby Overland, the first motor car in Banff. Its performance soon convinced him that the future of the tourist business would rely on motorized transport and in early in 1916 his company, recently renamed Brewster Transport Company, proudly accepted delivery of a carload of Overland touring cars. As a consequence, another historic change took place when the Bow Livery, acquired in the same deal as the Mount Royal Hotel, was unceremoniously made over into a garage. Other local businessmen quickly followed Jim's lead, although on a smaller scale, and by 1919 there were sixty livery car licenses being issued annually in the park.

Because of its isolation and more limited development, Jasper did not feel the effects of the internal combustion age as quickly or as fully as did Banff, but all the signs were there that it eventually would. Some work was done during the war years upgrading the Maligne Canyon trail to road status and beginning construction on a road to the newly named Mount Edith Cavell at the mouth of the Whirlpool Valley. Then, in the summer of 1920, Jack Brewster shipped in the first car by rail, and the government began to give consideration to the idea of building a road from Edmonton using, in part, the abandoned railroad grade made available by the consolidation of the GTP and CNR lines from Edson to Moose Lake in 1916. It would be many years before this project would come to fruition, but in the meantime several other vehicles were brought in to use on the roads in the town and its vicinity. In 1921 the government began to issue its first automobile permits and chauffeur's licenses in Jasper Park.

The effect of the automobile's widespread acceptance on guiding and outfitting is difficult to gauge. Understandably, its most direct influence was on the carriage trade as tally-hos and buggies soon began to disappear in favour of cars, but it appears to have had some direct effect on the trail business as well. Perhaps the major one was the change resulting from the way in which outfitters perceived the automobile and its future. The enthusiasm with which tourists, residents and governments alike embraced motorized transport made it seem likely that roads would soon penetrate to the most isolated of mountain valleys and that every tourist would shun the horse for the car. These fears would ultimately prove groundless, but at the time many trailmen decided to hedge their bets and develop other business interests that could be run in conjunction with their guiding and outfitting operations.

One who in later years freely admitted that the advent of motorized tourism impelled him into making one of the most important decisions in his life was Jimmy Simpson. While out on one of his first trips for Wilson in 1897 he had visited Bow Lake and had been impressed with the scenery and the excellent camping area available along its northeastern shore. Wilcox, who had visited the lake in 1895 with Peyto, had been similarly impressed and even at that early date predicted that it would become a favourite with tourists and that "a comfortable building, erected in a tasteful and artistic manner" would stand near its shore. Whether the two ever discussed this idea is unknown, but it is likely that Jimmy had the same thought more than once in the dozens of times he camped at the spot in the next two decades. Therefore, it was only natural when he began to contemplate the indefinite future of the horse in the post-war years that he would begin to give consideration to some development. While a hotel or bungalow camp on the proportions of those of the CPR was beyond his means, a large cabin that could be used in his outfitting operations and added on to as future conditions warranted was feasible. In 1920 he applied to the Parks Branch for a lease of five acres of land at his old camping spot but was informed that he would first have to carry out $5,000 worth of improvements. This he set out to accomplish, the first task being the cutting of enough logs to build a cabin of the proportions desired. Finding the logs at the altitude somewhat stunted, he had to be creative in his planning and settled on a design of a building that was octagonal in shape, with each side being about ten feet long. Once the initial log work was completed, it was necessary to have lumber, doors, windows and other hardware to complete the job, and these had to be packed over the notorious muskegy trail up the Bow River from Laggan. Finally, by late 1922, Jimmy had completed sufficient work to be granted a lease, and the next summer he was able to greet his first guests, Dr. J. Monroe Thorington and William S. Ladd, two American alpinists who he was guiding on a mountaineering expedition to the Columbia Icefield.

Jimmy christened the lodge "Num-Ti-Jah," the Indian word for the pine marten which abounded in the area, and eventually its development proved more auspicious than he could have foreseen. With the construction of the Banff-Jasper Highway during the depression years it became one of few places where lodging could be found between Lake Louise and Jasper. Because of the expected influx of tourists when the highway completed, he began work on a second lodge in 1937. Also made of logs, this building was much larger in scale, containing twenty-four rooms. On its completion the old lodge was turned into his personal retreat, or "ram pasture," where many of his later years were spent painting, reading and reminiscing about his days on the trail.

At Jasper, the veteran outfitters also took steps to ensure that they could earn a livelihood in an uncertain future. Those most closely associated with the appearance of the automobile were the Otto brothers, who like Jim Brewster in Banff realized that it was destined to play an important role in the future of tourism. Over the years they had acquired many teams and buggies in addition to their outfitting stock and equipment. Immediately after the war the teams were used in the operation of a tie camp they had established at the outlet of Moab Lake in the Whirlpool Valley and on road construction, while the buggies were employed transporting tourists over the rough road to the tent camp at Lac Beauvert. Early in 1921 they added a large open motor bus, which was probably converted from a tally-ho, and in the succeeding few years obtained seven livery cars. Then in 1923 they began construction of Mountain Motors, Jasper's first garage and the future site of a General Motors dealership and their livery headquarters.

Fred Brewster turned much of his attention to the further development of the tent camp venture on his return from the war. In 1915 the GTP had agreed with Brewster and Moore and their partners to become involved in the camp and, although little had been done during the war years, they were interested in moving forward in the post-war period. The company cooperated with the railway in the building of the first log dining room in 1921 and in 1922 erected the first cabins on the sites until then occupied by board floor tents. By that time Fred was the sole owner of the business, Colonel Moore having left the company to return to Banff in 1919 and Jack Brewster having decided to leave his brother and establish his own outfitting concern in Jasper. After helping to build the first unit of the log building that would eventually become Jasper Park Lodge, Fred was in turn made a tempting offer for his interest by the new Canadian National Railways, a nationalized company that had absorbed the old GTP and CNR lines. When he accepted the offer in 1923, he wisely retained the rights to the guiding and outfitting done from the location, and it soon became the central focus of his trail business and the key to his future success.

The Jasper outfitter who would become involved in the most diverse interests after the war was Curly Phillips. Given his upbringing in the Ontario lake country and his avowed love of water travel, it was not surprising that foremost among them would be a boat business, which would take on several aspects as time went on. While he had made boats for his own use for a number of years, in the early twenties he decided to get into boat building in a larger way. A workshop was set up in Jasper and, with the help of his father and brother, he began to turn out beautifully finished cedar and canvas canoes, specially adapted for poling and tracking, as well as larger made-to-order freight canoes, which could be fitted with inboard or outboard motors. By the mid-twenties he had compiled a fair inventory of these boats and began to use them to ferry passengers across Medicine and Maligne Lakes, and, as they became very popular with tourists, in 1930 he received a concession from the government allowing him exclusive rights to operate boats on these waters as well as Beaver, Mina and Mona Lakes. Also in the mid-twenties, he began a project that appealed to him more than any other — the provision and guiding of power boat trips up the Athabasca to Whitecourt and down the Peace River from Summit Lake to Peace River Crossing.

Curly was also involved in two other innovative ventures, one concentrating on the summer and the other the winter season. The first was an irrigated market garden worked with the assistance of his brother Harry, packer Art Allan and local climbing guide Joseph Saladana. Initiated in the summer of 1924 on Lewis Swift's property, the garden produced a variety of produce which was trucked over the old railroad grade to Jasper and sold to the town's residents. However, because it was subject to the vagaries of early mountain frosts and required daily attention, it did not prove profitable and was abandoned after two years.

The second enterprise, started in the winter of 1924-25, was to meet a similar fate. Because of the popularity at the time of romantic stories about trappers travelling by dog team in cold northern climates, Curly surmised that there would be some people who would like to experience the life for themselves. With his skills as a trapper and love for dog sledding as well as an abundance of experience with tourists, he felt that he would be perfectly qualified to provide such a service. Evolving from this concept was the creation of a "dude trapline" which, as his advertising material claimed, would provide a picture of what trapping was all about:

Most everyone is familiar with the term as applied in the West to the city man, of "dude", and from which is derived the terms "dude ranch" and "dude wrangler". To this I am going to add an entirely new one in my "dude trapline". It is a new idea which grew partly out of the many inquiries I have had in the last few years from city people who wanted to take a trip by dog-team, and to have the experience of winter travel in the great Northland, and partly I must confess to a genuine love of the life that has such an appeal to me. And incidentally to help others to do the same, and show them the real thing. Not the lurid faked up romance, but as it really is when placed on a commercial basis, and means of making a living.[2]

For the preceding few winters he had been running a trapline from north of Hinton to the Old Man River and then northeasterly across the Hay, Berland and Little Smoky Rivers. Here he chose to inaugurate his scheme and at first the response proved excellent, but after three years clients had become hard to come by and it was discontinued.

Apart from its influence on many outfitters' decisions to diversify their interests, the automobile brought about another interesting change which affected them. This related to the type of tourist visiting the parks after they became accessible by road. The day of the wealthy tourist-explorer, who wished to visit unexplored lakes, valleys and mountains and could afford to hire men and outfit for several months at a time, was drawing to a close. In his place came a tourist, likely from a middle-class background, who would more likely wish to see the maximum amount of country in the minimum time and at the least expense possible. Many of this new breed, if they wished to go out on the trail at all, demanded that their outings be inexpensive and of short duration. Trips of this nature, many outfitters soon found, were just not a paying proposition. This was attested to by Phillips's complaint to a prospective customer in 1925, when he was feeling a bit glum about the future:

> . . . *The average tourist business never pays in July and August unless you can book big parties for long trips. If you are going to give first class service you have to keep good reliable men on the payroll all the time and if you cannot keep them busy you are bound to lose. So I have decided to leave my horses out on the range this summer. Last summer I lost $1500 in July and August, so this season I am taking no chances. It would cost me around $200 to get an outfit in and fitted up for your party and to take them back to the range afterwards. And all I would take in on one week's trip for the horses use would be $210, which is too small a margin to make it worthwhile. . . . The day of the packtrain is pretty well over, as the tourist of today wants speed and the only way to get it is where there is good roads and motor cars. . . . We have wonderful country here and I have spent 17 years building up an outfit and a business only to find when got to the top that there was nothing there and no possible future to the business.*[3]

Because of problems of this nature it was not until the mid-twenties that many outfitting businesses were back to their pre-war levels of business, even though by 1920 visitor statistics had recovered from their wartime doldrums.

Despite the fact that guiding and outfitting had some drawbacks as an avocation in the immediate post-war years, there were, nonetheless, some new operators who came into the field. While some of these were new faces on the scene, most were men who had worked for one of the older outfitters and decided to strike out on their own. They included Jim Boyce, Pat Brewster, Tex Wood, George Harrison, Soapy Smith and Bill Potts along the Canadian Pacific line and Jack Brewster, Bert Wilkins and Jack Hargreaves along the Canadian National line. The consideration was usually monetary in nature, as the $60 to $70 a month they made working for one of the other outfitters did not seem like much compared with the returns apparently to be had from running their own pack string. In the early twenties a typical price for outfitting a party of two would vary anywhere from $25 to $40 per day depending on the length of the trip and the number of men and horses required.

Most of these concerns had an advantage in their small size. As Phillips's complaint pointed out, during the early twenties the major outfitters sometimes lost money because they had to keep large numbers of men on the payroll whether they were on the tail or not, a problem avoided by most of the new people. They usually had only enough horses to handle one or two parties at a time and did much of the guiding themselves, cutting the hired staff to a minimum. Because of this they were often quite able to make a profit handling the types of trip that many tourists were interested in. It was sadly ironic that men such as Stephens and Yates had departed the scene before this situation occurred, as these conditions would have accommodated their desires quite admirably.

The predictable result of the many new guiding and outfitting interests making their appearance were complaints that too many trail businesses were being allowed to establish in the parks. It seemed to the veteran outfitters that their men were taking advantage of them, accompanying the cream of the parties for a year of two as a guide and then, after becoming familiar with these clients, making arrangements to outfit them on their own. Such practices could eventually prove ruinous for everyone, and in an effort to correct these and other abuses eleven of the leading Banff area outfitting concerns held a meeting in May, 1922. It resulted in the formation of the Rocky Mountain Outfitters Association, whose

objective was "to have one official body who will be empowered
to negotiate with the dominion and provincial governments in all
matters pertaining to the outfitting business through the Rocky
Mountains, such as the inter-provincial recognition of guides'
licenses, betterment of trails in the park, game and fishing regulations etc."[4] Although the initial meeting was composed only of
Banff area interests, the association's secretary, L. S. Crosby of
Brewster Transport, was instructed to communicate with the major
outfitters in other areas of the Rockies, including Jasper,
Windermere and Waterton, to invite their cooperation. Some
response was received and the organization continued to function
for a few years, with its name being amended to the Rocky
Mountain Guides' Association. After its demise later in the twen-
ties it would not be until 1944 that the new Alberta Licensed
Outfitters was formed to look after the interests of trailmen.

The departure of several veteran outfitters and guides from the
scene and their replacement by new faces, the appearance of widespread motorized tourist transport and the creation of an official
trailman's organization provided clear indications that the pioneer
age of trail life in the Rockies was drawing to a close. Perhaps the
most important manifestation, though, was the appearance of a
new type of trail trip that was becoming popular in the twenties,
the conducted trail ride. Essentially, this was composed of a large
group of riders travelling a specified number of days over a pre-
determined route and usually, but not always, stopping at pre-
arranged camping spots. To a great degree, the outfitters' involvement in these rides was an attempt to meet and make a profit from
the post-war tourists' desires.

The earliest and perhaps least structured of these conducted
trail rides were the "Off The Beaten Track" trips arranged and conducted by Caroline B. Hinman. Born in Cincinnati but living most
of her life in Summit, New Jersey, Hinman served from 1915 to
1921 as the secretary of the Summit Board of Education. Finding
she had an all-consuming passion for travel, she participated in a
conducted tour of Europe and was so taken with the idea that she
arranged a tour of her own to the continent in 1914. Prior to this,

however, she had visited the Canadian Rockies during the Alpine Club of Canada camps at Cathedral Mountain and Mount Robson in 1913 and had been impressed with what she saw. In 1915 she made a second visit, this time accompanying Mary Jobe and other friends to Mount Sir Alexander under the guidance of Curly Phillips. With the continent closed to travel due to the war, in 1916 she took a party to Glacier Park, Montana and it proved so successful that in 1917 she decided to try a similar trip through the Canadian Rockies. Composed of well-educated teen-aged girls from wealthy American families, as all her conducted groups were, the party of ten was outfitted by Jimmy Simpson for a three-week trip to Mount Assiniboine, Sawback Lake and the Ptarmigan Valley. Impressed with Jimmy's services, she came back to Banff in 1919 and was again outfitted by him, this time on a trip north of the Saskatchewan as far as Nigel Pass.

The guides and packers working on these trips found the experience to be a little out of the ordinary. Not only were they required to camp some distance away from the girls but often felt they were coming under the close scrutiny of the chaperones in order to head off any possible handy-panky. On one occasion, a packer had a few of the girls out on a boat ride on a mountain lake when he noticed the glint of the sun catching glass on a nearby ridge. Using his binoculars he was amazed to see someone ensconced on a lofty perch observing his every move with a similar optical aid.

The first two Hinman trips in the Canadian Rockies proved so successful that they inaugurated several decades of similar outings. For the period 1920-22 Curly Phillips was the recipient of the business with excursions covering the entire area within Jasper Park and the environs of Mount Robson. Then in 1923 the tours began the first of sixteen summers under the guidance of Jim Boyce, who had been successively cook and guide on the first two trips outfitted by Simpson. Miss Hinman had been so taken with him that after he started in business for himself she would rarely go out with anyone else. It was during these years on the trail with Boyce that he tabbed her with the nickname "Timberline Kate" because of her penchant for choosing a campsite with a good view near timberline or on a high pass. Hinman's "Off The Beaten Track" tours in the Rockies eventually expanded to include up to three different groups each summer and, in addition to travel by pack train, began to include boat trips in the thirties and automobile trips in the forties.

At the opposite end of the spectrum from the Hinman tours were the "Banff To Mount Assiniboine Walking and Riding Tours" which were highly structured in their route and itinerary. A. O. Wheeler had for many years given consideration to the idea of permanent camps in the remoter regions of the mountains. By 1920 he was able to use his influence to convince Commissioner of Dominion Parks J. B. Harkin of the desirability of such camps, and quickly acquired a lease of some property at the Middle Springs in Banff as well as a sublease on the Alpine Club's holding at Lake Magog near Mount Assiniboine. He then approached Ralph Rink, a Swedish trailman who had worked for Brewsters at Lake Louise in 1912 and had done some guiding in the Kootenay country, with an offer to become both the Alpine Club's official outfitter and a partner in a horse transport business for his proposed camps. Rink accepted and was backed by Wheeler in the establishment of Ralph Rink and Company, with the outfit being run under the name of the Alpine Pack Train.

Wheeler's idea for the walking and riding tour was to make a circuit — from Banff up the Spray Valley and Bryant Creek to Assiniboine and then returning by way of Sunshine Meadows and Healy Creek — necessitating having a number of camps en route. Government permission was also granted for these and they were located at the former Eau Claire lumber camp seven miles up the Spray River from Banff, at Goat Pass near Lower Spray Lake, at Trail Centre near Spray Falls above Upper Spray Lake, and at Sunshine on the open meadows near the head of Sunshine Creek. The distance between camps varied from seven to sixteen miles, with the latter being judged the maximum for a hiker or rider unused to the rigours of mountain travel. Upon entering into his agreement with Wheeler in the spring of 1920, Rink's first task was to build the cabins and corrals at the two permanent sites of Middle Springs and Assiniboine, while Wheeler turned his attention to the promotion of the tours in the press:

If you are worn and tired from the daily grind of life's battle and routine existence; if you need revitalizing and a real rest; if you are nervous, neurotic or dyspeptic; come and try it for a week or two. The cure is certain and for the remainder of your life the pages of your memory's scrapbook will be replete with scenes and experiences that will occur again and again with the thrill of joy.[5]

The round-trip cost of the tour, which was to take four to five days, was set at $35, or $50 if a horse was desired. Horse could also be hired by the day at $3 each and baggage could be carried by pack horse at the rate of $1 per 40 pound lot or $3.60 for the whole trip. Provision could also be made for a longer stay at Assiniboine if the customer wished. In these circumstances, the tour was inaugurated in June, 1920 and for two seasons it proved quite popular. But by 1922 it was experiencing problems, not the least of which stemmed from Wheeler's allowing the idea to circulate that it was being run under the auspices of the Alpine Club. Some members of the club voiced their concern, and Wheeler's need to defend his actions to the club's executive on several occasions was undoubtedly damaging. Further difficulty developed because of the complaints of several outfitters that the incorporation of Rink's pack train with the tour constituted unfair competition. Their major concern was that the tour would act as a cover for outfitting longer trail trips, a practice not allowed by the terms of Wheeler's agreement with the government. As this is exactly what he intended doing, the resultant government restriction prohibiting horse trips beyond one day's journey from the tour camps was another serious blow. Because of these circumstances and competition from other conducted rides, attendance had dwindled to just twenty-nine participants by 1924 and by 1926 the tour had ceased entirely. Ralph Rink and Company disposed of its pack string and some of its equipment at auction in May, 1928, the partnership was dissolved and Rink went into business on his own, while Wheeler disposed of his lease agreements at Middle Springs and Mount Assiniboine to Pat Brewster in 1930.

A third scheme of conducted trail rides was inaugurated in 1924 by Jack Brewster. As the junior partner in Brewster and Moore, he had never received the recognition he deserved despite the fact that he had single-handedly kept the company afloat during the difficult war years. It was therefore not surprising when he left his brother Fred, bought up much of the Otto brothers' pack string and equipment and set up his own business in 1922. Although he had already established a reputation as one of the Rockies' foremost big game hunting guides, he soon realized he needed something to attract customers during the summer season. He hoped his idea for "The Glacier Trail," an annual pack train trip from Jasper to Lake Louise and return, would provide what was needed, even though the first year's effort proved pretty much a fiasco due to inexperience and lack of time. Thereafter, he allowed the pack train to proceed at a more leisurely pace, leaving Jasper at the beginning of July and arriving at Lake Louise three weeks later, and then starting the return trip with a new party at the beginning of August. Along the route, Jack established twelve camps, the major one located at Mount Castleguard where a three day layover allowed the group to explore the fringes of the Columbia Icefield. By 1927 "The Glacier Trail" was proving extremely popular using this format and continued to attract good patronage until the beginning of the depression.

Although the Hinman, Wheeler and Brewster conducted tours were important factors in post-war outfitting, they paled in significance compared with the ultimate in annual group trips in the mountains, the Trail Riders of the Canadian Rockies. The Trail Riders had their origin in a trip taken by a party of fourteen fishermen in 1923 under the guidance of Walter Nixon, a pioneer guide and outfitter of the Windermere district. Nixon, a native of Ontario, had come west and begun ranching in the upper Columbia Valley around 1905. He had also occcasionally served as game warden in the Kootenay River and Leanchoil districts, but most of his time was spent guiding. This work developed to the point where he had established an outfitting and guiding business at Invermere and had begun to take out several important parties, as the 1923 one was. It included: H. B. Clow, president of Rand McNally mapmakers; Reginald Townsend, editor of *Country Life in America* magazine; R. H. Palenske, a noted Chicago illustrator and artist; John Murray Gibbon, general publicity agent for the CPR; and Byron Harmon, by this time a well-established Banff commercial photographer.

The party set out from Lake Windermere and fished the Kootenay River until convinced by Clow to visit what he considered the most beautiful country in the mountains, the Wolverine Plateau near Tumbling Glacier. While camped there a summer snowstorm necessitated a layover of several days, and as they sat around the campfire passing the time the group began to discuss the future of trail riding. One of those present, likely Gibbon, suggested the idea of an order in which buttons of various grades could be awarded to those riding fifty, one hundred, five hundred, one thousand and two thousand, five hundred miles of mountain trails. All present agreed that it was a fine idea, and Gibbon was allotted the position of secretary-treasurer, in charge of promoting an organization.

Because of its obvious benefits to the CPR, which *de facto* became its patron, Gibbon threw the whole weight of his influential position behind the scheme and was able to elicit a tremendous response. Within one year the membership holding the various badges stood at well over two hundred people, many of them very distinguished and influential individuals. Among them were honourary president Charles D. Walcott and council members J. B. Harkin, W. T. Hornaday, Sir James Outram, Carl Rungius, Mary Vaux Walcott and Mary Schäffer Warren. The outfitting interests were likewise well represented with Jim and Bill Brewster, Jimmy Simpson, Bill Potts and George Harrison serving on the council.

The organization formulated a constitution, the stated aims of which included the improvement of old trails and the building of new ones, the study and conservation of bird and animal life, the preservation of the National Parks of Canada for the use of the public, and the publication and distribution of maps of existing and proposed trails. However, the main objective was to be encouragement of travel by horseback through the Canadian Rockies, an objective to be achieved by means of an annual trail ride. Originally, the idea was to have a three day ride on an interesting trail, which officials would examine beforehand to select appropriate campsites, and then finish with an annual pow-wow and general meeting in a huge tent called the Sun Dance Lodge. This would be erected at a suitable location, preferably in proximity to one of the CPR bungalow camps or hotels. The outfitting and guiding would be placed in the hands of the Rocky Mountain Guides' Association on the understanding that they would give the best rates possible. This turned out to be approximately $10 per day per person.

After the first year's ride in the Yoho Valley, the response proved so overwhelming that it was necessary to have both three and five day rides and to break the groups into "squadrons," which would start at different points and rendezvous at the site of the pow-wow. In addition, Fred Brewster organized a Jasper group in 1925, the first enrollees being Lewis Swift and the visiting Field Marshall Earl Haig and Countess Haig. But even the squadron idea did not prove capable of handling all comers, and it was soon necessary to have more extended trips lasting from eight to twenty-five days in addition to the three and five day "official" rides. Phil Moore, under whose direction the rides fell in the mid-twenties, also secured the government's permission in 1927 to build cabins at location suitable to allow the Trail Riders to start circle rides, much in the mode of Wheeler's tours.

These rides were unquestionably valuable business-wise for the various outfitters in the Rocky Mountain Guides' Association. Those benefitting most directly were Bill Potts, Walter Nixon, Pat Brewster, Soapy Smith and Fred Brewster, who not only took out the official rides but made their outfits available to those wishing private rides afterwards. These customers were not inconsiderable, since by 1929 the Trail Riders could count some 1,500 members with over 100 of them holding the 2,500 mile badge. In fact, during that year the officials of the Trail Riders claimed, with some justification, that it was largely due to their organization that the outfitters and guides, who only a few years previously were being driven out of business by the motor car, were once again working at capacity.

Although the creation of the Trail Riders of the Canadian Rockies played a key role in the revitalization of guiding and outfitting, it also marked the end of the pioneer era in that business at Banff and Jasper. The organization's executive was very conscious of this from the outset, and decided to pay tribute to the work of those who had opened up the country and had thereby made their travels through the mountains possible. In planning the first annual ride held in the Yoho Valley in July, 1924, they decided that it would be appropriate to invite Tom Wilson, the man who had started it all, as their special guest. Furthermore, his historic contribution was to be recognized by the unveiling of a bronze plaque mounted on a large boulder at the mouth of the valley bearing the inscription:

Tom Wilson
Trail Blazer of
the Canadian Rockies
Lake Louise 1882
Emerald Lake 1882

Tom agreed to attend and on reaching the camp for the official inauguration ceremonies on July 17th was greeted with speeches of welcome from Colonel Phil Moore and Mrs. Mary Vaux Walcott. Called upon to respond, he stated "I am not accustomed to speaking extemporaneously unless a cayuse has stepped on my foot." Undoubtedly, his mind was full of the images of earlier times, such as those forty years earlier when he had taken his own first prospecting trip up the same valley as the hordes of riders would travel on the morrow. Yes, the old days on the trail were gone forever.

An early camp at Swift's homestead in the Athabasca Valley

The Mumm party in camp, 1909. Back (l. to r.) — A. L. Mumm, L. S. Amery, Moritz Inderbinen and John Yates. Front — Geoffrey Hastings (second left) and James Shand-Harvey (second right)

Fred Stephens

Adam Joachim

Donald "Curly" Phillips

Jack Brewster in the Brewster and Moore corrals at Jasper, 1914

ACC-Smithsonian party, 1911 — (l. to r.) A. O. Wheeler, Curly Phillips, Harry Blagden, J. H. Riley, Charles Walcott jr., George Kinney (sitting), James Shand-Harvey and Casey Jones

Mary Jobe

Phillips's flying trestle bridge

The Brewster-Fay party chopping through downed timber

245

*James Oliver Curwood with Closson Otto at Otto Bros. corral in
Jasper, ca. 1915. Jack and Mrs. Jack Otto at rear*

War amputee Joe Woodworth tightening the diamond

Caroline Hinman

Fred Brewster

Curly Phillips guiding a Caroline Himan party near the head of the Southesk River, 1921

Walter Nixon leading the Gibbon party over
Wolverine Plateau, 1923

Tom Wilson at the unveiling of his plaque at the first Trail
Riders of the Canadian Rockies camp in the Yoho Valley, 1924

Epilogue

A lthough the end of the pioneer era of guiding and outfitting at Banff and Jasper saw significant changes in the profession, it did not mean the end to the careers of all the early trailmen in these areas. Along with several newcomers, some of the old guard continued to follow the trail for at least part of their livelihoods, usually combining it with some other aspect of the tourism business.

Jimmy Simpson continued to build on his reputation as the foremost outfitter in the Banff area, drawing from a wealth of clientele built up over many years. Mountaineers such as J. Monroe Thorington and William S. Ladd continued to seek him out, as did hunters hearing of his prowess from others of the same ilk. After the completion of the original lodge at Bow Lake in 1922, he gradually began to shift the focus of his operations away from Banff to Bow Lake. In the twenties he used it as a base camp for the hunting and climbing expeditions he took out from Banff and Lake Louise, but with the building of the new lodge in the thirties it became his main headquarters. Saddle horses were kept for lodge guests who wished day or short overnight trips, but the pack outfit was also kept in trim for those wishing the old-style trail trips into the mountains' farther recesses. Jimmy continued to guide some of these himself, particularly the hunting trips and the increasingly numerous trips by biologists studying the parks' wildlife, but as age crept up on him after the Second World War he began to turn responsibility over to his son, Jim jr. Even at that, though, he continued to accompany parties out as cook until he was well into his seventies.

Pat Brewster also rated as one of the principal outfitters working out of Banff by the late-twenties. After having worked for Brewster Brothers and Brewster Transport in Banff and Brewster and Moore in Jasper, he finally achieved a modicum of independence in 1925. Returning from the war, he had gone back to work for his brother Jim, handling the company's interests at Glacier for five years until the closing of Glacier House by the CPR with the building of the Connaught Tunnel. At that point he had approached his brother about the possibility of leasing all Brewster Transport's outfitting interests, as they had become rather burdensome to the company at a time when it was aggressively expanding into motorized transport. As the company's trail business had been allowed to languish for several years, Jim agreed, and Pat immediately began to rebuild it under the name of Brewster's Mountain Pack Trains. Because the lease included the CPR outfitting concessions, Pat was provided with an increasing supply of customers as the twenties progressed and eventually had to build up his pack string to huge proportions. The record year proved to be 1928 when he had 488 head of horses working out of Banff, Lake Louise and Field. Soon afterward, business began to plummet with the onset of the depression and operations were drastically reduced, and by the mid-thirties he had to be content with the more limited business he could garner from such customers as the Alpine Club, the Trail Riders and a few loyal hunters. Later he began a series of permanent camps established at Hillsdale, Egypt Lake and Sunburst Lake which both complemented and served as bases for his outfitting activities for many years afterwards.

Jim Boyce was a third outfitter who successfully began to work out of Banff in the twenties. A native of Pembroke, Ontario who had come to Banff in 1911 to join his father Joe, a successful trail-building contractor, he had begun working on the trail for Simpson in 1916. Soon he had gained a reputation as a trail cook, producing as light and toothsome bannock as ever to emerge from a campfire reflector, and he gained a great following among his employer's customers. In 1921 he and Max Brooks, a fellow employee of Simpson's, decided to form a partnership of their own, and after purchasing some of Soapy Smith's stock began business as Boyce and Brooks. This was dissolved in 1924, by which point Jim had become the main supplier of services for Caroline Hinman's conducted trail trips. These provided a basis for an expansion of the business as they continued to grow in popularity, at their height requiring him to supply up to fifty-five horses for each outing. He also had to be prepared to go far afield in these trips, on one occasion trailing a group out of Banff as far north as Mount Robson. During the thirties, like most of his confreres, his business suffered a setback, and he became involved in such other businesses as managing Skoki Ski Lodge, running a dog team and working on highway construction. Eventually, he became involved more actively in the hotel business, building the lodge in Lake Louise that would become the Post Hotel, but also kept his hand in at the trail business until disposing of his last horses in 1952.

Not all those engaged in guiding and outfitting along the CPR chose Banff as their headquarters. Both to the west and east along the line former Brewster men, including Tex Wood, George Harrison, Bill Potts and Soapy Smith, successfully carried on the profession.

Tex Wood had left Brewsters in 1915 to join the warden service, being posted to Peyto's Healy Creek district while Bill served overseas. One of his duties was rendering assistance to the distinguished geologist Dr. Charles D. Walcott of the Smithsonian Institution, who was investigating the Cambrian geology of the Rockies and was the discoverer of the famous Burgess Shales. In 1919 Tex decided to leave the wardens and upon acquiring an outfit began to regularly escort Walcott and his wife, the former Mary Vaux, on their summer expedition out from Lake Louise. These trips were supplemented by contracts from both the Smithsonian and the American Museum of Natural History and by a large clientele of New York lawyers whom he annually took on hunting trips. Except for a brief period in 1923-24, which was spent working on the movies at Hollywood, he ran his outfit primarily out of Lake Louise until 1938. Finding the country becoming too crowded for his liking at that point, he left for the Windermere district and opened a dude ranch for young boys from wealthy American families.

George Harrison, undoubtedly Brewsters' most loyal and competent guide, also chose the war years as the time to sever his connection with the company. He had spent the years from 1910 to 1915 as head guide at Lake Louise and then had been transferred to Glacier when the company had acquired the CPR concession from Syd Baker. Because the area appealed to him, Harrison decided that it would be a perfect locale for his own business, and in 1918, after a career of sixteen years with Brewsters, he made his move. His reputation as a hunting guide gained through long years of experience immediately brought him many parties he had handled for his former employer. Fortunately, after the closing of Glacier House, he was able to obtain the lease on the old CPR section house at Glacier, which he used as a headquarters until his retirement in 1945.

Bill Potts began his first efforts at outfitting in conjunction with two other returned war veterans, his brother Wattie and Stan Carr, and with the assistance of his brother-in-law Frank Wellman. Wellman had purchased the Morley Trading Company store and moved his family to Morley prior to the war, after having operated the Park Dairy in Banff from 1907 to 1913. Later he had disposed of the store and had acquired the old Dave McDougall ranch near Morley, from where he had guided and outfitted the occasional party. In the spring of 1918 he made an agreement with Jimmy Simpson and Tom Wilson, to whom John Wilson's share in the Kootenay Plains livestock had reverted, to purchase 140 head of horses. Once these were rounded up and moved to his ranch, Wellman donated a number of them and his supply of outfitting equipment to Bill and his partners so that they could establish the Potts Outfitting Company. Wattie remained with the company only a year and Carr slightly longer, departing for a three-and-a-half year stint in California in 1921 and then returning to work on the trail in the Yellowhead district. Bill Potts, left to run the operation himself, continued to maintain his headquarters at Morley, although he often leased livery facilities at Banff as well. Despite the support his business received from the Trail Riders, he decided to leave guiding and outfitting in the thirties in favour of a position with the warden service, eventually becoming supervising warden of Banff National Park.

Soapy Smith, like Harrison, was one of Brewsters' most loyal employees, serving respectively as harness maker, cook, packer and guide from 1905 to 1922. During this period he had continued to spend the winter months at his Jumping Pound ranch after coming in from his summer's work in the mountains. However, in 1922, after Frank Wellman had died in the 1919 flu epidemic, he was able to buy a piece of the Wellman property near the Kananaskis River and began a new ranch, known as the Rafter 6. For a time he abandoned the trail in order to concentrate on raising horses, but soon began to take parties out on his own. His most notable trip was in 1924 when he outfitted and guided Amercian writer Lewis R. Freeman and Byron Harmon on a trip to attempt the first complete photographic coverage of the Columbia Icefield. Assisted by Ulysse LaCasse and Bob Baptie, he successfully led the party and his pack train across the Saskatchewan Glacier, a feat given wide coverage in Freeman's subsequent article in *National Geographic Magazine* and in his book *On The Roof Of The Rockies*. Thereafter, Soapy remained active in guiding and outfitting, particularly with the Trail Riders, until two years before his death in 1948.

Along the Canadian National line, the picture was much the same. Some of the long-time outfitters in the area continued to make at least part of their living from the trail, and they were joined by a few newcomers. The major outfitting interests in the area after 1925 included Curly Phillips, Fred Brewster, Jack Brewster, Hargreaves Brothers, Jack Hargreaves, Alex Wylie and Stan Clark.

Curly Phillips married in 1923, and although he continued to outfit parties, he seldom accompanied them himself. Many of his former clients continued to seek out his services, including the Alpine Club and Miss Hinman, but they were taken care of by his well-seasoned guides, usually Adam Joachim or Dave Moberly, while he devoted most of his attention to boat trips. These and his winter trapline kept him busy until the mid-thirties when, in line with his progressive thinking, he began formulating a new scheme. This was an idea for using airplanes to get hunters into previously inaccessible areas, and in 1937 he proved it was feasible by flying two American hunters from Finlay Forks across the Lloyd George range to Tuchodi Lake. Intending to devote more attention to such enterprises, he sold most of his outfit to Bert Wilkins on returning from this trip. Sadly, he never got the opportunity to pursue his plans, as in March of the following year, despite three decades of experience at winter travel in the mountains, he fell victim to an avalanche while scouting out the possibilities for a ski camp near Elysium Pass.

Fred Brewster's activities in the early-twenties continued to be centred around the developments at Jasper Park Lodge, which he used as the headquarters for his outfitting operations. As the clientele at the lodge increased, his Sky Line Trail Rides to Maligne Lake gained in popularity, and in 1928 he decided to expand his business, leasing a parcel of land at Medicine Lake with the railroad's assistance. Here he constructed the Medicine Lake Chalet, the first in what would become a system of camps and chalets known as Fred Brewster's Rocky Mountain Camps. As time went on these included: Maligne Lake Chalet and Tonquin Valley Camp, used for riding, hiking, boating and fishing; camps in the Little and Big Shovel Passes and at Tekarra Basin, operated in conjunction with the Sky Line Trail Rides; and the Black Cat Ranch on Solomon Creek outside the park's eastern boundary, employed for big game hunting trips. Fred was also one of the early enthusiasts of skiing in the area, becoming an original member and president of the Jasper Ski Club in 1926, and he later began to use some of his trail facilities and chalets for winter ski camps. After Phillips's death he acquired the boat concessions at Maligne and Medicine Lakes and continued to run them in conjunction with his outfitting interests until his retirement in 1962.

Jack Brewster, although he continued to maintain Jasper as his headquarters, went much further afield in pursuit of his business interests. His reputation as one of western Canada's foremost big game hunting guides kept him constantly on the move in search of new and productive territory, and eventually he developed trips into the Cassiar country of British Columbia for this purpose. But on the completion of the Banff-Jasper Highway in the late-thirties he also focused some attention on the area formerly encompassed in his "Glacier Trail" trips. After overseeing the construction of the Columbia Icefield Chalet for the Brewster Transport Company, he began offering saddle horse service in the summer and hunting trips in the fall into the Brazeau country. Then, because of his skill at log work, he was asked to assist in the building of the Alaska Highway during the Second World War, holding the position of superintendent of camp and hospital construction at Whitehorse for three years. Shortly after the war he returned to his boyhood home of Banff and built one of the town's first motels, the Brewster Motel, on the site of his father's original lease on Moose Street and Banff Avenue, operating it until his death in 1951.

Jack Hargreaves was, perhaps, the most successful of the new guides and outfitters who established at Jasper, his appearance there being related to earlier developments at Mount Robson in an enterprise known as Hargreaves Brothers. Jack and his three brothers — Frank, George and Roy — had spent much of their youth travelling around the country with their rather footloose father. George and Roy had been the first to leave home, and in 1905 they had been involved in the cutting of a trail from Golden to Tête Jaune Cache. Jack, on the other hand, had first come to Jasper at age eighteen to play hockey in the winter of 1913-14. The next summer he had begun to work for Otto Brothers and in the winter of 1917 had accompanied Phillips and Miss Jobe on their trip to the Wapiti. After serving overseas in the war he had returned and headed for Mount Robson, where his brother Frank had filed on a homestead with an eye towards involvement in the tourist business. Together they erected several log buildings as well as a small store and before long were joined first by their brother George and later by Roy. The four soon began to outfit and guide parties, using about seventy head of horses and concentrating mainly on Berg Lake. Although they carried on business under the name of Hargreaves Brothers, each kept ownership of his part of the outfit, and the arrangement came to an end in 1924 when Jack decided to pull out. He moved on to Jasper, purchased some horses and equipment from Ralph James of Pocahontas, and began to take out hunting parties in 1927. Thereafter, both he and Hargreaves Brothers ran separate outfits for many years, Jack himself having up to eighty-five horses on the trail at one time.

Alex Wylie, although he had not worked for any of the established outfitters, was well-acquainted with packing in the mountains by the time he began his own outfit in 1918. After coming to Canada from his native Scotland at age five, he had spent his youth in Edmonton and had begun freighting for the Hudson's Bay Company to Athabaska Landing in 1898. In 1905 he had left for the mountains, intending to take a holiday but ending up working for N. H. Jock and Jack Gregg, pioneer ranchers at Prairie Creek. Jock had obtained a contract with the GTP and, in 1906, Alex had helped him freight supplies to the McLeod River and then pack them on to Prairie Creek. The next year he packed for the railway, making around trip from Swift's through to Tête Jaune Cache and back every eight days with a twenty-three horse pack string. After that he had worked with survey parties on the GTP until 1910, when he had hired on as a packer for a government survey of the Coal Branch region. During the war years, Alex had raised horses on his family's ranch at Nisku, south of Edmonton, and at its end had looked around for a good situation for using them, eventually settling on Jasper. While never a large outfitter, in the years before his retirement in 1939 he achieved some success with day trip tourists and sometimes combined his horses with another outfitter's string to take larger parties on longer treks. For a number of years he also had the job of delivering Jasper's water supply, hauling it from the outlet of Cabin Lake with two teams drawing water tanks.

Stan Clark had one of the most interesting backgrounds of those becoming involved in the trail business at Jasper in the early twenties. After graduating from college, where he was captain of the football team, he had entered the employ of the Canadian Forestry Service. Soon he had been promoted to superintendent of Rocky Mountain Forest Reserve and had done most of the pioneer work in establishing the Athabasca Forest Reserve north of Jasper. At the outbreak of the war, he had immediately enlisted and, with his training and background, was placed in charge of British forestry operations in France. Upon returning from overseas he had obtained a parcel of land across the Athabasca River from Entrance and began setting up a large horse and cattle ranch. In 1922 he was approached by Major Townsend Whelen, a leading ballistics expert with the United States Army, with a request to accompany him on a sheep hunt in the country west of the Smoky River. Although he wasn't intending on getting into the guiding and outfitting line, the success of this trip convinced him to do so. Whelen wrote the account of their hunt in a three-part series entitled "In Virgin Game Mountains of the North" which appeared in *Outdoor Life* magazine in 1923 and 1924. Because of the author's reputation, Clark was soon inundated with requests from other hunters and continued to be a successful big game guide for several years afterwards.

******

Regardless of how and when they got into the guiding and outfitting life, where they established themselves or how long they stayed with it, all of those individuals involved in the pioneer days of the profession had something in common. The blood of the trail ran strong in their veins, and as long as they lived they were never able to get the memory of those exciting and challenging days out of their minds. Then, like the explorers that had preceded them, they were driven to seek just beyond the next ridge, they were privileged to live in closest contact with nature in some of the most magnificent country which God had created on earth, and they were able to share a camaraderie with their fellow travellers that was the lot of few men. All reminisced freely about their experiences and the way of life, but perhaps the man to best articulate their feelings for the "good old days" was Tom Wilson, with whom the whole story had begun.

Tom had become disillusioned with the mountains by the end of the First World War, mainly because of his continued inability to obtain title to the Kootenay Plains ranches. Resigning his positions of justice of the peace and police magistrate, which he had held for several years, he moved to Vancouver in 1920. Soon discovering that city life did not agree with him, he went on to Enderby in the Okanagan Valley, where he intended on retiring permanently. But the old lure of the mountains proved too strong. After his visit to attend the initiation of the Trail Riders in 1924, he began to realize just how much he missed the trails and peaks of his younger days, and in January, 1927 returned to Banff with the promise of work from John Murray Gibbon on behalf of his old employer, the CPR. Until his death in 1933 he became "local colour" at the Banff Springs Hotel and the Chateau Lake Louise, entertaining guests and newspaper reporters with stories and tales of the early days drawn from his vast repertoire of trail lore. One of these reminiscences concerned his days spent packing with Major Rogers on the railway survey and ended with a poem he liked to call "Memories of Golden Days:"

Good old days on the trail and evenings around the campfire,
And when the coffee pot upset just as it was beginning to boil,
And the sugar and salt got wet,
And sometimes the beans went sour and the bacon musty,
And the wind blew sparks in your eyes and ashes on your blankets,
And the butt of the biggest bough hit the small of your back,
And the mosquitoes almost crowded you out of your tent,
And you heard the horse bell getting fainter and fainter,
And you knew damn well they would be five miles away in the morning,
But just the same, O Lord, how I wish I could live them all over again.

Notes

Notes

Chapter I

[1] Whyte Museum of the Canadian Rockies Archives (WMCRA), Copy of Wilson scrapbook, newsclipping, n.d. Much of the information about Tom Wilson's early life is contained in newsarticles written by journalists after interviewing him in the late twenties when he was performing public relations duties for the CPR at the Banff Springs Hotel and Chateau Lake Louise. These interviews often included a good sprinkling of "tall tales" and some of Wilson's claims must therefore be viewed with a degree of skepticism.

[2] Thomas E. Wilson, *Trail Blazer of the Canadian Rockies* (Calgary: Glenbow Alberta Institute, 1972), p. 19.

[3] Wilson scrapbook, Letter from Tom Wilson to J. B. Harkin, 1924.

[4] *Ibid.*, Ina Burns, "Mountain Miracle," *Calgary Herald*, n.d.

[5] In his book, Fleming identifies the packer as George Wilson, but Tom's later recollections of accompanying the party make it seem likely it was him.

[6] Sandford Fleming, *England and Canada, A Summer Tour Between Old and New Westminster* (London: Sampson, Low, Marston, Searle and Rivington, 1884), p. 243.

[7] *Ibid.*, pp. 248-49.

[8] *Ibid.*, p. 258.

[9] Wilson scrapbook, J. E. Middleton, "Eastern Tenderfoot Meets Tom Wilson," *Toronto Mail and Empire*, September 8, 1930.

[10] *Ibid.*

[11] Sandford Fleming, "Memories of the Mountains," *Canadian Alpine Journal*, I, (1907), p. 32.

[12] Walter D. Wilcox, *The Rockies of Canada*, (New York: The Knickerbocker Press, 1916), pp. 115-16.

[13] Glenbow Museum Archives (GMA), Wilson Papers, Barrett to Wilson, November 1, 1924.

[14] Walter D. Wilcox, "Early Days in the Canadian Rockies," *American Alpine Journal*, IV, (1941), p. 177.

Chapter II

[1] Wilson Papers, Wilcox to Wilson, Janury 18, 1930.

[2] WMCRA, Tape recorded interview with James Simpson, March 9, 1969.

[3] *Ibid.*

[4] Wilcox, "Early Days. . . .," p. 181.

[5] Wilcox, *The Rockies of Canada*, p. 120.

[6] Jimmy Simpson, Sr., "Peyto. . . of Peyto Lake," *Canadian Golden West*, VI, (Winter, 1971), p. 31.

[7] Ralph Edwards, *The Trail to the Charmed Land*, (Saskatoon: H. R. Larsen Publishing Company, 1949), p. 12.

[8] Walter D. Wilcox, *Camping in the Canadian Rockies*, (New York: G. P. Putnam's Sons, 1897), pp. 170-74.

[9] *Ibid.*, p. 214.

[10] *Ibid.*, p. 209.

[11] *Appalachia*, I, (June, 1876), p. 1.

[12] Philip S. Abbot, "The First Ascent of Mount Hector, Canadian Rockies," *Appalachia*, VIII, (January, 1896), p. 2.

[13] *Ibid.*, p. 3.

[14] Princeton University Archives (PUA), Thompson-Little Collection, Abbot to Fay, October 17, 1895 (copies available at WMCRA).

Notes

[15] Stanley Washburn, *Trails, Trappers and Tenderfeet In the New Empire of Western Canada,* (New York: Henry Holt and Company, 1912), p. 6.

[16] PUA, J. Monroe Thorington Collection, Simpson to Thorington, November 18, 1968 (copies available at WMCRA).

[17] Washburn, p. 175.

[18] Martin Nordegg, "Pioneering in Canada, 1906-1924," (memoirs of Martin Nordegg, nd.), p. 36.

[19] Thompson-Little Collection (Supplement), Wilcox to Thorington, December 5, 1944.

Chapter III

[1] Charles E. Fay, "The Casualty on Mount Lefroy," *Appalachia,* VIII, (November, 1896), p. 150.

[2] Thompson-Little Collection, Abbot to Wilson, June 28, 1896.

[3] *Ibid.,* p. 228.

[4] Wilcox, "Early Days. . .," p. 188.

[5] H. E. M. Stutfield and J. N. Collie, *Climbs and Explorations in the Canadian Rockies,* (London: Longmans, Green and Co., 1903), pp. 26-27.

[6] *Ibid.,* pp. 41-42.

[7] WMCRA, Tom Wilson, "A short history of the early work in developing the resorts and tourist trade in the Canadian Pacific Rockies," p. 2. Wilson wrote this manuscript in the late-twenties to point out all the work he had done for the CPR for which he had never received credit or reimbursement.

[8] Wilson scrapbook, Wilson to Harkin, November 30, 1922 and n.d., 1924.

[9] Edwards, p. 35-36.

[10] Charles E. Fay, "Old Times in the Canadian Alps," *Canadian Alpine Journal,* XII, (1922), p. 101. The time reference is an allusion to the hour and day of Abbot's fall in 1896.

[11] R. F. Curtis, "The Making of Abbot Pass," *Appalachia*, IX, (1899-1901), p. 36.

[12] Thompson-Little Collection, Fay to Thompson, August 17, 1898.

[13] Charles L. Noyes, "Mount Balfour and the Waputehk Snowfield," *Appalachia*, IX, (1899-1901), p. 31.

[14] Stutfield and Collie, p.84.

[15] J. Norman Collie, "Climbing in the Canadian Rockies," *The Alpine Journal*, XIX, (1898-99), p. 454.

[16] *Ibid.*, p.p. 457-58.

[17] Stutfield and Collie, p. 135.

[18] *Ibid.*, p. 97

[19] WMCRA, Excerpts from a diary by J. Norman Collie, 1900.

[20] Thompson-Little Collection (Supplement), Stephens to Wilcox, December 31, 1902.

[21] Thorington Collection, Simpson to Thorington, October 26, 1968.

Chapter IV

[1] *Calgary Daily Herald*, December 3, 1901.

[2] Thorington Collection, Simpson to Thorington, December 4, 1968 and November 18, 1968.

[3] Scott Polar Institute, Diary of Edward Whymper, July 27, 1901. (Copies available at WMCRA)

[4] *Ibid.*, August 8, 1901.

[5] Wilson Papers, Whymper to Wilson, August 9, 1901.

[6] A. O. Wheeler, "Some Memories of Edward Whymper, " *Canadian Alpine Journal*, XXVIII, (1941), p. 84.

Notes

[7] Wilson Papers, Contract between T. E. Wilson, Field, B. C., Liveryman and the CPR, 1902.

[8] GMA, Memoirs of Charles Lumley, p. 3.

[9] WMCRA, Tape recorded interview with Jack Fuller, February 6, 1969.

[10] WMCRA, Unpublished manuscript, "Mountain Men," by N. "Tex" Vernon-Wood.

[11] Thorington Collection, Simpson to Thorington, December 23, 1968 and July 30, 1969.

[12] Thompson-Little Collection, Collie to Thompson, March 10 and 13, 1902.

[13] Stutfield and Collie, pp. 296-97.

[14] Thorington Collection, Simpson to Thorington, October 26, 1968.

Chapter V

[1] Wilson Papers, Whymper to Wilson, May 29, 1905.

[2] Stutfield and Collie, p. 247.

[3] W. B. Mitchell, *Trail Life in the Canadian Rockies*, (New York: The MacMillan Co., 1924), p. 196.

[4] Thorington Collection, Simpson to Thorington, July 30, 1969.

[5] *Ibid.*

[6] Wilson Papers, Fay to Wilson, April 4, 1898.

[7] *Ibid.*, Oliver to Wilson, April 7, 1908.

[8] Newsclipping, "Canada's Mountain Beauty Spot," n.n., March, 1906.

[9] Wilson Papers, Wheeler to Mrs. Wilson, September 27, 1933.

[10] *Ibid.*, Wheeler to Wilson, June 8, 1906.

[11] Yoho Camp Circular, *Canadian Alpine Journal*, I, (1907), pp. 169-70.

[12] A. O. Wheeler, "The Origin and Founding of the Alpine Club of Canada," *Canadian Alpine Journal*, XXVII, (1938), p. 94.

[13] Frank Yeigh, "Canada's First Alpine Club Camp," *Canadian Alpine Journal*, I, (1907), p. 55.

[14] Alpine Club of Canada Archives, Minutes of the meeting of the Alpine Club of Canada held at the Yoho Camp, July 11, 1906.

[15] *Ibid.*, Minutes of the annual meeting of the Alpine Club of Canada, 1909, President's Address.

[16] Report of 1910 Camp, *Canadian Alpine Journal*, III, (1911), pp. 189, 195.

Chapter VI

[1] Washburn, p. 135.

[2] A. P. Coleman, *The Canadian Rockies, New and Old Trails*, (London; T. Fisher Unwin, 1911), p. 347.

[3] George P. Kinney and Donald Phillips, "To The Top Of Mount Robson," *Canadian Alpine Journal*, II, (1910), p. 40.

[4] J. Monroe Thorington (ed.), *Where Clouds Can Go*, (New York City: The American Alpine Club, 1935), p. 320.

[5] Canada, Department of the Interior, *Annual Report*, 1915, Part V, p.65.

[6] J. E. C. Eaton, "An Expedition To The Freshfield Group," *Canadian Alpine Journal*, III, (1911), p. 2.

[7] WMCRA, Untitled manuscript concerning a trip to Maligne Lake in 1911 by Mary T. S. Schäffer, p. 27.

[8] Jasper-Yellowhead Historical Society, "Reminiscing," by Fred Brewster.

[9] Canada, Department of the Interior, *Annual Report*, 1915, Part V, p. 65.

Chapter VII

[1] *Banff Crag and Canyon*, August 14, 1909

Notes

[2] WMCRA, Tape recorded interview with Tex Vernon-Wood and Stan Carr, August 18, 1970.

[3] Robert Frothingham, "Bighorns on the Brazeau," *Field and Stream*, March, 1917, p. 385.

[4] William N. Beach, "Land of Heart's Desire," *Field and Stream*, August, 1920, p. 376.

[5] Simpson's ram was the world's record until 1952 when a new system of determining record sheep heads, taking into account such points as symmetry and massiveness as well as the length of curl, was instituted by Boone and Crockett. At that time a head taken by Martin Bovey of Minneapolis in 1924 while hunting with pioneer outfitter and guide Bert Riggall of Waterton Lakes jumped from fourth to first place.

[6] WMCRA, Letter from Mary S. Warren to Wilson, n.d.

[7] Mary T. S. Schäffer, *Old Indian Trails of the Canadian Rockies*, (New York: The Knickerbocker Press, 1911), pp. 4-5.

[8] Mrs. Charles Schäffer, "The Valley of the Saskatchewan with Horse and Camera," *Bulletin of the Geographical Society of Philadelphia*, Vol. V, No. 2, (April, 1907), pp. 37-38.

[9] WMCRA, Mary Schäffer Warren Collection, Diary of Mollie Adams, July 7, 1908.

[10] *Ibid.*, July 28, 1908.

[11] WMCRA, Letter from Mary S. Warren to Zillmer, February 28, 1928.

[12] Mitchell, p. 78.

[13] WMCRA, Mabel Brinkley Collection, "Bill Peyto," unpublished manuscript.

Chapter VIII

[1] J. Norman Collie, "On the Canadian Rocky Mountains North Of The Yellow Head Pass," *The Alpine Journal*, XXVI, (1911), p. 11.

[2] *Ibid,,* p. 17.

[3] A. O. Wheeler, "The Alpine Club of Canada's Expedition to Jasper Park, Yellow

Head Pass and Mount Robson Region, 1911," *Canadian Alpine Journal*, IV, (1912), p. 91.

[4] Thorington Collection, Simpson to Thorington, November 18, 1968.

[5] *Ibid.*, Kinney to Thorington, September 7, 1934.

[6] Donald Phillips, "Fitzhugh to Laggan," *Canadian Alpine Journal*, IV, (1912), p. 91.

[7] Thorington Collection, "Tracks Across My Trail, The Trapping Diaries of Donald (Curly) Phillips," ed. by J. Monroe Thorington, April 4, 1911.

[8] WMCRA, Fred Brewster Collection, "Diary of a Trip from Jasper to Hudson's Hope, Peace River" by S. Prescott Fay, July 25, 1914.

[9] *Ibid.*, August 13, 1914.

[10] *Ibid.*, October, 2, 1914.

[11] Mary L. Jobe, "The Expedition to 'Mt. Kitchi'," *Canadian Alpine Journal*, VI, (1914-15), p. 200.

[12] WMCRA, Arthur Conan Doyle, "The Athabaska Trail," quoted from a Caroline Hinman advertising pamphlet, 1925.

Chapter IX

[1] *Banff Crag and Canyon*, August 7, 1920.

[2] Thorington Collection, advertising leaflet, "Introducing Donald 'Curly' Phillips 'Dude Trapline'," 1924-25.

[3] *Ibid.*, Phillips to Woodward, May 17, 1925.

[4] *Banff Crag and Canyon*, May 6, 1922.

[5] Newsclipping, n.n., May 15, 1920.

Index

Index

Index

Photographic Credits

Whyte Museum of the Canadian Rockies Archives Wilson
Collection: title, 87 (bottom), 89 (top), 90 (top), 168 (top), 169 (top
left), 171 (top left), 172 (top left & bottom), 243 (top left), 248 (bot-
tom); Paris Collection: 85, 87 (top); Vaux Collection: 89 (bottom),
167; Simpson Collection: 91, 169 (top right), 172 (top right); ACC
Collection: 170 (bottom), 242 (top & bottom), 245 (top left): Byron
Harmon Coll: 244 (bottom), 245 (top right), 248 (top); Hinman
Collection:243 (top right and bottom), 246 (bottom); 247 (top left);
Other collections: 86 (top & bottom), 88, 168 (bottom), 169 (bottom), 170 (top), 171 (top right and bottom), 173, 247 (top right
and bottom)
Jasper Yellowhead Historical Society 90 (bottom), 244 (top), 245
(bottom), 246 (top)